Core Collection for Children and Young Adults

Rachel E. Schwedt
and
Janice A. DeLong

THE SCARECROW PRESS, INC.
Lanham, Maryland • Toronto • Plymouth, UK
2008

SCARECROW PRESS, INC.

Published in the United States of America
by Scarecrow Press, Inc.
A wholly owned subsidiary of
The Rowman & Littlefield Publishing Group, Inc.
4501 Forbes Boulevard, Suite 200, Lanham, Maryland 20706
www.scarecrowpress.com

Estover Road
Plymouth PL6 7PY
United Kingdom

British Library Cataloguing in Publication Information Available

Library of Congress Cataloging-in-Publication Data

Schwedt, Rachel E., 1944-
  Core collection for children and young adults / Rachel E. Schwedt and Janice A.
DeLong.
     p. cm.
  Includes indexes.
  ISBN-13: 978-0-8108-6115-2 (cloth : alk. paper)
  ISBN-10: 0-8108-6115-1 (cloth : alk. paper)
  ISBN-13: 978-0-8108-6649-2 (electronic)
  ISBN-10: 0-8108-6649-8 (electronic)
  1. Children's literature—Bibliography. 2. Young adult literature—Bibliography.
3. Children—Books and reading—United States—Bibliography. 4. Teenagers—Books
and reading—United States—Bibliography. 5. School libraries—United States—Book
lists. 6. Children's libraries—United States—Book lists. I. DeLong, Janice, 1943-
II. Title.
  Z1037.S378 2008
  011.62—dc22
                                                                      2008015070

⊚™ The paper used in this publication meets the minimum requirements of
American National Standard for Information Sciences—Permanence of Paper
for Printed Library Materials, ANSI/NISO Z39.48-1992.
Manufactured in the United States of America

To our children, with whom we shared the love of reading,
we dedicate this book.
To Alan and Julie: thanks for understanding my passion. (RS)
To Beth, Mike, Lynne, and Kara: may you continue to be biblioholics. (JD)

Contents

Acknowledgments

We express our gratitude to Sandra Bondy for her tireless research, efficient editing, enthusiastic encouragement, and cheerful spirit. Without her knowledge of children's books and her technological skill, the process would have been a lot less fun.

Introduction

With thousands of new volumes lining the shelves of bookstores, abundant advertisements, and innumerable online reviews, how does the concerned adult select literature that is of quality, yet speaks to young audiences where they live? How can works be found that demonstrate positive character themes without sermonizing? These critical questions were addressed in our first book, *Core Collection for Small Libraries: An Annotated Bibliography of Books for Children and Young Adults*, published in 1997. In this second collaboration, following the first in its goals, we have found even greater challenges because of the sheer quantity of material available to readers from ages four to eighteen.

Titles in the earlier book were chosen from personal experience in the classroom and library, or from selections that had garnered excellent professional reviews. In the ten years since the publication of *Core Collection for Small Libraries*, awards to writers and illustrators of children's publications have grown along with the number of these works. Recent research reveals that nearly every state in the union and many foreign countries highlight excellence through such honors. These awards seemed to be a logical standard by which choices could be made. Thus the criterion for inclusion in *Core Collection for Children and Young Adults* became the winning of at least one award (although most entries were the recipients of many). The Classics chapter stands as an exception to this requirement with titles that have remained in print for at least fifty years and therefore are books of distinction in their own right.

Specific criteria have been established for each genre. Contemporary fiction must portray daily life with its challenges while ending with hope. Fantasy books should stretch the imagination without appealing to the dark side of young minds. Historical fiction needs to accurately reflect the past without bias. Nonfiction must relate factual information while entertaining youthful readers. Picture books should bring to children the perfect balance of text and illustration. Poetry, by definition, must take the abstract and make it concrete. Traditional literature should reflect the culture from which it arises and underscore the power of story.

Organization of this work follows a similar format as that of *Core Collection for Small Libraries*. In this second volume, however, classics have been unified under one chapter heading. In contrast, multicultural works are now interwoven throughout the text, instead of having their own separate designation. For easy access, specific culture groups are referenced in the annotations as well as in the subject index.

Within each chapter entries are arranged alphabetically by author. As in volume one, Related Subjects headings refer to topics included in each title. Character Themes, as in the earlier work, alert readers to values expressed through plot or other literary elements. New to this edition is the listing of awards won by the entry. Full bibliographic information is provided including suggested grade levels for the audience. Four separate indexes provide access to pertinent information. Index A lists titles, authors, translators, editors, and illustrators. Index B is a comprehensive list of awards referenced. Index C names character themes reflected in each volume. Index D includes related subject terms used in each annotation.

Within these pages are summaries of more than 350 titles that represent significant contributions to the field of children's and young adult literature. Many titles are copyrighted since 1994, but none have been repeated in *Core Collection for Children and Young Adults* that were reviewed in *Core Collection for Small Libraries*. A core collection, by its very nature, eliminates some titles that may be favorites of the authors and readers alike. We have chosen to omit information about books or series of books that have already received copious publicity. Most educators, parents, and youth are already saturated with information about these stories.

There are few joys that compare with introducing a child or adolescent to a book that may change his or her life. With the current aggressive marketing of juvenile books, more adults are also discovering the pleasure of reading and collecting stories originally intended for a younger audience.

We believe that *Core Collection for Children and Young Adults* will provide concise, readable guidance for fans of all ages.

CHAPTER ONE

Classic Books

By definition, classic books are those that have endured. They have remained in print from one generation to the next, proving themselves to be
relevant and rewarding to those who read them. They touch on themes important to young people, such as the desire for independence versus the need
for the love and approval of others, or the pull of fantasy versus the restric-
tions of reality. At the same time, these titles display variety, originality, and
careful craftsmanship. This excellence of expression has gained classic titles
the approval of adults as well as children. Their appeal never seems to fade,
for readers are often drawn back to revisit them at later ages. The pleasant
memories they evoke encourage adults to share their enthusiasm for special
tales with children, thus ensuring the continuation of the titles' popularity.

Classic books strengthen the spirits of those who read them. They effectively draw the reader into the lives of the characters so that they share the
feelings, the struggles, and the victories portrayed. They are written well
enough to challenge the reader intellectually and spiritually, and can exert
great influence on the lives of those who partake of their pages. Yearly, there
are many excellent titles published for young people. Some of these may
eventually make their way onto the illustrious lists of works that have earned
the right to be called "classic," but often their themes lie in the reality that
children see around them every day. Reading the classics affords the young
person a broader, richer perspective, illustrating to them that the struggles
and joys of the human spirit are the same from generation to generation.

Alcott, Louisa May, *Eight Cousins*. Puffin Classics, 1995 (orig. 1875). ISBN: 0140374566 (paperback) (Grades 7–10)
When young Rose Campbell is left an orphan after her father's death, she is pale, shy, and frail. Moving to "Aunt Hill," which is home to her six aunts and seven active boy cousins, is somewhat intimidating for the young teen. Into this mix dashes her new guardian, Uncle Alex, who wishes to try an experiment for one year with the health and well-being of the orphan. Dr. Alex prescribes fresh air, no regular school, play with the seven lively lads, and milk to drink. This is the story of that year and the metamorphosis not only of Rose, but of her cousins, her maid Phebe, and Uncle Alex, as well. Dire predictions of some of the aunts are found to be groundless, and readers will almost feel their own cheeks blossom as the delightful tale of Rose and her relatives unfolds. Alcott's story continues in the sequel, *Rose in Bloom*.
Related Subjects: 1800s, Family—Nontraditional, Family—Relationships, Orphans
Character Themes: Joy, Kindness, Love, Sharing, Unity

Bailey, Carolyn Sherwin, *Miss Hickory*. Lithographs by Ruth Gannett. Viking Press, 1974 (orig. 1946). ISBN: 0670479403 (hardcover) (Grades 3–6)
Created with a hickory-nut head and an apple-twig body, diminutive Miss Hickory is a diligent housekeeper, and competent provider, who is completely content in her tiny corncob house. Upheaval comes to her snug little world when the family who gave her birth moves away from the New Hampshire countryside to Boston for the school year so that daughter Ann can attend school. Left alone, and feeling bereft, the brave little doll is befriended by Crow, and Mr. T. Willard-Brown, the barn cat. Independence and ingenuity, with just a bit of help from others, gives Miss Hickory the edge she needs to survive the winter. Readers are entertained by her antics and those of other animals, while learning about seasons, habitats, and natural adaptation. Although the end is a bit shocking, it is realistic and symbolically beautiful. A natural companion book to this volume would be Robert Lawson's *Rabbit Hill*.
Related Subjects: Dolls, Friendship, Habitats, New England, New Hampshire
Character Themes: Adaptation, Cooperation, Ingenuity, Survival

Brown, Margaret Wise, *The Runaway Bunny*. Illustrated by Clement Hurd. HarperCollins, 1942. ISBN: 0061074292 (board book) (Grades PreK–3)
When little bunny decides to run away from home, he calmly announces his plans to his mother. With gentle creativity, Mother Bunny advises her ad-

venturous son that wherever he goes and whatever he becomes, she will be there ahead of him to offer security and protection. The furry little prodigal-to-be eventually makes the wise decision and the story concludes with love and a carrot. Brown's sparse text serves as a cliff-hanger to keep the pages turning. Clement Hurd's bright full-page color illustrations alternate with expressive black-and-white drawings enhancing the joy of the journey. This board book edition offers the thrill of ownership for the very young audience. The story offers peace and a smile to readers and listeners of all ages.

Related Subjects: Adventure, Fantasy, Rabbits, Runaways

Character Themes: Family love, Imagination, Joy, Love—Maternal

Carlson, Natalie Savage, *The Family Under the Bridge*. Illustrated by Garth Williams. HarperCollins, 2007 (orig. 1958). ISBN: 0060209917 (hardcover) (Grades 3–6)

Armand, the hobo, lives a carefree life in Paris. Having made a home under one of the many bridges along the river, and with few possessions to his name, he has no rent to pay and no need to seek work. One day, as he approaches the bridge where he lives, he is horrified to find three young children huddled in his space. Guarding against the demands of love, he wants only to see these intruders gone, but the children's obvious need and their open trust overcome his reluctance to share his life with others. Slowly, the idea of working to support his adopted family seems less distasteful as the children and their mother fill a larger portion of his formerly empty heart.

Related Subjects: Death of parent, Family—Single parent, Gypsies, Homelessness, Paris

Character Themes: Family love, Giving, Ingenuity, Responsibility, Unselfishness, Work ethic

Craik, Dinah Maria Mulock, *The Little Lame Prince and His Travelling Cloak*. Buccaneer Books, 1991 (orig. 1875). ISBN: 0899667627 (hardcover) (Grades 5–9)

Locked up in a lonely tower after his uncle has usurped the throne of Nomansland, the lame Prince Dolor sees only the woman known to him as Nurse. As he grows, so does his desire for more companionship. One day as he is wishing aloud for a friend, a little gray lady appears in his room. Her gifts to him include a cloak that can take him across the country like a magic carpet, spectacles which show him faraway objects, and silver ears through which he can hear distant sounds. In his adventures on his wonderful cloak, he learns much about his country and the troubles of the people. Finally restored to his rightful throne, Prince Dolor uses the understanding he has gained through his travels to rule with wisdom and kindness.

Related Subjects: Orphans, Overcoming adversity, Special needs—Physical disabilities
Character Themes: Empathy, Generosity, Wisdom

Estes, Eleanor (author and illustrator), *Ginger Pye*. An Odyssey/Harcourt Brace Young Classic, 2000 (orig. 1951). ISBN: 0152025057 (paperback) (Grades 3–6)
Jerry Pye wants a little yellow puppy more than anything and both sister Rachel and small Uncle Benny agree to help Jerry earn enough money to get exactly the dog he desires. The entire Pye family falls in love with Ginger, from the day he joins the family. All goes well, even with Gracie-the-cat, until Thanksgiving Day when the beloved pet disappears. Searching brings no results although there is a mysterious suspect who has only been seen by his or her yellow hat. All ends well as patience, diligence, hope, and collective sleuthing earn their reward.
Related Subjects: 1940s, Dogs, Pets
Character Themes: Diligence, Hope, Humor

Estes, Eleanor (author and illustrator), *The Moffats*. Harcourt, 1941. ISBN: 0152025413 (paperback) (Grades 4–6)
The Sixtieth Anniversary Edition of this beloved story will be enjoyed by the twenty-first-century audience just as surely as it was by their parents or grandparents. Widowed Mrs. Moffat's struggles with budget and the dual roles of parenting demonstrate timeless issues with which adult readers as well as children will identify. Introspective little Janey, the narrator, tells of the antics of her siblings, young Rufus, active Joe, and accomplished Sylvie. The Moffats' travels by foot, sled, or horse and carriage seem just as adventurous to contemporary readers as travel by modern skating. Neighbors are kindly or cranky; peers are staunch friends or annoying pests—relationships that do not vary with time. Although vocabulary is a bit elevated when compared with contemporary texts, young readers should be able to rise to the occasion with good humor. Runaway kindergartners, a real live ghost, and a near head-on trolley collision create action throughout this nostalgic delight.
Related Subjects: 1940s, Family—Single parent
Character Themes: Cooperation, Family love, Ingenuity, Loyalty

Forbes, Kathryn, *Mama's Bank Account*. Harcourt, Brace & World, 1943. Harvest/HBJ, 1968. ISBN: 0156563770 (hardcover) (Grades 6–12)
Warm family love and unity fill the pages of Kathryn Forbes's classic tale of Norwegian immigrants making a place for themselves in America in the

early 1900s. Facing financial crisis, sickness, and the needs of her children with unflagging determination, Mama's ingenious solutions sometimes place the family in humorous situations. Her honesty and loyalty to others is an example for all to follow whether young or old. This little gem is as relevant today as when it was first written.

Related Subjects: 1900s, Family, Immigration—Norwegian, Norwegian-Americans, San Francisco

Character Themes: Courage, Family love, Humor, Ingenuity

Gruelle, Johnny (author and illustrator), *Raggedy Ann Stories*. Simon & Schuster Books for Young Readers, 1993 (orig. 1918). ISBN: 0027375854 (hardcover) (Grades PreK–3)

Since their creation in the early 1900s, Raggedy Ann and Raggedy Andy have achieved icon status in the world of American toys. This collection of stories is a reprinting of the first tales told, with authentic dialogue and illustrations. In these pages, Ann establishes her reputation as the wisest of nursery toys solving problems in her head stuffed with cotton, guided by her heart full of love. Adventures include the French doll, Uncle Clem the Scottish doll, Fido the real live dog, and other beloved toys. Young Marcella, the "Mama," narrowly misses discovering that her toys come to life the minute adventure calls and no humans are around to see. Finding a happy lesson in every difficulty, Ann becomes the role model for the nursery toys as well as for young readers. More than ninety years old, Ann has gained fans from all over the world with her stories of cooperation, adventure, diversity, and general goodwill for all.

Related Subjects: Childhood, Diversity, Dolls, Exploring, Friendship, Toys

Character Themes: Boldness, Friendliness, Humor, Joy, Spunk, Survival

Kastner, Erich, *Emil and the Detectives*. Scholastic, 1985 (orig. 1930). ISBN: 0590405713 (paperback) (Grades 4–8)

When Emil's mother sends him to Berlin with a large sum of money for his grandmother, he pins the money to the inside of his jacket as a precaution. But when he falls asleep on the train, his seatmate, Herr Grundeis, steals the money and escapes. Waking up, Emil determines to find this man and reclaim his stolen goods. Befriended by a local boy who gathers his friends to help, Emil and the children create a plan to confound the thief and see that justice is done. They lurk in the hotel where Grundeis is staying; they stand by the phone to forward reports of his whereabouts; and finally they overcome him with sheer force of numbers. Mystery, intrigue, chase scenes, likeable characters, and the hero-gets-the-reward ending make this a classic to read and reread.

Related Subjects: Friendship, Germany, Mysteries, Problem solving
Character Themes: Cooperation, Determination, Humor, Teamwork

Keene, Carolyn, *The Secret of the Old Clock.* **Grosset & Dunlap, 1987 (orig. 1930). ISBN: 0448095017 (hardcover) (Grades 5–9)**
This account of Nancy Drew and her sleuthing skills is the first in the series of mystery stories that spans several generations. Nancy is introduced to her audience as an unaffected socialite who is always concerned about the welfare of others. The young detective is snubbed and insulted by her peers, the Topham sisters, who have fallen into wealth as a result of the death of a lonely old man, Josiah Crowley. Both Nancy and her lawyer father believe that the windfall is illegal, and that another more recent will exists that provides for the bounteous inheritance to be shared with several needy relatives. With her trademark determination and courage, Nancy sets out to find the document which she believes to be hidden in a family heirloom, the mantle clock. Adventure, logic, resourcefulness, and humor await readers as they meet this traditionally famous teenage investigator.
Related Subjects: Adventure, Friendship, Mysteries
Character Themes: Cleverness, Courage, Generosity, Resourcefulness

Kingsley, Charles, *The Water Babies* **(abridged). Puffin Books, 1994 (orig. 1863). ISBN: 0140367365 (paperback) (Grades 6–12)**
When an ill-treated young chimney sweep, Tom, enters the great Harthover Hall, he has no way of knowing that his entire life is about to be transformed. Mistaken for a thief, and chased by nearly everyone who can run, little Tom is pursued to the limit of his endurance and seeks the water as a refuge. Immediately, Tom takes the form of a water baby, and it is then that his real adventures begin. Author Charles Kingsley uses the medium of story to teach lessons of tolerance, forgiveness, courage, and transformation. This classic tale has offered pleasure and self-examination for generations of readers, and its timeless truths still touch the hearts of the twenty-first-century audience.
Related Subjects: Adventure, England, Sea, Victorian era
Character Themes: Courage, Forgiveness, Humility, Purity

Kipling, Rudyard, *The Jungle Book.* **Tor Books, 1992 (orig. 1893). ISBN: 0812504690 (paperback) (Grades 5–9)**
Although best known for its tale of the child Mowgli, who was raised in the jungle by wolves, a black panther, and a bear, *The Jungle Book* is really a collection of several stories written about the country of India. The most popular of these tales, besides the story of Mowgli, are *Rikki-Tikki-Tavi* and *Toomai*

of the Elephants. Rikki-Tikki-Tavi is a mongoose who saves his family from the evil cobras Nag and Nagaina. Toomai is a young elephant handler who is granted a privilege that few men ever see when he views the legendary elephants' dance. These stories have remained popular not only for their great adventure set in exotic places, but also for the moral lessons buried within.
Related Subjects: Elephants, Feral children, India, Mongooses
Character Themes: Courage, Loyalty

Lang, Andrew (editor), *The Red Fairy Book*. Illustrated by H. J. Ford and Lancelot Speed, Dover, 1996 (orig. 1890). ISBN: 048621673X (paperback) (Grades 7–12)
This volume represents the enormously popular retelling of folktales from around the world in the series entitled *The Rainbow Fairy Stories*. Collected and refurbished by Andrew Lang and his wife in the late 1800s, these classics house most of the fairy tales beloved by contemporary readers. *The Red Fairy Book* contains thirty-seven stories from French, German, Danish, Russian, Romanian, and Norse sources. Dover Publications has brought these wellsprings of entertainment and culture to contemporary readers in unabridged form, with original illustrations and sturdy bindings. Familiar tales including "Jack in the Beanstalk," "Rapunzel," and "The Twelve Dancing Princesses" are joined by such lesser-known stories as "Kari Woodengown" (a Scandinavian Cinderella story), "The Three Princesses of Whiteland," and "The True History of Little Goldenhood" (a variation of "Little Red Riding Hood"), among others. This particular volume is reported to have been a favorite of J. R. R. Tolkien.
Related Subjects: Folk literature, Heroes, Storytelling
Character Themes: Courage, Love, Loyalty, Perseverance

Latham, Jean Lee, *Carry On, Mr. Bowditch*. Illustrated by John O'Hara Cosgrave II. Houghton Mifflin, 1955. ISBN: 0618250743 (paperback) (Grades 7–12)
American children from poor families had little opportunity for advancement in social class or worldly goods in the 1770s. Nathaniel Bowditch had fewer advantages than many. Being bereft of his mother at age twelve, and having a father who never really recovered his joy of life after losing his ship at sea, Nat had little to look forward to as an indentured servant. However, resilient and intelligent, young Bowditch was possessed with a passion for math and used its logic to reason himself into the wide world of education, sailing, and discovery. With minimal education but gracious masters, Nat earned a reputation for efficiency and bold adventurousness, eventually

being awarded a Master of Arts by Harvard University for his brilliant contributions to math and oceanography. This biography, though it reads like a
novel, will inspire contemporary readers to follow their dreams and believe
in their talents and abilities, regardless of social status or wealth.

Related Subjects: Adventures, Indenture, Mathematics, Nathaniel
Bowditch, Sailing, Sea

Character Themes: Adventure, Cleverness, Discipline, Family love, Inspiration, Knowledge, Resilience

**Lawson, Robert (author and illustrator), *Rabbit Hill*. Puffin Books, 1977
(orig. 1944). ISBN: 014031010X (paperback) (Grades 1–4)**
When the little animals on The Hill hear that New Folks are coming to the
Big House, they are all aflutter. Questions and dire predictions fly thick and
fast among rabbits, moles, skunks, deer, and mice. Whether the humans will
have dogs or cats, and whether they will plant a garden or put out traps are
issues holding great significance among the wild and inquisitive animals that
populate the woods and fields. As a repairman and a landscaper begin to
make changes in the house and yard, the animals are encouraged about the
kind of New Folks who are coming to live on their hill. This fantasy story
that places the child reader right alongside Little Georgie, the adventurous
bunny, and Phewie, the skunk, encourages care of the environment while offering memorable entertainment.

Related Subjects: Ecology, Nature, Rabbits, Wildlife

Character Themes: Compassion, Cooperation, Humor

**Lenski, Lois (author and illustrator), *Blueberry Corners*. J. B. Lippincott
Co., 1940. No ISBN. (hardcover) (Grades 5–8)**
Lois Lenski narrates and illustrates the lives of Becky Griswold and her seven
brothers and sisters as they share the adventures of village life in the mid-
1800s. Poverty is their constant companion as each wears hand-me-downs
and enjoys meager, though adequate, fare at mealtime. Being children of the
parson has its own special joys and hardships, especially when their father op-
poses almost all forms of entertainment that their friends enjoy. However,
Aunt Leteshy, Great-Aunt Mehitable, and even a prissy little rich girl, Julie
Ann Janeway, help to share the circus, personal wealth, and the first-ever-
celebrated Christmas with the Griswolds. This warmhearted classic expresses
values that will reach across the generations and touch contemporary readers just as it did their parents, or even grandparents. Themes of family unity,
generosity, sharing, and thrift are as significant to current audiences as to
those of the past.

Related Subjects: 1800s, Connecticut, Family, Villages
Character Themes: Family loyalty, Generosity, Sharing, Thrift

Lewis, C. S., *Out of the Silent Planet.* Scribner Paperback Fiction/Simon
& Schuster, 1996 (orig. 1938). ISBN: 0684823802 (paperback) (Grades
10–12)
When philologist and Cambridge scholar Dr. Ransom is kidnapped by an old
school adversary, he is forced to embark on an outer-space adventure. He
dares not hope that he will ever arrive back home in England. Armed with a
spirit of adventure, Ransom is teachable, intelligent, and has a knack for
learning new languages. Each talent or character trait proves invaluable when
he finds himself in a completely alien culture. Having escaped his human cap-
tors, who hoped to offer him as a sacrifice to appease the "gods" of the planet,
the lone adventurer forges ahead with nothing but wit and determination as
guides. As Ransom ventures deeper into unknown territory, he learns to communicate with three diverse native populations. Eventually, he even comes to
recognize that Earth's culture may be more savage than that of the alien. This
is the first volume of the Space Trilogy and introduces themes that will keep
the science fiction fan enthralled throughout the series.
Related Subjects: Science fiction, Space travel
Character Themes: Courage, Honor, Respect

Lewis, C. S., *The Voyage of the Dawn Treader.* Illustrated by Pauline
Baynes. HarperTrophy, 2000 (orig. 1952). ISBN: 0064471071 (paper-
back) (Grades 6–12)
Lucy and Edmund Pevensie, brother and sister first introduced to readers in
The Lion, The Witch, and The Wardrobe, are visiting their detestable cousin,
Eustace Scrubb, when the magic of Narnia literally draws all three children
into a sea journey of epic proportions. Edmund and Lucy revisit their
friends Prince Caspian and Reepicheep the valiant warrior mouse, as they
become valuable crew members of the seaworthy vessel the *Dawn Treader.*
Eustace, spoiled, skeptical, and cynical at first, discovers the power of
Aslan's magic as he embarks on his own journey of self-discovery. Caspian's
quest is to find seven lords who were friends of his father and he is determined to solve the mystery of their fates as he moves into uncharted waters. Reepicheep eagerly awaits his own passage into Aslan's country. This
fifth volume of *The Chronicles of Narnia* is a classic quest story with enduring truths awaiting all readers.
Related Subjects: Adventure, Friendship, Quests, Sea, Voyages
Character Themes: Cooperation, Courage, Faith, Honor, Loyalty

Lovelace, Maud Hart, *Betsy-Tacy*. Illustrated by Lois Lenski. HarperTrophy/ HarperCollins, 1940. ISBN: 0064400964 (paperback) (Grades K–4)

Betsy and Tacy can hardly remember a time when they were not best friends. They spend so much time together that neighbors begin to think of them as a unit, Betsy-Tacy. In a setting where children can freely roam streets and fields without adult supervision, Lovelace writes of adventures that are fun while still safe. The two little girls go to school together the first day, take picnics alone, ride with the milkman, and even create a business venture in partnership. Without electricity, without cars, without indoor plumbing, the stories still bristle with activity and humor. The timeless themes of loyalty, adventure, compromise, and simple fun have appeal for the twenty-first-century audience, as well as to parents and grandparents who may read the chapters aloud to the younger listeners. This is the first in a series that later adds Tib, a third member of the close-knit little group.

Related Subjects: 1940s, Family, Friendship
Character Themes: Humor, Sharing

McCloskey, Robert (author and illustrator), *Blueberries for Sal*. Viking Press, 1948. ISBN: 0670175919 (hardcover) (Grades K–2)

When Sal goes berry picking with her mother, she becomes absorbed in discovering and eating the tasty fruit. Suddenly she finds herself following behind a mother bear instead of her parent. A baby bear does the same and is soon following after Sal's mother instead of his own. All comes right in the end as mothers and children reunite. Although the blue-and-white illustrations place the story in the time period when it was written, their charm will capture contemporary children's hearts. Science topics introduced include hibernation and geography. Some explanation of what it means to be canning fruit may be needed but overall the tale has timeless appeal.

Related Subjects: Bears, Food, Geography, Hibernation, Maine, Mother-daughter relationships, Parents
Character Themes: Curiosity, Family love, Humor

Menotti, Gian Carlo, *Amahl and the Night Visitors*. Illustrated by Michele Lemieux. HarperCollins, 1986 (orig. 1951). ISBN: 0688054269 (hardcover) (Grades 7–12)

Amahl's body is slowed by crippled legs, but his imagination knows no such limitations. Used to his fantastic tales, Amahl's impoverished mother initially discounts his claims that there are three kings standing at their door. As she sees they are real, and offers them hospitality in her humble home,

she struggles with jealousy over the riches being taken to this unknown child they seek. When Amahl makes the ultimate sacrifice, mother and son experience a miracle beyond their deepest hopes. This poignant story has become a Christmas classic alongside *The Gift of the Magi* and *A Christmas Carol*.
Related Subjects: Christmas, Miracles, Opera, Poverty, Special needs—Physical disabilities
Character Themes: Faith, Family love, Religious faith, Sacrifice

Montgomery, L. M., *Emily of New Moon*. Bantam Books, 1993 (orig. 1923). ISBN: 055323370X (paperback) (Grades 6–12)
Although her father tells Emily on his deathbed that she was a "child of . . . happiness," the little orphan finds it difficult to live at her new home at New Moon farm without him. Her stiff, stern Aunt Elizabeth is difficult to please, but childlike Uncle Jimmy and gentle Aunt Laura make life almost pleasant at New Moon. As Emily falls in love with her new home, special school friends enter her world: wild-hearted Ilse, intensely loyal Perry, and gentle Teddy. The foursome unites to bring adventures never expected to New Moon. This is the first book in the Emily trilogy, and readers may want to have the sequel, *Emily Climbs*, available to begin when the last page of this book is completed. Although not as well known as the indomitable redhead of *Anne of Green Gables* fame, Emily is every bit as winsome in her own way.
Related Subjects: Canada, Creative writing, Friendship, Orphans, Prince Edward Island
Character Themes: Creativity, Hope, Humor, Talent

Moody, Ralph, *Little Britches: Father and I Were Ranchers*. University of Nebraska Press, 1991 (orig. 1950). ISBN: 0803281781 (paperback) (Grades 5–9)
When Ralph's father becomes ill, the family moves west to settle on a rented ranch in Colorado. Together they face windstorms, wild horses, and wars over water. However, with hard work and ingenuity, they manage to eat well, send the children to school, and live in dignity and honor. The writing style is simple, but the straightforward messages it conveys about character building are ageless. Ralph is a tough, brave young man who finds himself in many hilarious situations. This autobiographical adventure presents a true portrait of life in the West in the early 1900s.
Related Subjects: 1900s, Colorado, Death—Parent, Frontier and pioneer life, Ranching
Character Themes: Courage, Family love, Honesty, Ingenuity, Work ethic

Selden, George, *The Cricket in Times Square*. Illustrated by Garth Williams. Yearling, 1970 (orig. 1960). ISBN: 0440415632 (paperback) (Grades 3–8)

Accidentally transported to New York City in a picnic basket, a tiny Connecticut cricket named Chester is found by a young boy whose parents operate a struggling newsstand at the Times Square subway station. Befriended by two other denizens of the subway tunnels, namely Tucker the mouse and Harry the cat, Chester experiences many adventures. Their schemes cause near disaster to the Bellinis, but in the end bring new success to the nearly bankrupt family. This fanciful tale of friendship between a cricket, a mouse, and a cat, with delightful illustrations by Garth Williams, will enchant young readers.
Related Subjects: Cats, Crickets, Friendship, Mice, New York City, Subways
Character Themes: Giving, Sacrifice

Seuss, Dr. (author and illustrator), *Horton Hears a Who*. Random House, 1954. ISBN: 0394800788 (hardcover) (Grades K–4)

Hearing a very small voice as he is bathing one day changes the perspective and life of Horton the elephant. Immediately, Horton becomes the champion of the very small, nearly invisible, inhabitants of Whoville, facing down his peers, even when they become aggressive and abusive to the gentle giant. His mantra, "A person's a person no matter how small," is recited repeatedly to the unbelievers as Horton endures injustices for the sake of those too small to defend themselves. Eventually, right prevails, and all have learned important, though harrowing, lessons. The theme has myriad meanings among any who are different or disenfranchised.
Related Subjects: Adoption, Elephants, Social issues, Special needs—Children
Character Themes: Courage, Diligence, Loyalty

Sewell, Anna, *Black Beauty*. Children's Classics, 1998 (orig. 1877). ISBN: 0517189585 (hardcover) (Grades 3–9)

Born in nineteenth-century England, Black Beauty begins life in pleasant surroundings, spending much of her early years as a riding and carriage horse. When circumstances force her to be sold, Beauty finds herself pulling a town cab, where she begins to experience the abusive treatment afforded many horses during the turn of the century. Sold to masters both kind and cruel, her life is filled with adventure and memorable friends such as Ginger the horse and Jerry the cabbie. Forthright in its description of the maltreatment suffered by this beautiful animal, *Black Beauty* nevertheless remains a strong voice for kindness and caring for those who cannot care for themselves.

Related Subjects: 1800s, Abuse—Animal, England, Horses
Character Themes: Kindness, Love—Pets

Sidney, Margaret, *Five Little Peppers and How They Grew.* **Illustrated by William Sharp. Grosset & Dunlap, 1963 (orig. 1948). ISBN: 0448054590 (hardcover) (Grades 4–6)**
Adversity seems to bring out the best in these spirited children as they help support their widowed mother. Ben does odd jobs for neighbors while Polly battles with the old wood stove to prepare meals for the little family. Together these older siblings watch over the younger Joel, Davie, and Phronsie, until a bout with the measles puts them in bed and threatens Polly's eyesight. Friends and neighbors lend invaluable aid, and a new friend, Jasper King, enriches their lives and brings unexpected benefits to these adventurous children.
Related Subjects: 1900s, Family—Single parent, Illness, Poverty, Pride, Siblings
Character Themes: Family love, Ingenuity, Overcoming adversity, Resilience, Responsibility, Spunk

Steinbeck John, *The Red Pony.* **Illustrated by Wesley Dennis. Viking Press, 1966 (orig. 1937). ISBN: 067059184X (hardcover) (Grades 7–12)**
When he is ten years old, Jody Tiflin is given a beautiful red pony by his rather stern father. With the guidance of Billy Buck, the hired man, Jody spends all his spare time caring for and training his beloved horse, which he has named Gabilan. As his expertise and his friendship with the horse grows, so does Jody's self-confidence. One day Gabilan is left outside the barn and is caught in an unexpected rainstorm. He catches cold and despite the careful ministrations of Billy Buck and his young owner, he does not recover. This is just one of the challenging situations that Jody must face in this poignant coming-of-age story. The black-and-white illustrations of Wesley Dennis in this 1963 edition capture the essence of Steinbeck's tale of love and loss.
Related Subjects: Death, Father-son relationships, Grief, Horses, Ranching
Character Themes: Compassion, Discipline, Friendship, Love—Pets, Responsibility, Self-acceptance

Streatfeild, Noel, *Theater Shoes.* **Yearling, 2003 (orig. 1945), 1945. ISBN: 0679854347 (paperback) (Grades 5–8)**
Sorrel, Mark, and Holly Forbes are living with their rather emotionally distant grandfather while their father is engaged in the Navy. They are virtual orphans since their mother has been deceased for some time. Suddenly,

Grandfather dies and the children are whisked off to live with a grandmother they have never met, who is completely engrossed in her role as a formerly famous actress. Upon arrival at the large, though poorly furnished house, Sorrel, Mark, and Holly discover that all three of them are to be trained in the fine arts of drama, dance, and music, fields which are completely foreign to them. As each child finds his or her talent, meets new family members, and learns to scrimp through the rationing of World War II, young readers will also learn timeless lessons. Told largely from Sorrel's point of view, the story reveals the wonders of the wartime theater, the rigors of study and opening nights, and the thrill of each new triumph of the spirited Forbes children. This title is volume two in the classic *Shoes* series.

Related Subjects: England, Orphans, Theater, World War II
Character Themes: Cooperation, Diligence, Family loyalty, Independence, Respect for authority, Thrift

Tolkien, J. R. R., *The Fellowship of the Ring: Being the First Part of the Lord of the Rings.* **Houghton Mifflin, 1954. ISBN: 0618129030 (paperback) (Grades 6–12)**
Upon receiving the ring of power from his cousin, Bilbo, hobbit Frodo Baggins sets out on a quest to save the Shire from the power of Dark Lord, Sauron. At the beginning of his trek, only Merry, Pippin, and faithful Sam accompany Frodo. As they step further and further into danger, the little men are joined by wise Gandalf, brave Aragorn, sure-shot Legolas, testy but tough Gimli, and experienced warrior Boromir. Together, the varied party forms the Fellowship, with the goal of protecting Frodo as he carries the ring to its destruction. This initial installment of *The Lord of the Rings* has the distinction of introducing readers to heroes and villains that make this story of good versus evil the internationally acclaimed epic it has become. Richly layered in meaning and symbolism, this timeless tale lingers in the memory long after the last page is turned, whetting the appetite for the remaining volumes of the trilogy.

Related Subjects: Adventure, Fantasy, Heroes, Loneliness, Quests
Character Themes: Cooperation, Courage, Diligence, Faithfulness, Friendship, Honesty, Teamwork

Travers, P. L., *Mary Poppins.* **Illustrated by Mary Shepard. Harcourt, 1981 (orig. 1934). ISBN: 0152017178 (paperback) (Grades 3–6)**
Mary Poppins is a nanny like no other. Blowing in on a strong wind, she arrives at Number 17 Cherry Tree Lane in London to take over the care of the Banks children. Mary is stern, a bit vain, and always mysterious, but nothing is ever ordinary when she is around. Laughter makes tables set for tea float in

the air, zoo animals talk when the moon is full, and stars come Christmas shopping in the department store. With all the fantastic adventures, Mary brings order and security to Jane, Michael, and the twins, and though they remain a bit awed of her, they are truly sad when the wind changes and Mary must take her leave. Seven other titles continue the stories about this remarkable character.
Related Subjects: Fantasy, London, Nannies
Character Themes: Adventure, Humor

Twain, Mark, *The Adventures of Huckleberry Finn*. Illustrated by Richard Lauter. Adapted by Suzanne McCabe. Modern Publishing, 1999 (orig. 1884). ISBN: 0766607208 (hardcover) (Grades 4–8)
Abandoned Huckleberry Finn is adopted by the widow Douglas, who plans to educate the waif. When his abusive father suddenly appears and abducts him, the young adventurer decides that enough is enough. He wants neither "civilizing" nor beating, so he runs away and fakes his own death. While hiding on a deserted island, Huckleberry finds Jim, the runaway slave of Miss Watson. The two become fast friends and have many adventures as they join the Mississippi moving southward. Although Huck loves Jim, he is torn by a conflict of conscience and culture knowing that the black man is a runaway and assisting him is illegal. This volume is one of the Treasury of Illustrated Classics and has the advantage of brevity, while retaining the mood of Twain's text. Also missing are the racial epithets that will cause pain for African-Americans listening to or reading the story.
Related Subjects: 1800s, Abuse—Child, Adventure, Prejudice, Slavery
Character Themes: Courage, Friendship, Humor, Loyalty

Warner, Gertrude Chandler, *The Boxcar Children*. Illustrated by Kate Deal. A. Whitman, 1977 (orig. 1942). ISBN: 0807508527 (paperback) (Grades 4–8)
Jessie, Benny, Henry, and Violet are running away from a grandfather that they fear, but have yet to meet. All they know is that he did not like their deceased mother; therefore, the children do not like him. Hiding from all authority figures, the four fugitives find an abandoned train car, and ingeniously outfit it for survival, of sorts. Henry manages to secure a part-time job, and all is well until Violet becomes very ill. The resolution of the adventure is more than satisfactory, and leads on to many other stories of these youngsters, now loved by generations of readers. Courage, humor, and creativity are presented in easily read, page-turning format.
Related Subjects: Orphans, Survival

Character Themes: Cooperation, Family loyalty, Ingenuity, Love

Wiggin, Kate Douglas, *Rebecca of Sunny Brook Farm*. Illustrated by Peter Fiore. Children's Classics/Dilithium Press, 1993. ISBN: 0517092751 (hardcover) (Grades 6–10)

As ten-year-old Rebecca Rowena Randall's mother puts her on the stagecoach to send her to live with her spinster aunts, she observes, "Mirandy will have her hands full but I shouldn't wonder if it would be the making of Rebecca." During the next seven years, Rebecca is "made," by Aunt Miranda's rules, Aunt Jane's tenderness, and through her own integrity, intelligence, creativity, generosity, and wit. Lives of the aunts, as well as the entire community of Riverboro, Maine, are brightened by the sunny disposition and indomitable spirit of the dark-haired, part-Hispanic lass. This classic story has touched the hearts of millions of readers since the first publication in 1903, and was first immortalized by Shirley Temple in film—which, no doubt, would have scandalized Aunt Miranda, delighted Aunt Jane, and amazed Rebecca. For readers of the twenty-first century, Rebecca's spunk, enthusiasm for life, and desire to do what is right serve as much-needed inspiration, far outshining many role models readily available to contemporary children and young adults.

Related Subjects: 1900s, Family—Nontraditional, Maine, Prejudice

Character Themes: Creativity, Humor, Individuality, Respect

CHAPTER TWO

Contemporary Fiction

Writers of realistic fiction attempt to tell a story that entertains, while reflecting the everyday experiences of readers. They capture life in a way that causes the audience to become involved with the plot, and to feel as if the characters are, indeed, acquaintances. Writers of contemporary realistic fiction choose the current time for their setting, building a bridge of experience connecting reader and protagonist. Such cohesion has the potential to open doors to delight in reading, and thus create a lifelong reader.

Characters, themselves, face familiar challenges presented in daily life. Authors of children's realism differ in their approach to resolution of conflict. Some have the child tackle the conflict of the story and solve his or her own problems. Others create a bond between a caring adult and the young protagonist to bring about resolution as a team.

Contemporary realistic fiction covers a variety of subgenres. Domestic stories include both the traditional family with father, mother, and child, and a variety of nontraditional households of extended, single parent, surrogate, or foster families. Books about peer influence, both positive and negative, abound in the realistic genre. Cultural diversity introduces characters from a variety of ethnic or regional backgrounds, sometimes in family settings, sometimes as they attempt survival alone in harsh environments. Animal stories in realistic settings portray normal behavior as expected of the species in nature. Sports stories reflect conflicts faced by young people who value physical activity more highly than most other aspects of life, or for whom competition creates a challenge. Mysteries with modern settings also fall into the realistic genre, and have the extra bonus of encouraging reluctant readers to continue turning pages to the end of the book.

Realistic fiction may cover any topic that is a part of the experience of contemporary children and teens. Since this genre imitates life, awards given reflect the ability of an author to combine absorbing plots with the daily problems, joys, conflicts, and resulting growth of the protagonist. Some are humorous, some are profound, but all portray situations that might really happen just down the street. Since life often presents formidable odds to child and young adult readers, the best contemporary stories offer resolutions resounding with hope.

Bauer, Joan, *Backwater*. Putman, 1999. ISBN: 0399231412 (hardcover) (Grades 9–12)
Ivy Breedlove often feels isolated in her large, aggressive family and completely misunderstood by her father. For generations, lawyer has followed lawyer, but Ivy longs to become a historian, breaking with tradition. Her only kindred spirit, it seems, is Aunt Josephine, who has been missing from the family circle for years. Ivy is driven to find Aunt Jo to complete a personal genealogy as well as to gain a greater understanding of herself. A wilderness trek in the dead of winter, a devastating snowstorm, and a wolf help to reunite aunt and niece. Father and daughter also find common ground.
Awards: *Los Angeles Times* Book Prize, Society of School Librarians International Honor Book Award
Related Subjects: Father-daughter relationships, Genealogy, Storms—Snow
Character Themes: Courage, Individuality, Perseverance, Respect

Bauer, Joan, *Hope Was Here*. Putnam, 2002. ISBN: 0698119517 (paperback) (Grades 8-12)
Deserted at birth by her mother, Hope, a.k.a. "Tulip" as named by her mother, lives with her waitress aunt. All of her life, Hope has known the significance of work, integrity, and a sense of humor. Leaving New York City to work as waitresses in a small Wisconsin town has its special challenges. However, with Hope's practice of living up to her name, and the resilience of Aunt Addie, courage and success are achieved. The story includes layers of character-building insights and psychological survival techniques, and concludes with joy, yet not with a fairy-tale ending.
Awards: ALSC Notable Children's Book, ALA Best Book for Young Adults, Christopher Award, Newbery Honor, Young Reader's Choice Award (Pacific Northwest Library Association)
Related Subjects: Bibliotherapy, Cancer, Family—Single parent, Waitressing
Character Themes: Cooperation, Courage, Humor, Integrity, Joy, Survival

Bauer, Joan, *Rules of the Road.* **Puffin Books, 1998. ISBN: 0698118286 (paperback) (Grades 9–12)**
Summer has arrived and Jenna Boller is ready for a break from school. She prizes highly her newly acquired driver's license and her part-time job as shoe salesperson. However, the blight on her life is her errant father's alcoholism and the disappointment he always leaves in his wake. When chagrin over his disgusting drunken display of paternal interest intersects with Jenna's success in selling shoes, the surprising results change her life forever. "Vacation" takes on new meaning as Jenna sees much of the country from the driver's seat of a Cadillac while discovering her own untapped talents and strengths, despite her dysfunctional family.
Awards: ALA Best Book for Young Adults, BCCB Blue Ribbon Book, Golden Kite Award, Thumbs Up Award (Michigan)
Related Subjects: Alcoholism, Cross-generational relationships, Family—Dysfunctional, Teenage driving
Character Themes: Courage, Humor, Ingenuity, Resilience, Responsibility

Birdsall, Jeanne, *The Penderwicks.* **Knopf Books for Young Readers, 2005. ISBN: 0375831436 (hardcover) (Grades 4–8)**
When the Penderwick family, consisting of Father, four girls, and Hound, arrive at Arundel for their summer vacation, they fall in love with their cottage, but quickly fall out of the good graces of its owner. Mrs. Tifton, the wealthy matron, is the very antithesis of Mr. Penderwick and his lively daughters, and she has no desire to broaden her horizons. Furthermore, she is incensed at the effect she believes the fun-loving sisters are beginning to have on her son, Jeffrey. Mrs. Tifton's maternal solution is to pack Jeffrey off to a military school, but the girls have other ideas. This is a heartwarming story of adventure, misguided soccer balls, preteen crushes, and grieving family members helping each other to cope with the death of the wife and mother. Readers will love to hate, and love to love the memorable characters—including Hound.
Awards: National Book Award, *Publishers Weekly* Best Book of the Year, *School Library Journal* Best Book of the Year, Texas Bluebonnet Award
Related Subjects: Family—Single parent, Grief, Vacations
Character Themes: Cooperation, Family unity

Boyce, Frank Cottrell, *Framed.* **Macmillan Children's Books, 2006 (orig. 2005). ISBN: 0060734035 (hardcover) (Grades 4–6)**
Dylan Hughes is the only boy in his elementary school and the oldest son in his family. Both of these distinctive roles require survival skills of the highest social order. Dylan's passion for soccer, and for anything with an engine,

often go unfulfilled in his female-dominated culture. However, his assets of being both organized and creative stand him in good stead as he helps to keep the family garage running, especially after his dad leaves to find work in a larger city. Mystery and adventure find Dylan when carloads of strangers move to the top of the mountain outside the village of Manod and business begins to thrive at Snowdonia Oasis Auto Marvel. Stolen paintings, baby chickens, and a missing Mini Cooper provide wild adventures for Dylan and the entire wacky Hughes family. Subtle lessons about the power of art on those who least expect it are scattered throughout this humorous novel.

Awards: Manchester Book Award (UK), Whitbread Book Award: Children's Shortlist (UK)

Related Subjects: Art, Villages, Wales

Character Themes: Cooperation, Family loyalty, Humor, Ingenuity

Burnford, Sheila, *The Incredible Journey*. Illustrated by Carl Burger. Little, Brown & Co., 1960. No ISBN (hardcover) (Grades 5–8)

Trekking 250 miles across the Canadian wilderness to return home to their owners, three domestic animals encounter adventure, danger, and kindness in their fight to survive. Luath, a young Labrador retriever, Tao, a Siamese cat, and Bodger, a bull terrier, combine their instincts and abilities to protect each other from starvation, cold, flood, and wild animals. Together they demonstrate the value of mutual love and support.

Awards: Canadian Library Association Book of the Year, William Allen White Children's Book Award (Kansas), Young Reader's Choice Award (Pacific Northwest Library Association)

Related Subjects: Animals, Cats, Dogs, Pets, Survival, Wilderness

Character Themes: Cooperation, Determination, Friendship, Initiative, Loyalty

Byars, Betsy, *The Midnight Fox*. Puffin Books, 1968. ISBN: 0140314504 (paperback) (Grades 4–8)

With humor and sensitivity, Byars recounts the metamorphosis of city-dwelling, nine-year-old Tom, who goes practically kicking and screaming to spend two months in the country. While his parents are biking across Europe, Tom is sent to stay with his aunt, uncle, and overly dramatic teenage cousin on their farm. Leaving his best friend, Petie, behind in the city, Tom envisions himself compelled to rise before dawn to help with all kinds of farming feats, at which he will surely fail. Fearing change and disliking outdoor life, Tom holds little hope for anything pleasant during this interlude in his life. However, as the story opens, Tom shares with readers, in flashback, what he remembers about that summer five years ago, and the mysterious black fox that changed him forever. City and country dwellers alike will find Tom's journey with the fox intriguing and compelling.

Awards: Library of Congress Children's Book of the Year

Related Subjects: Animals, Family, Foxes, Rural life

Character Themes: Curiosity, Empathy, Observation, Respect for nature

X **Byars, Betsy, *Wanted . . . Mud Blossom*. Illustrated by Jacqueline Rogers. Dell Publishing Co., 1996. ISBN: 0440407613 (paperback) (Grades 3–7)**

Joy almost overwhelms him when Junior Blossom has the honor of taking home the class hamster, Scooty, for a weekend. To make the little pet feel comfortable, Junior creates a small private outdoor run for him. Trouble arises when Scooty vanishes and Pap's dog, Blossom, is found sniffing suspiciously at the scene of the disappearance. Nothing short of a trial to decide the fate of the presumed canine criminal will satisfy the family. For fans of the Blossom family series, this rollicking addition provides action from all of the favorite characters: Mad Mary, Vern and Michael, Maggie and Ralphie, Pap, and of course, Mud. This is one more Byars creation that is not to be missed.

Awards: ALSC Notable Children's Book, Edgar Award, Horn Book Fanfare Selection

Related Subjects: Dogs, Family—Single parent, Hamsters, Mysteries, Pets

Character Themes: Humor, Justice, Responsibility, Trust

Cleary, Beverly, *Ramona and Her Father*. Avon Camelot, 1975. ISBN: 0380709163 (paperback) (Grades 4–7)

As Christmas approaches, Ramona diligently creates an ambitious wish list. However, when her father loses his job, priorities, finances, and moods change. Even the cat, Picky-picky, must adjust to less expensive food that is not to his taste. With her usual hilarious practicality, Ramona sets about to solve everyone's problems, often creating more in the process. Young audiences will relate to the Ramona-sized crises of having to eat leftovers and not having her mother at her beck and call. There is also the question of what to do with a father who is home all day, smoking cigarettes. As is most appropriate, joy comes to Ramona's world just in the nick of Christmastime, and a realistically satisfying conclusion is enjoyed by all.

Awards: ALSC Notable Children's Book, Land of Enchantment Award (New Mexico), Newbery Honor, *School Library Journal* Best Book of the Year, Young Reader's Choice Award (Pacific Northwest Library Association)

Related Subjects: Family, Father-daughter relationships, Unemployment
Character Themes: Family love, Humor

Clements, Andrew, *Frindle.* **Illustrated by Brian Selznick. Simon & Schuster Children's Publishing, 1996. ISBN: 0689806698 (hardcover) (Grades 4–7)**
Nick Allen is the kind of student who always has perfect attendance, but his teachers may wish that he didn't. Not the smartest, not a troublemaker, Nick is just creative and charismatic enough to achieve a following that enables him to accomplish anything he chooses. In this case, he has chosen to call a pen a "frindle" because his fifth-grade teacher, Mrs. Granger, has said that "we, the people" create words. This quickly read novel highlights creativity, respect, challenge, and words, and is ultimately about . . . chess. Readers will not discern until the final pages just who has won the right to declare "Checkmate," and a more pleasing ending cannot be imagined. "Award-winning" seems to be an understatement, since this small jewel has garnered more than thirty honors.
Awards: Charlie May Simon Children's Book Award (Arkansas), North Carolina Children's Book Award, Prairie Pasque Award (South Dakota), Rebecca Caudill Young Readers Book Award (Illinois), Rhode Island Children's Book Award, Sasquatch Reading Award (Washington), William Allen White Children's Book Award (Kansas)
Related Subjects: Inventions, School, Teachers, Vocabulary
Character Themes: Creativity, Humor, Individuality, Leadership, Respect

Couloumbis, Audry, *Getting Near to Baby.* **G. P. Putnam's Sons, 1999. ISBN: 039923389X (hardcover) (Grades 8–12)**
Followed by Little Sister, Willa Jo climbs up to the roof of Aunt Patty's house, and despite everyone's coaxing cannot seem to make herself come down. Through flashbacks, the reader learns of Baby's death from drinking tainted water at the carnival and the resulting grief that has overwhelmed the family. Somehow the children feel that sitting on the roof will bring them nearer to the baby they have lost. Although she cares deeply, bossy, misguided Aunt Patty is unable to connect with the sorrowing girls. A cast of unlikely neighbors and sensible Uncle Hob lighten the mood and help to bring the girls to understanding and acceptance. In the end, they reconcile with their aunt, reunite with their mother, and find healing through their love for each other.
Awards: Newbery Honor
Related Subjects: Death, Family, Grief, Self-concept, Siblings
Character Themes: Forgiveness, Responsibility

Creech, Sharon, *Granny Torelli Makes Soup*. Illustrated by Chris Raschka. Scholastic, 2003. ISBN: 0439648750 (hardcover) (Grades 4–6)
This warm and funny tale dishes up just the right recipe to soothe the wounds that come from childhood arguments. Listening to Rosie's recital of disagreement with her best friend Bailey, Granny Torelli weaves in stories of her up-and-down relationship with Pardo from the old country. While creating wonderful dishes to please the palate, Granny dispenses just the right amount of wisdom in bite-sized pieces.
Awards: Sequoya Book Award (Oklahoma)
Related Subjects: Bibliotherapy, Cooking, Cross-generational relationships, Food, Literature
Character Themes: Friendship, Honesty, Humor

Creech, Sharon, *Walk Two Moons*. HarperCollins, 1994. ISBN: 0060233346 (hardcover) (Grades 7–12)
On a trip to Idaho with her grandparents, thirteen-year-old Salamanca Tree Hiddle spins a tale to keep them all entertained. Her story features Phoebe Winterbottom, whose mother has disappeared. As the journey and the story unfold, it becomes apparent that Salamanca's own life parallels that of her outrageous heroine. One day her mother left for Idaho, promising to return before the tulips bloomed. Salamanca hopes to reach their destination before her mother's birthday in order to bring her back home. Although Sal's journey does not accomplish the desired results, this young adolescent comes to terms with the truth about her mother and begins to understand herself. The story is humorous and poignant, with many unexpected plot twists.
Awards: Heartland Award, NCTE Notable Children's Books in the Language Arts, Newbery Medal, Sequoyah Book Award (Oklahoma)
Related Subjects: Abandonment, Cross-generational relationships, Death, Family, Idaho, Loss of parent, Native Americans
Character Themes: Family strength, Humor, Inventiveness, Self-image

Curtis, Christopher Paul, *The Watsons Go to Birmingham—1963*. Delacorte Press, 1995. ISBN: 0385321759 (hardcover) (Grades 6–12)
The title of this book does not prepare the reader for the humor nor for the tragic realities that infuse its pages. Told by ten-year-old Kenny, the story abounds in detail important to any fourth-grader. Those living in colder climates can relate to having part of their bodies frozen to metal or having their parents bundle them up in so many coats they can hardly walk. What sets the "Weird Watsons" apart is the love between the parents and the loyalty among family members. When Byron pushes the limits of his parents' tolerance too far, Mom and Dad head south to deliver him to the care of Grandma

Sands for the summer. The contrast between the hilarious family antics in Chicago and the racial hatred encountered in Birmingham give great emotional impact to the book. This book would pair well with *Through My Eyes* by Ruby Bridges.

Awards: ALA Best Book for Young Adults, California Young Readers Medal, Claudia Lewis Award, Coretta Scott King Award, Golden Kite Award, Newbery Honor

Related Subjects: Alabama, Cross-cultural relations, Grief, Siblings, Tolerance

Character Themes: Friendship, Humor, Responsibility, Self-acceptance

DiCamillo, Kate, *Because of Winn Dixie*. Scholastic, 2000. ISBN: 043925051X (paperback) (Grades 4–8)
When India Opal Buloni and her preacher father move to the Friendly Corners Trailer Park in Naomi, Florida, neither could possibly guess how much a stray dog will change their lives. Deserted by their wife and mother, both Opal and her dad are grieving privately, until a dog, named "Winn Dixie" by Opal, crashes into her heart and transforms the relationship of father and daughter. Summer in a small town is a tricky time to get to know new people, but Winn Dixie makes friends in his own way and almost literally drags his lonely little owner along. An ex-prisoner, an aristocratic but solitary librarian, a reclusive alcoholic, and assorted children enter the lives of Opal and her father before the summer ends, all because of Winn Dixie.

Awards: Blue Hen Book Award (Delaware), Golden Archer Award (Wisconsin), Indian Paintbrush Book (Wyoming), Maine Student Book Award, Mitten Award (Michigan), Newbery Honor, West Virginia Children's Book Award

Related Subjects: Alcoholism, Dogs, Family—Single parent, Father-daughter relationships

Character Themes: Acceptance, Friendliness, Humor, Tolerance

Ellis, Deborah, *The Breadwinner: An Afghan Child in a War Torn Land*. Scholastic, 2000. ISBN: 0439446333 (paperback) (Grades 6–9)
Parvana's family lives in Kabul in a bombed-out apartment building. Her father, once a history teacher, makes his living from a blanket in the marketplace reading letters and documents for people who do not know how to read or write. When he is arrested for the crime of having a foreign education, there is no one to provide an income for the family. Filling the gap by disguising herself as a boy, Parvana takes her father's place in the market reading and selling the few special possessions they had been able to save. While

Parvana works, her mother secretly holds classes for girls and writes for an underground newspaper to tell of the cruelty suffered at the hands of the Taliban. There is danger and adventure in this story based on stories heard in the Afghan refugee camps, and some graphic description.

Awards: Hackmatack Children's Choice Award (Canada), Jane Addams Children's Book Award, Manitoba Young Readers' Choice Award (Canada), Middle East Book Award, Rebecca Caudill Young Readers Book Award (Illinois)

Related Subjects: Afghanistan, Family—Relationships, Taliban

Character Themes: Courage, Family loyalty, Ingenuity, Overcoming adversity, Sacrifice

Fenner, Carol, *Yolanda's Genius*. Scholastic, 1995. ISBN: 059098859X (paperback) (Grades 3–6)

When their widowed mother moves Yolanda and her brother Andrew to the Chicago suburbs to escape the problems of the inner-city schools, their adjustment is difficult. Yolanda copes more easily by performing well in her studies. Six-year-old Andrew however, has trouble learning to read until his speech teacher begins to relate his reading to musical terms. Convinced that her sibling is a musical genius, Yolanda struggles to make his talent known. Using all of her mental acuity and physical strength, she schemes to protect them both and to convince those around her that she is right about her brother's unusual talent.

Awards: Newbery Honor

Related Subjects: African-Americans, Bullies, Family—Single parent, Problem solving, Prodigy, School, Siblings, Talent

Character Themes: Coping, Family loyalty, Genius, Resourcefulness, Spunk

Fine, Anne, *Flour Babies*. Bantam Doubleday Dell Books for Young Readers, 1992. ISBN: 0440219418 (paperback) (Grades 8–12)

When Room 8, the designated location for underachievers and troublemakers, chooses The Flour Baby Experiment for Dr. Devoy's science fair, Simon Martin is elated. He has overheard his often cynical teacher, Mr. Cassidy, say that at the end of the project the teen misfits will break the bags all over the room in one glorious mess. However, as the other boys lose any sense of parenthood with their charges, Simon becomes increasingly attentive. Writing judiciously in his journal, fiercely protecting "her," even patting her, Simon obviously has developed an almost human attachment to his project. Sneaking a peek over Simon's shoulder as he writes, Mr. Cassidy discovers that deep psychological issues are coming out of storage and being solved on paper as Simon discovers the demands of fatherhood. This is a poignant, funny,

realistic, and unique adventure into the mind of a boy who has sold himself short, just because he believes his dad has seen him as unworthy.
Awards: ALSC Notable Children's Book, Boston Globe-Horn Book Honor Award, Carnegie Medal (UK), Whitbread Book Award: Children (UK)
Related Subjects: Babysitting, Family—Single parent, Father-son relationships
Character Themes: Duty, Humor, Self-acceptance

Fine, Anne, *Jamie and Angus Stories*. Illustrated by Penny Dale. Candlewick Press, 2002. ISBN: 0763618624 (hardcover) (Grades K–3)
When Jamie first spies Angus, the Highland bull, in a toy shop window, he knows that the little animal must come home with him. Although it is love at first sight, Jamie cannot take possession until Christmas morning. However, when ownership becomes a reality, bonds strengthen as the two playmates are never separated, even at the babysitter's wedding. Angus survives a mishap in the washer and loses his silky appearance, but not Jamie's adoration. At bedtime, when Uncle Edward instructs the little bull in jumping lessons, Angus is a good sport. When Jamie must spend some time in the hospital, Angus does not snitch at a misdeed committed by his young human friend. Finally, on the day that Jamie chooses to act like an adult for twenty-four hours, Angus patiently endures. Charming illustrations pair perfectly with the whimsical text to entertain children and adults alike. Doubtless, readers will become fans and hope for more stories of the adventures of Jamie and Angus.
Awards: Boston Globe-Horn Book Award
Related Subjects: Family—Relationships, Toys
Character Themes: Creativity, Imagination

Fleischman, Paul, *Seedfolks*. Illustrated by Judy Pedersen. Joanna Cotler, 1997. ISBN: 0060274719. (hardcover) (Grades 5–9)
When Kim, a young Vietnamese girl, plants a few seeds in an abandoned lot, she is joined by neighbors of Hispanic, Korean, Haitian, and African-American descent who are determined to turn this vacant lot into a community garden. Challenges abound, but government apathy, vandalism, and racial prejudice are overcome as attitudes change and friendships are forged. Thirteen distinct narrators from diverse backgrounds tell this story of an inner-city neighborhood moving from suspicion to cooperation and joint purpose.
Awards: ALA Best Books for Young Adults, Buckeye Children's Book Award, (Ohio), IRA Teachers' Choices, Jane Addams Children's Book

Award Honor, Jefferson Cup Honor Award (Virginia), NCTE Notable Children's Book Trade Book in the Language Arts
Related Subjects: Cross-cultural relations, Diversity, Gardening, Urban life
Character Themes: Cooperation, Friendship, Perseverance

Fusco, Kimberly Newton, *Tending to Grace*. Alfred A. Knopf, 2004. ISBN: 0375828621 (hardcover) (Grades 8–12)
Used to being the caregiver for her irresponsible mother, Cornelia is resentful when Lenore goes to Las Vegas with her latest boyfriend, leaving her daughter to live with crusty, eccentric Aunt Agatha. Her aunt's backwoods cottage is filled with cobwebs and dirty dishes, and it doesn't even have an indoor bathroom. As the teen and her aunt battle it out, a genuine mutual respect begins to grow. Slowly the stone that is hard and strong deep inside of Cornelia begins to soften and she starts to overcome the stuttering that has kept her silent for many years. Fusco tells her story in short chapters of first-person narration.
Awards: ALA Best Book for Young Adults, *Booklist* Top 10 First Novel for Youth, IRA Notable Book
Related Subjects: Cross-generational relationships, Family—Dysfunctional, Mother-daughter relationships, Rejection, Self-concept, Stuttering
Character Themes: Coping, Friendship, Overcoming adversity, Self-acceptance

Gantos, Jack, *Joey Pigza Loses Control*. HarperTrophy/HarperCollins, 2000. ISBN: 0064410226 (paperback) (Grades 4–8)
When Joey and his dog, Pablo, visit his dad and grandma for six weeks in the summer, Joey has high hopes for some father-son bonding time. However, Carter Pigza is just as wired as his ADHD child, without realizing just how much either of them needs medication. Feeling that he is freeing Joey from the bondage of chemicals, Carter flushes the patches that keep Joey on course, instructing him to be a man and learn to live in the real world. Although he is a Little League baseball coach, Joey's father has no real understanding of his son's needs, and the visit is a comedy of chemistry. Joey learns valuable lessons, however, and comes to a greater appreciation of the life that he has with his mom and Pablo. Poignant and humorous, this story of three generations offers valuable insights to all families. This is the second in the Joey Pigza series.
Awards: ALSC Notable Children's Book, *Booklist* Editors' Choice, Horn Book Fanfare, Maine Student Book Award, Newbery Honor, *School Library Journal* Best Book

Related Subjects: Baseball, Family—Single parent, Learning disabilities
Character Themes: Hope, Perseverance, Tolerance

Garland, Sherry, *The Silent Storm*. Harcourt Brace, 1993. ISBN: 015200016X (paperback) (Grades 6–10)
Thirteen-year-old Alyssa has not spoken since being rescued from a storm at sea that took the lives of both her parents. Ridiculed at school because of her handicap, the teen has developed aggressive behavior, while internally she is desperate to communicate. Living with her grandfather provides a safe haven for Alyssa to reflect on the mystery of her speech loss. Her greatest joy is riding her beloved horse, Stormy, and reveling in the wildness of the ocean. Facing the imminent landfall of Hurricane Berta, Alyssa rushes into her own personal storm. Her grandfather plans to sell his horses and move back to Scotland, leaving Alyssa with an aunt who has a completely different lifestyle from that to which she is accustomed. Determined to stay with her grandfather, Alyssa runs away and in the process finds an unlikely friend and ally. In the harrowing conclusion Alyssa is able to solve her mystery and find peace at last.
Awards: Junior Library Guild Selection, Lamplighter Award, New York Public Library Book for the Teen Age
Related Subjects: Cross-generational relationships, Family—Nontraditional, Hurricanes, Mutism—Elective, Special needs—Children, Storms
Character Themes: Courage, Determination, Friendship, Overcoming fears, Survival

George, Jean Craighead (author and illustrator), *On the Far Side of the Mountain*. Puffin Books, 1990. ISBN: 0140342486 (paperback) (Grades 6–12)
Readers may have already met Sam Gribley in Jean Craighead George's award-winning novel, *My Side of the Mountain*, as he began his adventure of living alone in the Catskill Mountains. Two years later, fourteen-year-old Alice, Sam's sister, joins him, but on her own turf, and under her own terms. This is the story of Alice's adventures. Most of the time, Sam and Alice work well together; however, each occasionally needs to act independently. When Alice suddenly disappears, leaving Sam only a note, the loyal brother sets off across the mountains to find her. Readers will enjoy tracking Alice and her adopted pig, Crystal, as Sam reads the signs left behind by the two fugitives. Along the way, each sibling has his or her own narrow escapes, and works in cooperation with nature to survive. Information gleaned about living off natural foods, fish, and water may inspire young readers in their own camping adventures.

Awards: Washington Irving Children's Book Choice Award (New York)
Related Subjects: Adventure, Birds—Falcons, Camping, Catskill Mountains, Endangered species, Mountains, Nature, Outdoor life, Siblings
Character Themes: Independence, Ingenuity, Resourcefulness

Giff, Patricia Reilly, *Pictures of Hollis Woods.* **Wendy Lamb Books, 2002. ISBN: 0385326556 (hardcover) (Grades 5–8)**
In flashback, readers are introduced to Hollis Woods, a ward of the state who has been bounced from one foster home to another since infancy. At twelve, Hollis was placed with the Regans. Although she knew that she had found her family, fear of abandonment overruled her good sense, and she ran away. Gifted as an artist, Hollis always carried with her pictures of the beloved family so that she would never really lose them. As the story opens, Josie Cahill, an aging artist, is taking the risk of accepting Hollis as her charge. Almost immediately, the two creative souls bond; however, Hollis notices that Josie's memory is slipping, and for the first time in her life, the child feels needed. This is an emotionally draining book, but one that brims with compassion, humor, and ultimately a completely satisfying conclusion.
Awards: ALA Best Book for Young Adults, Christopher Award, Newbery Honor, Rebecca Caudill Young Readers Book Award (Illinois)
Related Subjects: Aging, Art, Family—Fostercare, Self-concept
Character Themes: Creativity, Love, Responsibility, Trust

Gordon, Amy, *The Gorillas of Gill Park.* **Illustrated by Matthew Cordell. Scholastic, 2003. ISBN: 0439643120 (paperback) (Grades 5–8)**
Willy Wilson is transformed after spending the summer with his eccentric Aunt Bridget, the costume designer; this is the story of that summer. In his own home, Willy feels misunderstood and among his peers at school, rather like an outsider. However, almost from the moment that he arrives at Gill Park, which borders his aunt's apartment, Willy begins to feel the excitement of being alive. Gareth, the baseball coach; Liesl, the free-spirited orphan; Mitch Bloom, who lives in a tree—literally; and Otto Pettingill, the mysterious millionaire, all play vital roles in Willy's self-discovery. The music of Gill Park provides a perfect accompaniment to the drama of unfolding adolescence, related in first person. A great read for middle school students, this title is followed by *Return to Gill Park*.
Awards: Georgia Children's Book Award Finalist, Golden Kite Award, Land of Enchantment Award (New Mexico), Missouri Association of Librarians Award, Texas Bluebonnet Award Master List
Related Subjects: Baseball, Family—Nontraditional, Friendship, Music, Theater

Character Themes: Cooperation, Humor, Individuality, Loyalty, Perseverance

Hesse, Karen, _The Music of Dolphins._ Scholastic, 1996. ISBN: 0590897985 (paperback) (Grades 6–9)
Mila has been raised by dolphins from the age of four. Captured by the Coast Guard as an adolescent, Mila is placed in a research facility to be taught human language and behavior. Beginning with large print and simple words, the author uses more difficult vocabulary and smaller typeface as Mila's understanding of language increases. Mila learns quickly, adding music and computer skills to her growing understanding of human ways. Gradually, however, she begins to realize what a prisoner she is and longs to return to the freedom of the sea.
Awards: ALA Best Book for Young Adults, Keystone to Reading Book Award (Pennsylvania), _Publishers Weekly_ Best Book of the Year, _School Library Journal_ Best Book of the Year
Related Subjects: Diaries, Dolphins, Feral children
Character Themes: Honesty

Hiaasen, Carl, _Hoot._ Alfred A. Knopf, 2002. ISBN: 0375821813 (hardcover) (Grades 4–8)
Roy Eberhardt is not happy that his family has moved from Montana to Florida. As the new student at school, he is tormented daily by Dana Matherson, the local bully. Then one day as Dana is pushing his face against the window of the school bus, Roy spies a boy running barefoot away from school instead of toward it, and his curiosity is aroused. As he snoops around to find out the identity of this mysterious person, Roy's investigation leads him into an amazing adventure involving the mysterious boy, Beatrice the Bear, endangered burrowing owls, Mother Paula's All-American Pancake House, and a whole cast of humorous and quirky characters. This is an amusing story with an ecological message.
Awards: ALA Best Book for Young Adults, Grand Canyon Young Reader Award (Arizona), Massachusetts Children's Book Award, Newbery Honor, Nutmeg Award (Connecticut), Rebecca Caudill Young Readers Book Award (Illinois), Rhode Island Teen Book Award
Related Subjects: Birds—Owls, Bullies, Conservation, Family—Dysfunctional, Habitats, Runaways
Character Themes: Appreciation of nature, Cooperation, Determination, Inventiveness

Horowitz, Anthony, *Stormbreaker.* **Speak/Penguin Group, 2000. ISBN: 0142406112 (paperback) (Grades 7–12)**
Orphaned at fourteen by the death of his uncle, Alex Rider is almost immediately plunged into a world of intrigue, adventure, and constant danger. Having lost both his parents in an airplane crash, Alex has lived most of his life with his father's brother, Ian, who he has believed to be a banker. The automobile crash that took his uncle's life seems a bit suspicious to Alex, and he is even more bewildered upon discovering that Ian was a high-profile international spy. The teen is even more bewildered when the Company approaches him to complete Ian's final case. At head-spinning speed, Alex is catapulted into the sinister world of international intrigue. This fast-paced novel is the first of the Alex Rider series, and is predicted to addict readers of all ages. The best plan is to have *Point Blank*, the sequel, at hand when finished.
Awards: Beehive Award (Utah), *New York Times* Best Seller
Related Subjects: Orphans, Survival, Technology, Terrorism
Character Themes: Courage, Creativity, Independence, Ingenuity

Hunt, Irene, *Up a Road Slowly.* **Follett Publishing Company, 1966. ISBN: 0695490095 (hardcover) (Grades 5–9)**
After the death of their mother, seven-year-old Julie and her brother Chris are sent to live with their Aunt Cordelia, a spinster schoolteacher. Overwhelmed at first by grief and the drastic changes in her situation, Julie slowly learns to love and appreciate the kind nurture and firm direction her aunt provides. Through the tragedy of a schoolmate's death and the disappointment of a first love gone wrong, she learns that life is not fair. However, rides in the woods on her horse, times around the fireplace with her aunt, and the love of family and friends like Danny Trevort build in Julie a loving security that enables her to triumph over the heartbreaks of life and her own tendency to rebellion.
Awards: Newbery Medal
Related Subjects: Family—Extended, Loss of parent, Prejudice, Relationships—Family, Self-concept
Character Themes: Coping, Self-acceptance, Wisdom

Korman, Gordon, *No More Dead Dogs.* **Scholastic, 2000. ISBN: 0439329485 (paperback) (Grades 5–8)**
Wallace Wallace, the accidental hero of the final game of football season, became a celebrity because fate handed him the ball at the right time, and in

the right place. Just as the new season is beginning, Wallace is given detention by Mr. Fogelman because he has written a negative review of the English teacher's favorite book, *Old Shep, My Pal*, stating that all dog stories end
in death. Detention means no football practice. Steadfast, Wally will not
stretch the truth about his view of the book, not even for the fame of football. Since Mr. Fogelman is directing the middle school play based on the
book, attending rehearsals and being useful become part of Wally's punish-
ment. With hilarious and amazing table-turning results, Wallace finds himself in charge of the drama and at great odds with his football teammates. Using the first person voices of Wallace, aspiring actress Rachel Turner, her
boy-crazy friend Trudi Davis, and the beleaguered Mr. Fogelman, Korman
takes readers inside the slapstick tragicomedy that IS middle school. This little novel will ring true with all readers who long for a dog story that ends
with excitement, and a hero who will not compromise.
Awards: Young Reader's Choice Award (Pacific Northwest Library Association)
Related Subjects: Football, Music, Theater
Character Themes: Creativity, Humor, Loyalty

**Little, Jean, *Willow and Twig*. Viking, 2000. ISBN: 0670888567 (hard-
cover) (Grades 5–8)**
Eleven-year-old Willow and her emotionally disturbed four-year-old brother
Twig have the same mother, but different fathers. Overwhelmed by life, their
drug-addicted mother leaves them in the care of an elderly neighbor and
never returns. When their neighbor dies, the children are sent to live with
the grandmother who Willow believes has disowned them. Through all their
difficulties, Willow displays great loyalty toward Twig and despite great odds,
the children find a real home for the first time. With all of the mounting
problems, the book could be depressing, but Little's characters unfold naturally and the problems, though never downplayed, are resolved optimisti-
cally.
Awards: CLA Book of the Year for Children: Finalist (Canada), Mr.
Christie's Book Award (Canada)
Related Subjects: Cross-generational relationships, Mutism, Orphans,
Prejudice, Survival
Character Themes: Determination, Family love, Loyalty

**Lord, Cynthia, *Rules*. Scholastic, 2006. ISBN: 0439443822 (hardcover)
(Grades 5–12)**
Twelve-year-old Catherine has discovered a method of more or less normal-
izing life with her younger autistic brother, David. Although life can never

be just like that of her friends because of David's erratic and often noisy behavior, Catherine commits to writing a set of rules that solidifies David's understanding of social skills. As Catherine patiently reminds David that he should knock before opening the bathroom door, and that he should not put toys in the fish tank, she finds herself developing her own set of life rules. The rule about saying hello to others who say hello first provides opportunity for growth in two very different friendships, as Catherine learns what is most valuable in life, and what is not. This compelling novel is a must-read for families with children of special needs. Entire classrooms could greatly benefit from this story, written with authentic voice out of the author's own experience.

Awards: Great Stone Face Award (New Hampshire), Newbery Honor, Schneider Family Book Award

Related Subjects: Autism, Bibliotherapy, Friendship, Special needs—Physical disabilities, Special needs—Mental disabilities, Special needs—Siblings

Character Themes: Acceptance, Adaptation, Initiative, Family loyalty, Love

MacDonald, Amy, *No More Nasty*. Illustrated by Cat Bowman Smith. Farrar, Straus & Giroux, 2001. ISBN: 0374355290 (hardcover) (Grades 3–6)

Simon's fifth-grade class is proud of its reputation as incorrigible, sending substitute teachers to an early retirement. Simon is mortified, however, when he realizes that their newest substitute is none other than Mrs. Matilda Maxwell, his eccentric great-aunt. From her first day in class, Aunt Mattie turns things upside down, foiling the children's tricks, challenging their minds, and writing herself detentions. She even has the audacity to think that the class can win the school's annual science fair. With great humor, the author challenges readers to look at learning from a new perspective.

Awards: "Children's Choice" lists in twelve states, West Virginia Children's Book Award

Related Subjects: Family, School, Teachers

Character Themes: Creativity, Humor, Self-acceptance

MacLachlan, Patricia, *Arthur, For the Very First Time*. Illustrated by Lloyd Bloom, Scholastic, 1980. ISBN: 0590465309 (paperback) (Grades 4–7)

As Arthur's parents struggle with the tension of expecting a second child, they decide to send the ten-year-old to spend the summer on a farm with Great-Aunt Elda and Great-Uncle Wrisby. Arthur is an observer, not a doer, and a keeper of copious notes on significant facts that he sees, learns, or wonders about. As the summer progresses, Arthur finds friendship with a neighbor waif, Moira, who reminds him of a starling; Pauline the hen, who responds to conversations in French; and a very pregnant pig, Bernadette, who requires a song before she will cooperate, even with her beloved Wrisby. Moira, a girl of action, chides Arthur to *do* something instead of just watching life from a safe distance. What they do together changes Arthur forever. This slim volume is a gem that remains in the reader's heart long after the final page is turned, showing the same tenderness as MacLachlan's Newbery winner *Sarah, Plain and Tall*.

Awards: Golden Kite Award

Related Subjects: Cross-generational relationships, Family—Nontraditional, Farm life, Pigs

Character Themes: Cooperation, Courage, Friendship, Initiative

Martin, Ann M., *A Corner of the Universe*. Scholastic, 2002. ISBN: 0439388805 (hardcover) (Grades 5–9)
When Hattie turns twelve, her Uncle Adam comes to live with the family, turning everything in their comfortable life upside down. Uncle Adam's mental problems bring the family embarrassment while his outlandish actions and childlike behavior cause many to reject him. Hattie is drawn by his exuberance and his affection, but worries that she might be like him. The cruel reaction of others who make fun of him causes Hattie to become protective of her uncle and to grow in understanding of the difficulties he faces.

Awards: Newbery Honor, William Allen White Children's Book Award (Kansas)

Related Subjects: Family—Relationships, Friendship, Special needs—Mental disabilities

Character Themes: Courage, Empathy, Understanding

McDaniel, Lurlene, *Angels Watching Over Me*. Bantam Books, 1996. ISBN: 0553567241 (paperback) (Grades 9–12)
As Christmas approaches, sixteen-year-old Leah Lewis-Hall finds herself alone and under the care of an unknown doctor while her mother honeymoons in Japan with husband number five. Since there is no plausible explanation for the broken finger that has hospitalized her, Leah's doctor keeps her for observation. New to the area and friendless, the teen welcomes interaction with her five-year-old Amish roommate, Rebekah. As the days pass, Leah becomes friends with Charity and Ethan, Rebekah's older sister and brother. In the warmth of their religious faith, Leah begins to lose some

of her cynicism. When the dire diagnosis is given, her now-present mother becomes nearly hysterical, but recognizes that significant changes must be made in her relationship with her daughter. Leah is further encouraged by Gabriella, a mysterious visitor who has touched her spirit and given her comfort and hope. This is the first in McDaniel's *Angels* trilogy.

Awards: Soaring Eagle Book Award (Wyoming)

Related Subjects: Amish, Christmas, Family—Relationships, Illness, Mother-daughter relationships, Religion

Character Themes: Devotion, Friendship, Love, Patience

Mikaelsen, Ben, *Touching Spirit Bear*. HarperTrophy, 2001. ISBN: 038080560X (paperback) (Grades 8–12)

After venting his anger on classmate Peter Driscal, Cole Matthews is facing a term in prison. Known as a bully, he has gone too far this time, putting his victim in the hospital with multiple injuries and life-threatening brain damage. When parole officer Garvey offers an alternative called Circle Justice, based on his Tlingit Indian traditions, Cole accepts the plan to escape prison time. Banished for one year to an island in Alaska, he faces life-threatening events including an attack by a gigantic white bear, which leaves him near death. Facing his own mortality helps Cole to turn the corner and begin to strive for healing and survival of his spirit as well as his body. Mikaelsen's description of the young man's mauling by the bear is excruciatingly real, but adds to the emotional impact of Cole's journey from anger to wholeness. This book would be excellent to use in conjunction with Gary Paulsen's *Hatchet*.

Awards: ALA Best Book for Young Adults, Beehive Award (Utah), California Young Readers Medal, Nevada Young Readers' Award, William Allen White Children's Book Award (Kansas)

Related Subjects: Abuse—Child, Alaska, Anger, Bears, Bullies, Native Americans—Tlingit, Rehabilitation, Restitution, Survival

Character Themes: Forgiveness, Giving, Obedience, Responsibility, Self-control

Mori, Kyoko, *Shizuko's Daughter*. Ballantine Books, 1993. ISBN: 0449704335 (paperback) (Grades 10–12)

When Shizuko Okuda commits suicide, her twelve year-old daughter Yuki is left to adjust to life with a father who cares little for her welfare and a stepmother who bitterly resents her. Yuki's experience shows how the strictures of Japanese custom contribute to her comfort as well as her lonely confinement. There is no easy Cinderella ending for Yuki, but there are people who reach out to her and encourage her in her search for forgiveness and self-acceptance. Rich in cultural detail and emotionally moving, this story should appeal to adolescents struggling with difficult situations in their own lives.

Awards: ALA Best Book for Young Adults, Horn Book Fanfare Book, *New York Times* Notable Book, Outstanding Book for the College Board

Related Subjects: Abuse—Child, Cross-generational relationships, Grief, Japan, Relationships—Family, Suicide, Track and field

Character Themes: Forgiveness, Respect for elders, Self-acceptance

Naidoo, Beverly, *The Other Side of Truth*. HarperCollins, 2000. ISBN: 0060296283 (hardcover) (Grades 9–12)

Because Sade and Femi's father writes openly about the corruption in his country of Nigeria, agents of the military government shoot their mother. Afraid for the children's safety, their father arranges for them to be smuggled into England. Abandoned at the London airport, the brother and sister find themselves in the care of English government agencies and foster families. When she begins to attend school, Sade is confronted with pressures from bullying classmates similar to those faced by her father in Nigeria. She finds that she must make difficult choices for herself. When the children's father attempts to join them in London, he is imprisoned for illegal immigration and the family must fight to be reunited. Memories of her mother's wise sayings lend strength to Sade during these difficult days of sorrow and uncertainty. Through her sympathetic characters, Naidoo effectively portrays the anguish experienced by the world's refugees.

Awards: CBC/NCSS Notable Children's Trade Book in Social Studies, Carnegie Medal, IRA Teachers' Choices, *School Library Journal* Best Book

Related Subjects: Abandonment, Death of parent, Family, Fear, London, Nigeria, Prejudice, Refugees—Political, Siblings

Character Themes: Courage, Determination, Family loyalty, Honesty, Self-respect

Namioka, Lensey, *Yang the Eldest and His Odd Jobs*. Illustrated by Kees de Kiefte. Little, Brown & Company, 2000. ISBN: 0316590118 (hardcover) (Grades 3–5)

The strange buzzing Yang the Eldest hears as he plays his violin spells disaster. Repairing or replacing the instrument will cost a great deal of money. To raise funds, he tries everything from babysitting to playing in the park. Slowly, making money begins to take precedence over his music. Distressed by the Eldest Brother's change of focus, his family lovingly leads him back to resume the pursuit of his great musical gift. Told by younger sister Mary, this touching and humorous story explores the cultural differences Chinese fam-

ilies face when they come to America. Readers may also enjoy other stories about the Yang family, including *Yang the Youngest and His Terrible Ear*.
Awards: Akron Symphony Orchestra Award (Ohio)
Related Subjects: Asian-Americans, Diversity, Music, Siblings, Violins
Character Themes: Discipline, Family love, Persistence

Park, Barbara, *Skinnybones*. Random House Fiction, 1997 (orig. 1982). ISBN: 069788792X (paperback) (Grades 4–8)
Being the smallest player on his baseball team does not stop Alex Franovitch from ordering a size large uniform—perhaps that is the size of his sense of humor and bravado. With the same aplomb, Alex is not deterred from submitting his entry to the Kitty Fritters cat food contest just because the form is missing. His solution is to dump the entire bag of Fritters on the kitchen floor, and blame the cat for the mess. Just such a penchant for mischief gets Alex into big trouble. Boasting once too often of his own imagined prowess, Alex finds himself in public competition with boy wonder, classmate, and pitching ace T. J. Stoner, who originally nicknamed him "Skinnybones." Relying on his unique methods of attacking problems, Skinnybones survives the trial by public humiliation, and even steals the spotlight, briefly, from Stoner. The updated edition of this amusing story will produce chuckles from baseball fans and all who like to see a bully get his due. Barbara Park, winner of fifteen Children's Choice Awards, is at her best in this revised edition of the eighties classic.
Awards: Beehive Award (Utah), Georgia Children's Book Award, Maud Heart Lovelace Book Award (Minnesota), Tennessee Volunteer State Book Award, Texas Bluebonnet Award
Related Subjects: Athletes, Baseball, Bullies
Character Themes: Creativity, Humor

Paterson, Katherine, *The Same Stuff as Stars*. Clarion Books, 2002. ISBN: 0618247440 (hardcover) (Grades 5–9)
At eleven years old, Angel Morgan is the adult in her family. Daddy is in jail and her mother Verna is irresponsible. It is Angel who looks after her little brother Bernie. When Verna abandons the children at their grandmother's in rural Vermont, Angel has the added burden of caring for the cantankerous old woman. In the midst of this hardship, solace is found in friendship with the "star man" next door, and in Miss Liza, the town librarian. "Santy Claus," as her grandmother calls their neighbor, leaves food and chopped wood on grandma's doorstep and introduces Angel to the wonders of astronomy. As the brother and sister make a new life for themselves in this difficult place,

Angel is encouraged to persevere when she learns that she is made of the same stuff as stars. Angel is a resilient and intelligent young heroine who steadfastly works to keep her family together.

Awards: ABA Book Sense Pick, Jane Addams Children's Book Award, Mitten Honor Award (Michigan), *Publishers Weekly* Best Book of the Year
Related Subjects: Abandonment, Astronomy, Cross-generational relationships, Grandparents, Mother-daughter relationships, Poverty, Siblings
Character Themes: Family loyalty, Resilience, Self-reliance

Paulsen, Gary, *Brian's Winter*. Delacorte Press, 1996. ISBN: 0385321988 (hardcover) (Grades 6–10)
Written as a result of fan mail asking the author what would have happened if his hero, Brian Robeson from the classic book *Hatchet*, had not been rescued before winter, this sequel is nearly a guidebook for survival. Readers live with Brian through the fall season, which is fairly carefree except for a major encounter with a bear and a rather humorous one with a skunk. Suddenly, signs of winter appear, and the young city dweller must get serious about his situation. Having learned much about the woods during his solitary summer, Brian prepares his home for the winter as he watches and listens to what nature communicates. Remembering school lessons on how bows and arrowheads are made stands him in good stead when the only other hunting weapon he has fails. Observing the wolves, he learns how to mark his territory. This is an altogether satisfying story that is accurately told by a woodsman with intimate knowledge of nature's whims and blessings. This contemporary novel would be an excellent companion to a historical fiction novel with a similar theme.

Awards: Garden State Teen Book Award (New Jersey), Golden Archer Award (Wisconsin), IRA Young Adults' Choice
Related Subjects: Ecology, Nature, Survival
Character Themes: Endurance, Ingenuity, Maturity

Paulsen, Gary, *The Haymeadow*. Illustrated by Ruth Wright Paulsen. A Yearling Book, 1992. ISBN: 0440409233 (paperback) (Grades 5–10)
Fourteen-year-old John Barron seems incapable of pleasing his widowed father. John believes that if his mother were alive, there would be less tension in their home. However, his mother died when he was only three years old. When John has the task of herding six thousand sheep to the mountain pasture for the summer, he is intimidated, yet relieved to be away from home. At least he will not be in conflict with his father, and anything seems less complex than that relationship. Not anticipating flooded streams, attacking

coyotes, and injured dogs, John's greatest hope for the summer is that he will finally please his father. This is a story that speaks to all fathers and teenage sons, whether ranchers or businessmen. Some language and references to violent acts may require adult discretion.

Awards: ALA Best Book for Young Adults, Kentucky Bluegrass Award, Maine Student Book Award, William Allen White Children's Book Award (Kansas)

Related Subjects: Family—Relationships, Ranching, Wyoming

Character Themes: Coping, Independence, Survival

Philbrick, Rodman, *The Mighty* (orig. *Freak the Mighty*). Scholastic, 1993. ISBN: 0590110225 (paperback) (Grades 8–12)
Although to the local bullies, they are taunted as "Frankenstein and Igor," Maxwell Kane and his undersized but brilliant friend Kevin become the unstoppable unit of "Freak the Mighty." Max is indeed a gentle giant, often intimidated by difficult tasks, such as living with his well-meaning but sometimes bumbling grandparents. Kevin is tiny and can walk only with massive mechanical aid, yet he possesses an indomitable spirit and voice. Each boy fills a gap in the other and together they comprise a courageous team that lives long in the reader's memory. Each helps the other to overcome pain that no child should suffer, with humor and bravado, even in the face of death. A movie based on the book, *The Mighty*, is available.

Awards: ALA Best Book for Young Adults, California Young Readers Medal, Judy Lopez Memorial Award for Children's Literature Honor Book, Soaring Eagle Award (Wyoming)

Related Subjects: Abandonment, Bibliotherapy, Family—Nontraditional, Friendship, Special needs, Survival

Character Themes: Courage, Family love, Friendship, Self-acceptance

Polacco, Patricia (author and illustrator), *Mr. Lincoln's Way*. Scholastic, 2001. ISBN: 0439430119 (paperback) (Grades 2–6)
Taught prejudice by his father, Eugene Esterhause repeats the racist names he hears at home to his classmates at school. When his bullying lands him in Mr. Lincoln's office, the principal searches for a positive way to change "Mean Gene's" behavior. Discovering the boy's interest in birds, Mr. Lincoln enlists his help in designing a school atrium that will attract these animals to visit. Slowly the loving attention and nurture of the principal offer Eugene the opportunity to appreciate the differences in people and to learn to think for himself. This book offers a springboard for discussion of a number of important topics such as bullying and tolerance.

Awards: California Young Readers Medal: Picture Books for Older Readers, Pennsylvania Young Reader's Choice Award, South Carolina Children's Book Award
Related Subjects: African-Americans, Birds, Bullies, Prejudice, School, Teachers
Character Themes: Ingenuity, Tolerance

Robinson, Barbara, *The Best Christmas Pageant Ever*. Illustrated by Judith Gwyn Brown. Joanna Cotler, 1972. ISBN: 0060250437 (hardcover) (Grades 3–6)
Everyone is afraid of the Herdman children. With their father gone and their mother working two jobs, the children fend for themselves. To survive, they have learned to lie, steal, swear, and hit anyone who gets in their way. When the children decide to take over the major parts in the church's Christmas pageant, they turn everything upside down. Since the Herdmans have never heard the Christmas story before, they give it their own unusual interpretation. In the process the pageant becomes one of the most memorable the church has ever held.
Awards: ALSC Notable Children's Book, Georgia Children's Book Award, Library of Congress Children's Book of the Year, Young Hoosier Book Award (Indiana)
Related Subjects: Christmas, Family, Holidays, Siblings
Character Themes: Curiosity, Determination, Family loyalty, Humor

Ryan, Pam Munoz, *Becoming Naomi Leon*. Scholastic, 2004. ISBN: 0439856213 (paperback) (Grades 5–8)
Naomi Outlaw and her brother, Owen, have only faint memories of their parents, but adore their guardian, Gram. The joy that the three experience living in Baby Beluga, their small Airstream trailer, is rivaled only by their warmhearted neighbors at the Avocado Acres Trailer Rancho. With Gram, Owen's birth defects and emotional quirks, or the fact that Naomi's skin and hair are shades darker than that of her brother, do not seem to matter. They are a family. Entertainment is economical: Naomi has become proficient at carving animals out of soap, Gram watches television, and Owen breezes through his homework. Security reigns until the errant and neglectful mother, Terri Lynn, crashes back into their lives. The ensuing roller coaster of emotions may seem familiar to many young readers. No easy solutions lurk in these pages, but Naomi, Owen, and Gram learn valuable life lessons in their shared experiences.

Awards: ALSC Notable Children's Book, Americas Award, Parents' Choice Silver Honor Award, Pura Belpré Honor, Schneider Family Book Award, Tomás Rivera Mexican American Children's Book Award
Related Subjects: Abandonment, Bibliotherapy, Cross-generational relationships, Family—Biracial, Hispanic-American, Special needs
Character Themes: Cooperation, Creativity, Resilience, Survival

Smith, Robert Kimmel, *The War with Grandpa*. Illustrated by Richard Lauter. Delacorte Press, 1984. ISBN: 0385293127 (hardcover) (Grades 3–6)
Peter always loved visits with his grandparents. This time, however, Grandma has died and Grandpa is coming to stay. The only drawback is that his parents have decided that Grandpa is going to have Peter's room and Peter is being moved to the scary attic. Unable to accept this arrangement, Peter declares war, but Grandpa is pretty good at playing tricks himself. Written in the vocabulary and style of a fifth-grader, this story explores a problem that many families face. Love overrides hurt in this situation and a solution is found that is satisfactory to all.
Awards: Dorothy Canfield Fisher Children's Book Award (Vermont), IRA-CBC Children's Choices, Mark Twain Award (Missouri), Tennessee Volunteer State Book Award, William Allen White Children's Book Award (Kansas), Young Hoosier Book Award (Indiana)
Related Subjects: Communication, Cross-generational relationships, Family, Grandparents
Character Themes: Family love, Humor, Independence, Respect

Spinelli, Jerry, *Loser*. HarperCollins, 2002. ISBN: 0060001933 (hardcover) (Grades 4–8)
Donald Zinkoff doesn't fit in with the crowd, but he doesn't seem to care. He loves school and laughs at himself when his classmates make fun of his mistakes. In fourth grade, however, the teasing takes on a harder edge and a single bad mistake earns him the nickname of Loser. His family offers Donald continual support through his struggles and one tragic event gives this teen the opportunity to show just how courageous and unselfish he can be. Though Donald does not gain instant acceptance from his peers, he does come to terms with his own identity. This realistic story can give encouragement to those who are not always part of the popular crowd in school.
Awards: ABA Book Sense Pick, Dorothy Canfield Fisher Children's Book Award (Vermont), Great Lakes Book Award (Michigan), Great Stone Face

Award (New Hampshire), Judy Lopez Memorial Award for Children's Literature, Maine Student Book Award, Mark Twain Award (Missouri), Sasquatch Reading Award (Washington)
Related Subjects: Bullies, Failure, Family, School
Character Themes: Coping, Courage, Humor, Sacrifice, Self-acceptance

Stauffacher, Sue, *Donuthead*. Alfred A. Knopf, 2003. ISBN: 0375824685 (hardcover) (Grades 5–8)
Franklin Delano Donuthead is in a class by himself, or would like to be. Sensitive, analytical, alert, probably brilliant, but above all, anxious, Franklin observes life, rather than lives it. If warding off teasing bullies because of his name isn't enough to strengthen his character, readers will see his baseball-loving mom accomplishing that feat on her own. Franklin's only parent had one goal for him—playing in the majors; Franklin's goal is to stay as hygienically immaculate as possible at all cost, and at all times. Into this paradoxical family unit charges Sarah Kervick—neglected, rambunctious, and (in Franklin's opinion) flea infested. The unlikely little waif becomes the catalyst for delightful self-discovery in the Donuthead abode, and the target for abundant hilarious asides from Franklin. There is occasional use of graphic language.
Awards: Kentucky Bluegrass Award, Rhode Island Children's Book Award, William Allen White Children's Book Award (Kansas)
Related Subjects: Baseball, Family—Single parent, Obsessive-compulsive disorder
Character Themes: Compassion, Humor, Individuality

Tolan, Stephanie S., *Ordinary Miracles*. HarperTrophy/HarperCollins, 1999. ISBN: 0380733226 (paperback) (Grades 6–12)
Being an identical twin has advantages, but Mark Filkins has reached the point in his teenage life that he is weary of being a shadow of his domineering brother, Matthew. School classes, soccer team, church, and family find the two boys paired as naturally as bread and butter. However, when Mark makes friends with a Nobel Prize winner whom Matthew does not even know, the rift between the boys begins to widen. Science and faith clash, leaving both Matthew and Mark with monumental questions on opposing sides. Through family support and love, the brothers learn valuable lessons in life, love, belief, and individuality. This thought-provoking young adult novel, pitting age-old forces against each other, is worthy of parents' attention, as well as that of the target audience.
Awards: *Booklist* Editors' Choice

Related Subjects: Christians, Death, Religion, Science, Siblings—Twins
Character Themes: Family loyalty, Hope, Individuality, Religious faith

Wallace, Bill, *A Dog Called Kitty*. Pocket Books, 1980. ISBN: 0671770810 (paperback) (Grades 3–6)
Attacked by a rabid dog when he was very young, Ricky has developed a terrible fear of all kinds of dogs. When a starving puppy is dropped off at their farm, Ricky is determined not to let it stay, but his sympathy for the animal's pitiful plight eventually overcomes his reluctance. He begins to give it scraps from the table and slowly his all-consuming fear is overcome. Boy and dog become fast friends. When a pack of wild dogs attacks a young heifer in the field, the loyalty and strength of both animal and child are sorely tested. This is a dog story that should appeal to all ages.
Awards: Golden Sower Award (Nebraska), Sequoyah Book Award (Oklahoma), Texas Bluebonnet Award
Related Subjects: Bullies, Dogs, Family, Farm life, Fear, Pets
Character Themes: Courage, Humor, Responsibility

Wiles, Deborah, *Love, Ruby Lavender*. Gulliver Books/Harcourt, 2001. ISBN: 0152045686 (paperback) (Grades 4–8)
Ruby Lavender and her grandmother, Miss Eula, are inseparable, even leaving secret notes to be found in a special knothole when they are seeing each other daily. They plot schemes together, laugh together, and they have grieved together for the past year, since Ruby's grandfather drowned. So, it is not surprising that Ruby is shocked and angry when Miss Eula tells her as gently as possible that she is leaving Halleluia, Mississippi, for an undetermined amount of time, and going to meet her brand-new baby granddaughter in Hawaii. During the following weeks, Ruby learns to face life on her own with the help of her busy mom, some other rather unconventional characters, and a constant stream of letters both to and from Miss Eula, humorously written by both, and included in the text. This tender story reveals Ruby's wit and indomitable strength in the face of loss, the responsibility of raising ornery chickens, and the absence of her beloved grandmother and grandfather. It is a book too good to be missed by any granddaughter, or any reader who has grieved the loss of someone dear.
Awards: ALSC Notable Children's Book, NCTE Notable Children's Trade Book in the Language Arts, *Parent's Guide* Children's Media Award
Related Subjects: Chickens, Cross-generational relationships, Family—Single parent, Friendship, Grandparents, Grief
Character Themes: Family unity, Forgiveness, Humor, Survival, Teamwork

Williams, Vera B., *Something Special for Me*. Mulberry Books, 1983. ISBN: 0688065260 (paperback) (Grades 1–3)
Rosa, Mama, and Grandma make it a practice to put their extra coins in a money jar to save for special occasions. With Rosa's birthday rapidly approaching, Mama and Grandma decide it is time for her to use that money for something special. After a long day of shopping, Rosa has chosen and then rejected roller skates, a new dress, and even a new sleeping bag. Discouraged and confused, Rosa hears music coming from someone standing on the street corner. He is playing an accordion just like Grandma used to play. Suddenly the little girl knows exactly what will be the perfect gift.
Awards: Akron Symphony Orchestra Award (Ohio), ALSC Notable Children's Book
Related Subjects: Birthdays, Hispanic-Americans, Music
Character Themes: Family love, Sharing, Thrift

Wolff, Virginia Euwer, *The Mozart Season*. Scholastic, 1991. ISBN: 0590454455 (paperback) (Grades 6–8)
Allegra Shapiro has just completed a demanding softball season and plans to enjoy a relaxing summer. However, when violin instructor Mr. Kaplan informs her that she has qualified to enter the Ernest Bloch Competition for Young Musicians of Oregon, the ambitious eighth-grader realizes that her labor has just begun. Both Mr. Kaplan and her musician parents allow Allegra to choose whether she will compete. Without hesitation she plunges into rigorous practice; the summer is consumed with understanding the Mozart piece, and then making it her own. Because of her involvement with music, Allegra finds herself befriending a homeless man, and in her grand moment, paying homage to her great-grandmother who was lost in the Holocaust. Told in first-person narrative, this compelling novel reels readers in and holds hearts right to the final page. Wolff has produced a masterpiece, told simply but powerfully, that rivals her award-winning *Probably Still Nick Swansen*. This story is highly recommended for young adults dedicated to the performing arts.
Awards: ALA Best Book for Young Adults, ALSC Notable Children's Book
Related Subjects: Family—Relationships, Jews—Heritage, Music, Violins
Character Themes: Dedication, Friendship, Respect, Talent

Wolff, Virginia Euwer, *Probably Still Nick Swansen*. Simon Pulse, 2002. ISBN: 0689852266 (paperback) (Grades 10–12)
At sixteen, Nick Swansen wants to get his driver's license and have a date for the prom. However, as a special education student, Nick struggles with his

mental limitations. Although his parents respond to their son's issues with love and wisdom, they cannot change his circumstances. Written with realism and sensitivity, the story will move readers to both smiles and tears, creating a deeper understanding of children and teens who are mentally challenged.

Awards: ALA Best Book for Young Adults, *Booklist* Editors' Choice, *School Library Journal* Best Book, Sequoyah Book Award Master List (Oklahoma)
Related Subjects: Bibliotherapy, Psychology, Special needs—Mental disabilities
Character Themes: Coping, Creativity, Family love

Woodson, Jacqueline, *Miracle's Boys*. G. P. Putnam, 2000. ISBN: 0399231137 (hardcover) (Grades 7–12)
When both of their parents die, Charlie, Lafayette, and Tyree all carry a burden of guilt and struggle to cope each in his own way. Charlie feels responsible for the death of a dog he tried to rescue, Lafayette for his mother's death, and Tyree for his father's. As their emotions cycle through pain, anger, and despair, their mother's love works in them even after her death, keeping them together and bringing them to reconciliation and a determination to make it together.

Awards: Coretta Scott King Award, Tayshas Reading List (Texas)
Related Themes: Bibliotherapy, Orphans, Siblings, Urban life
Character Themes: Determination, Family loyalty, Sacrifice

Wyeth, Sharon Dennis, *A Piece of Heaven*. Dell Yearling, 2001. ISBN: 0440418690 (paperback) (Grades 4–6)
Haley's thirteenth birthday turns sour when her mother has a nervous breakdown and commits herself to the hospital. With her brother Otis spending most of his time on the streets, Haley is left to fend for herself. Answering an ad for a job to clean up the backyard of a local music teacher, Haley finds friendship and stability in her relationship with her new employer. Bringing order to Mr. Jackson's backyard helps her to create a piece of heaven in her own chaotic life. After Otis has trouble with the law and a social worker wants to put Haley in a group home, it is Mr. Jackson to whom she turns for strength to face her hardships.

Awards: New York Public Library Best Book for the Teen Age, Young Hoosier Book Award (Indiana)
Related Subjects: Abandonment, Family—Dysfunctional, Friendship, Siblings, Teachers, Urban life
Character Themes: Coping, Spunk

CHAPTER THREE

Fantasy

The child who reads fantasy enters worlds of magical settings, talking animals, toys that come to life, or creatures that seem to spring from outside his or her world. In these extraordinary places, the reader or listener chooses to believe the unbelievable, accept the unacceptable, and sometimes even see characters that are invisible. Could this experience possibly be healthy for an impressionable mind?

Without fantasy, Orville and Wilbur Wright would never have dreamed of flight, nor would Alexander Graham Bell have attempted to send words through the air in a wire. Fantasy encourages thinking of possibilities, not simply settling for experiencing the factual. Children are natural wellsprings of imagination. Responsible adults accept the privilege and pleasure of feeding youthful fantasies entertaining, enlightening, and enriching fare. In this section, books are recognized that reach across a range of reading abilities and interests, but all encourage young readers to dream, to consider, to believe beyond the realm of reality.

The discipline of children's literature divides fantasy into two main categories, complex and common. High or complex fantasy includes stories of adventure in which the destinies of entire civilizations are at stake. Conflict is created by a courageous hero, or savior figure, battling in some way against a seemingly overwhelming foe with evil intent that wants to gain power for itself. The second, and vastly different, category is simple or common fantasy. Talking toys, talking animals, and the worlds of little people belong in this adventure of a different sort. No earth-shattering change arises from conflict resolution, just wonderfully magical endings, with all made right for child, toy, animal, or very little person. Time-warp stories, in which the protagonist is magically moved forward or back in time, may fit into either complex or simple fantasy, depending on the theme of the story.

Awards given for this genre are sometimes based on the popularity of the book as determined by sales, the responses of children and young adults, or votes cast in a survey, as well as the quality of writing, as assessed by a panel of experts in the field. Modern fantasy often opens its pages with the familiarity of the real world, but moves seamlessly into the fantastic. Other stories will begin and end in the fantasy world. Whatever type of fantasy is selected, readers and listeners are in for a treat as they pretend, dream, and wonder, "What if . . ."

Alexander, Lloyd, *The Iron Ring*. Dutton Children's Books, 1997. ISBN: 0525455973 (hardcover) (Grades 6–12)
When young King Tamar is tricked into keeping a dreadful promise to the sinister, mysterious King Jaya, a wild and challenging journey ensues. On his quest, Tamar attracts a strange circle of friends, including a spirited and crafty monkey, a wise old sage, a beautiful young cow herder, and a complaining eagle that would try the patience of Job. As the youthful monarch moves toward his destination, he seems oblivious to danger, driven in his rush to judgment by honor alone, and in the end discovers who he was when he began, and who he has become at the amazing journey's conclusion. This memorable young adult novel is vintage Alexander—its subtle message is all about the passage through adolescence, and how hardship, humility, and help from others are essential in forging true character.
Awards: ALA Best Book for Young Adults, *Booklist* Top Ten Fantasy Novel for Young Readers
Related Subjects: Chivalry, Folk literature, India, Promises, Proverbs
Character Themes: Courage, Duty, Honesty, Honor, Humor, Respect, Responsibility, Wisdom

Armstrong, Alan, *Whittington*. Illustrated by S. D. Schindler. Random House, 2005. ISBN: 0375828648 (hardcover) (Grades 4–8)
Bernie and his wife, Marion, are surrogate parents for their orphaned grandchildren, Abby and Ben. A blue-collar worker of limited means, kindhearted Bernie also adopts unwanted animals, housing them in his barn. The rambling old shelter that serves as both a home for the animals and a source of comfort for the children provides the setting for this humble masterpiece. Whittington, a stray cat with legendary lineage, is desperately seeking a place

to sleep when he comes upon Bernie's barn, and he discovers much more than just a home. Whittington has just lost "his boy" to a school for special-needs children, and is still in mourning. Shortly after meeting Ben, the literary cat recognizes that his new boy has the all-too-familiar reading problems. The warp of the story is Whittington's recounting the adventures of his famous ancestor; the woof of the tale is Ben's struggle with the printed word. The final product is seamless, an enticing read-aloud or page-turning fantasy for individual reading.

Awards: ALSC Notable Children's Book, Newbery Honor
Related Subjects: Animals, Friendship, Reading, Special needs
Character Themes: Compassion, Humor, Perseverance

Avi, *Perloo the Bold.* **Illustrated by Marcy Reed. Scholastic, 1999. ISBN: 0590110039 (paperback) (Grades 8–12)**
Perloo the rabbit is content to stay in his cozy warren and study the history of his Montmer tribe while winter wails outside. However, he finds himself abruptly cast in the unlikely role of designated tribal leader. Worse yet, he must run for his life and is soon exiled in the land of his clan's enemy. Through adversity, Perloo discovers hidden courage, wisdom, and inner strength when called on to confront a conniving, vicious usurper who is determined to rule the Montmer village in his own dictatorial way. Perloo also gains unanticipated insights into the minds of the Felbarts, longtime foes of his tribe.

Awards: Black-Eyed Susan Book Award (Maryland), Great Stone Face Book Award (New Hampshire), Nutmeg Book Award (Connecticut), Sunshine State Young Readers Award (Florida)
Related Subjects: Animals, Government, Literature, Proverbs, Rabbits, Reading
Character Themes: Courage, Friendship, Loyalty, Responsibility

Barry, Dave, and Ridley Pearson, *Peter and the Starcatchers.* **Illustrated by Greg Call. Hyperion Paperbacks for Children, 2004. ISBN: 078684907X (paperback) (Grades 6–12)**
How did Captain Hook and Peter Pan become archenemies? This creative prequel might surprise James Barrie, the creator of the original Peter, as it enthralls contemporary readers of all ages. This is a story of miserable orphans, malicious sea captains, talking porpoises, stardust, the monstrous crocodile, Mr. Grin, and the daredevil courage of forever-young Peter. Readers learn how the invader of the nursery first came to fly, why he never ages, and how the Lost Boys came to be lost. Adventure abounds and when completed, this volume offers teaser pages for the next in the series.

Awards: Colorado Children's Book Award, Dorothy Canfield Fisher Children's Book Award Master List (Vermont), Grand Canyon Young Reader Award (Arizona), *New York Times* Best Seller, Young Reader's Choice Award (Pacific Northwest Library Association)
Related Subjects: Adventure, Orphans, Peter Pan, Pirates, Sea
Character Themes: Cooperation, Humor, Survival

Beck, Ian, *The Secret History of Tom Trueheart.* **Greenwillow, 2006. ISBN: 0061152102 (hardcover) (Grades 4–8)**
Tom's six older brothers are always being sent on great adventures in the Land of Stories. Given only a description of their character, they must meet the challenges set before them, creating the endings of their unfinished tales. When none of his brothers return in time for his twelfth birthday, Tom is sent to discover why their missions remain incomplete. Accompanied only by a friendly crow, Tom must prove that he too is worthy of the name Trueheart. Through Tom, readers see Cinderella, Snow White, Rapunzel, and other characters of traditional literature in a whole new light.
Awards: ABA Book Sense Pick, Highland Children's Book Award (UK)
Related Subjects: Adventure, Fairy tales, Family, Heroes
Character Themes: Courage, Humor, Loyalty

Cleary, Beverly, *The Mouse and the Motorcycle.* **Illustrated by Louis Darling. Cornerstone Books, 1989. ISBN: 1557361371 (hardcover) (Grades 3–6)**
Keith thinks that the time with his parents at the Mountain View Inn is going to be boring until he meets Ralph, a talking mouse, that has fallen in love with the boy's toy motorcycle. With Keith's help, the plucky mouse masters the skill of riding this exciting mode of transportation and new adventures begin. Zooming through hotel hallways, he dodges the dangers of two-legged adults, four-legged predators, and equally fearsome vacuum cleaners. When Keith becomes ill, it is the courageous effort of Ralph to retrieve an aspirin that brings the boy relief. In this tale, Cleary has crafted a delightful fantasy for young and old alike.
Awards: Great Stone Face Book Award (New Hampshire), William Allen White Children's Book Award (Kansas), Young Reader's Choice Award (Pacific Northwest Library Association)
Related Subjects: Adventure, Friendship, Mice
Character Themes: Humor, Ingenuity

DiCamillo, Kate, *The Miraculous Journey of Edward Tulane.* **Illustrated by Bagram Ibatoulline. Candlewick Press, 2006. ISBN: 0763625892 (hardcover) (Grades 3–6)**
Edward Tulane is a very beautiful and a very proud china rabbit. Why shouldn't he be with a little girl who adores him and gives him a custom-made wardrobe? Suddenly, however, Edward is launched on a journey that takes him from the bottom of the ocean to a garbage pile, a hobo camp, and to the arms of a dying child. Along the way he meets those who are warm-hearted and giving as well as those who are selfish and evil, but when his own heart is broken he comes to understand his need to receive love and his ability to give it. The exquisite illustrations add depth and poignancy to this timeless tale.
Awards: Boston Globe-Horn Book Award
Related Subjects: Adventure, Dolls, Emotions, Journeys, Pride, Rabbits, Redemption, Toys
Character Themes: Friendship, Giving, Humility, Love

DiCamillo, Kate, *The Tale of Despereaux: Being the Story of a Mouse, a Princess, Some Soup, and a Spool of Thread.* **Illustrated by Timothy Basil Ering. Candlewick Press, 2004. ISBN: 0763617229 (hardcover) (Grades 3–9)**
An especially small mouse with exceptionally large ears is the endearing hero of this fantasy. Ostracized by his community because he dares to love a princess, Despereaux refuses to give up his dream. When Chiaroscuro the rat devises a plan to kidnap the princess, Despereaux's love, courage, and ingenuity are put to the test. Complicating the plot are the yearnings of Miggery Sow, a dim-witted serving girl, to be a princess. Timothy Ering's charming pencil sketches add just the right touch.
Awards: Dorothy Canfield Fisher Children's Book Award (Vermont), Golden Archer Award (Wisconsin), Indian Paintbrush Book Award (Wyoming), Land of Enchantment Award (New Mexico), NCTE Notable Children's Book in Language Arts, Newbery Medal, Parents' Choice Silver Honor Award, Rhode Island Children's Book Award
Related Subjects: Abuse, Adventure, Heroes, Mice
Character Themes: Courage, Determination, Forgiveness, Love

Ferris, Jean, *Once Upon a Marigold.* **Harcourt, 2002. ISBN: 0152050841 (paperback) (Grades 6–12)**
At six years old, Christian chooses to leave a life that does not allow him the time to be himself. Running away from home and becoming lost in an

enchanted forest, Christian readily attaches himself to a kindhearted troll, Edric, and his dogs, Bub and Cate. After Edric tries unsuccessfully to persuade the child to allow him to find his parents, the tenderhearted little creature becomes a surrogate father. As the years pass, Christian finds himself enamored with Princess Marigold, his friend only through the telescope and by carrier pigeon. However, when the forest dweller discovers a plot to harm Marigold, he risks everything—including Ed, Bub, and Cate—to save her. Impossible intrigues, daring rescues, foiled murders, all peppered with Ed's malapropisms, result in a traditional fairy tale with just the right jolt of contemporary humor to make the whole story timeless.

Awards: ALA Best Book for Young Adults, Indian Paintbrush Book Award (Wyoming), Junior Library Guild Selection, Massachusetts Children's Book Award, Rhode Island Teen Book Award, *Smithsonian Magazine* Notable Book for Children

Related Subjects: Dogs, Family—Nontraditional, Inventions, Language, Postal service

Character Themes: Creativity, Determination, Friendship, Humor, Independence, Ingenuity, Love

Funke, Cornelia, *Inkheart*. Scholastic, 2005 (orig. 2003). ISBN: 0439709105 (paperback) (Grades 7–12)

Meggie wonders why her beloved father, whom she has always called "Mo," never reads aloud to her, especially since parent and child alike thrive on books, both for entertainment and for their livelihood. Mo is a bookbinder, specializing in the repair of antique volumes. Mysteriously, however, he and Meggie seem to live in the same house for only a year, and suddenly move on, reportedly because of an important client. Their secure world of two is inexplicably thrown into upheaval by the appearance of the eerie Dustfinger, an old acquaintance of Mo's. Riveting action, dreadful villains, and heroic acts of selflessness pervade this modern fantasy. This is a riveting story of devotion and courage, love and sacrifice, supported by the mesmerizing quality of the power of the printed word.

Awards: ALSC Notable Children's Book, Colorado Children's Book Award, Maine Student Book Honor Award, *Publishers Weekly* Best Children's Book, *New York Times* Best Seller

Related Subjects: Bookbinding, Father-daughter relationships, Family— Single parent, Good vs. evil, Survival

Character Themes: Cooperation, Courage, Family loyalty, Ingenuity, Trust

Funke, Cornelia, *The Thief Lord.* Scholastic, 2001 (orig. 2000). ISBN: 0439771323 (paperback) (Grades 5–8)
Reminiscent of *Oliver Twist*, this page-turner features orphans who triumph over both adversity and greedy adults. Two brothers, Prosper and Bo, narrowly escape being adopted by unpleasant relatives and have no place to live nor sustenance with which to survive. Making friends with a girl named Hornet, and other homeless boys, they come under the leadership of the enigmatic Thief Lord. Adventure, mystery, intrigue, and sweet revenge guide the plot to an impossible-to-predict conclusion. A compassionate private investigator, a fearless artist, and a convent of ingenious nuns round out the cast of characters in this fast-paced survival story. Romantic Venice forms the background, and much of the action takes place in or around the lovely but dangerous canals. As added attractions, the author includes a glossary, an afterword with facts about the city, and the story behind the story.
Awards: ABA Book Sense Pick, Garden State Teen Book Award (New Jersey), Great Lakes Books Honor Award (Michigan), Maine Student Book Honor Award, *New York Times* Best Seller, *School Library Journal* Best Book
Related Subjects: Friendship, Orphans, Venice
Character Themes: Compassion, Creativity, Loyalty

Hale, Shannon, *Enna Burning.* Bloomsbury Publishing, 2004. ISBN: 1582348898 (paperback) (Grades 8–12)
Young adult readers may have already met Enna in *Goose Girl*, as an aide and ally to Ani, the displaced princess. A sequel, this story takes place two years later, and Enna faces her own set of challenges. Her beloved Forest is endangered, and her brother Leifer uses his newly acquired art of fire-talking as a defense. When Enna discovers that she, too, can call fire into existence, she faces moral questions that are as contemporary as technology. Although the spirited teen promises herself that she will use her ability only for patriotic defense, she quickly becomes entangled with danger, destruction, and mind-boggling decisions. Enna fights an inner battle that speaks to all who have struggled with addiction. This powerful story carries a message for all teachers, parents, and teens.
Awards: Beehive Award finalist (Utah), New York Public Library Best Book for the Teen Age
Related Subjects: Addictions, Friendship, War
Character Themes: Courage, Discernment, Self-control

Hale, Shannon, *The Goose Girl*. Bloomsbury Publishing, 2005 (orig. 2003). ISBN: 1582349908 (paperback) (Grades 6–12)

As Princess Anidori-Kiladra Talianna Isilee, Crown Princess of Kildenree, grows up in her bustling castle-world, she is groomed, as the firstborn, to eventually become the monarch. Benevolent Ani, sensitive to the forces of nature, seems to have a special kinship with the wind, as she tenuously grasps through the stories told her by her favorite aunt. Indeed, it is this ancient folklore that later supplies the resources that Ani requires for survival. When it comes time for her to ascend the throne, Ani is devastated when the honor is instead bestowed upon her brother. Suddenly, she finds herself dispatched on a hazardous journey to become the wife of the Prince of Bayern, whom she has never met. En route, treachery overwhelms the young bride-to-be as her trusted handmaiden assumes the royal identity, and Ani barely escapes alive. Enlarging the folktale of the title, Hale creates a realistic protagonist who moves from the delicate, pampered princess to a sturdy tender of geese, and in the process gains the love of her peers as well as the loyalty of a mysterious member of the royal court who provides her salvation in the page-turning conclusion.

Awards: Beehive Award (Utah), Josette Frank Award, Lone Star Reading List (Texas)

Related Subjects: Betrayal, Folktales, Friendship, Good vs. evil, Journeys, Survival

Character Themes: Courage, Cooperation, Diligence, Duty, Humility

Hale, Shannon, *The Princess Academy*. Bloomsbury Publishing, 2005. ISBN: 1582349932 (hardcover) (Grades 7–12)

All of the teenage girls from Miri's mountain village are herded off to a new location for training to become candidates for the prince's bride. Though only fourteen, the diminutive Miri reluctantly goes along. Taught the basics of reading, math, history, courtly manners, and commerce, each girl responds from her own personality, and each dreams of becoming a princess. As time draws near for the prince to make his selection, competition becomes fierce and loyalties are tested. Then a band of cutthroats invades the school, holding hostage all who live there. With her characteristic logic, tempered by a touch of magic and a small gift of love, little Miri becomes a hero. The prince gets his bride, and all live happily, but with a delightful ending that will both satisfy and surprise.

Awards: ALSC Notable Children's Book; Irma Simonton Black and James H. Black Award for Excellence in Children's Literature (Bank Street), Newbery Honor

Related Subjects: Coming of age, Education, Family relationships, Loneliness, Friendship, Mining, Mountains, Villages
Character Themes: Courage, Wisdom

Hoeye, Michael, *Time Stops for No Mouse: A Hermux Tantamoq Adventure*. G. P. Putnam's Sons, 2002. ISBN: 0399238786 (hardcover) (Grades 8–12)
Watchmaker Hermux Tantamoq is a hardworking mouse who is thankful for ordinary things: donuts, coffee, and peaceful evenings at home with his pet ladybug. However, his quiet life takes a dramatic and adventurous turn when Ms. Linka Perflinger, dashing daredevil aviatrix, bursts into his repair shop, drops off a broken watch, and steals his heart. As a result of his infatuation with Ms. Perflinger, Hemux is led deeper and deeper into intrigue and danger—eventually attempting a daring rescue of his ladylove, discovering that he, too, is bold and brave. Hoeye's inventive style sweeps the reader so convincingly into the world of Hermux and his associates that she easily forgets that the hero is a mouse, living in a society "peopled" by animals.
Awards: Michael L. Printz Award
Related Subjects: Adventure, Mystery
Character Themes: Courage, Humor

Jacques, Brian, *Redwall*. Redwall Abbey Company Ltd. (England), Penguin Putnam Inc., 1986. ISBN: 0441005489 (paperback) (Grades 5–9)
Since *Redwall* made its debut, a super-successful series has arisen that retains the name of this internationally acclaimed first book. Readers are introduced to clumsy Matthias the mouse, hearty Constance the badger, the wise old mouse Abbot Mortimer, and others of Redwall Abbey as they enjoy pastoral lives of preserving peace, food, and a sense of community. Into this idyllic life charges Cluny the Scourge and his ruthless band of sea rats. The courage and cunning that follows introduces elementary readers and middle school fantasy lovers to all of the qualities of life that parents and caring teachers hope to instill in them, in the format of high adventure. Matthias matures, Constance leads, Abbot Mortimer guides, and Cluny comes to understand just how very thoroughly might does not make right. Most readers will want to continue reading more in this action-packed series. Websites galore are available, beginning with www.redwall.org, which even includes recipes for some delectable feasts.
Awards: *New York Times* Best Seller
Related Subjects: Adventure, Animals, Badgers, Birds, Food, Heroes, Mice
Character Themes: Boldness, Celebration, Cooperation, Courage, Faithfulness, Leadership

Kendall, Carol, *The Gammage Cup: A Novel of the Minnipins*. Illustrated by Erik Blegvad. Harcourt, 1959. ISBN: 0152024275 (hardcover) (Grades 4–9)

In the village of Slipper-on–the-Water, society is controlled by the "Periods" who are descendents of Fooley the Magnificent. To maintain the status of the town, they believe that everyone should wear the same color clothes and paint their front doors green. This tendency to "sameness" escalates when it is announced that a prize, the Gammage Cup, will be awarded to the most beautiful village in the Land Between the Mountains. Convinced that five freethinking citizens will ruin the town's opportunity to win the coveted cup, this hapless group is banished from the village. As the five outcasts set up housekeeping upriver from Slipper-on-the-Water, they discover that an ancient enemy has again infiltrated the land. The question is whether or not they will be able to persuade the other Minnipins of this impending danger in time to survive. Part social commentary and part simple fantasy, this story is full of wit and wisdom.

Awards: ALSC Notable Children's Book, Newbery Honor, Sequoyah Book Award (Oklahoma), William Allen White Children's Book Award (Kansas)

Related Subjects: Rejection, Self-expression, Social issues

Character Themes: Audacity, Courage, Friendship, Humor, Individuality, Teamwork, Wisdom

King-Smith, Dick, *Ace: The Very Important Pig*. Illustrated by Lynette Hemmant. Random House, 1990. ISBN: 0679819312 (paperback) (Grades 3–6)

Although he isn't really sure what "Market" means, when all of his siblings are sent to Market, Ace is certain that he does not want to go there. Plotting his survival in stages, the little piglet with the ace-shaped markings on his rump first endears himself to Farmer Tubbs, a neighbor of Farmer Hogget of *Babe* fame. Next, Ace forges a friendship with the house cat, Clarence. Finally, he manages a coup d'état of the snobbish corgi Megan, and gains unlimited access to the house, except at night when he sleeps in the barn with best friend Nanny the goat. Soon Ace is operating the controls of the television and choosing his favorite shows, which Clarence and Megan enjoy, as well. The seal of his triumph however, comes from his visit to the notorious Market, where his distinction emerges. This is a success story of "hoggish" proportions that will bring chuckles to adults and children alike.

Awards: IRA Children's Choices

Related Subjects: Animals, England, Farm life, Pigs

Character Themes: Friendship, Humor, Ingenuity

Mains, David, and Karen Mains, *Tales of the Resistance*. Illustrated by Jack Stockman. Lamplighter Publishing, 1986. ISBN: 1584740531 (hardcover) (Grades 3–9)
The Enchanted City is held in the grasp of the evil Fire-King who seals people's identity with his practice of branding. Scarboy, one of the many orphans who inhabit this dark place, has escaped to Great Park, where the True King has renamed him Hero. Through the stand-alone chapters that follow, Hero learns life principles that allow him to fulfill the promise of his new name. Colorful characters such as Naysayers, Doubletalk, Mercie, Heroic Taxi-drivers, Caretaker, dragons, and the Ranger Commander fill these tales of adventure, giving readers tools to overcome the temptations they face in everyday life. High-quality illustrations enhance the text. Those who enjoy this volume will want to continue the stories in *Tales of the Kingdom* and *Tales of the Restoration*.
Awards: Christian Book Award
Related Subjects: Good vs. evil, Orphans, Self-concept
Character Themes: Honor, Overcoming adversity, Sacrifice

Martin, Ann M., and Laura Godwin, *The Doll People*. Illustrated by Brian Selznick. Scholastic, 2000. ISBN: 0439329078. (paperback) (Grades 3–6)
Except for the disappearance of Auntie Sarah forty-five years before, life in the dollhouse has remained much the same since 1898 when the toy was purchased as a gift for young Gertrude Cox. The china doll family now belongs to Kate, the third generation of Gertrude's descendents. When young Annabelle, who is eight in doll years, discovers Auntie Sarah's personal journal, she begins to believe that perhaps this adventurous aunt is still somewhere in the big house. Defying the doll Code of Honor, which has bound her family to the confines of the dollhouse for one hundred years, Annabelle determines to search until she finds her long-lost relative. With the arrival of the Funcrafts, a family of plastic dolls purchased for Kate's younger sister Nora, Annabelle finds a friend to join in her adventures.
Awards: Kentucky Bluegrass Award, Massachusetts Children's Book Award, Maud Hart Lovelace Book Award (Minnesota), *Publishers Weekly* Best Children's Book
Related Subjects: Adventure, Dolls, Family—Relationships, Friendship, Mysteries
Character Themes: Courage, Family love

McAllister, M. I., *Urchin of the Riding Stars.* **Illustrated by Omar Rayyan. Hyperion, 2005. ISBN: 0786854871 (paperback) (Grades 3–9)**
On the night of the Riding Stars, a baby squirrel found on the beach of Mistmantle Island is taken under wing by Crispin, a captain in the king's inner circle. The day that the squirrel, Urchin, begins to work as a page for Crispin in the Tower, the King's son is found murdered and Crispin is blamed. An evil force has been unleashed on the peaceful island of Mistmantle that is threatening to overthrow good King Brushen and Queen Spindle. Work parties have been formed that are being pushed to work harder and harder, and a culling of babies that are born with any slight deformity has been ordered. Urchin's dedication to the innocence of his mentor, his courage, and his bravery will have a lot to do with whether or not his adopted island will be able to regain its freedom. This is book one in *The Mistmantle Chronicles.*
Awards: ALSC Notable Children's Book, Branford Boase Award
Related Subjects: Animals, Good vs. evil, Hedgehogs, Heroes, Moles, Otters, Squirrels, Swans
Character Themes: Cooperation, Courage, Initiative, Integrity, Loyalty, Survival

Oppel, Kenneth, *Airborn.* **EOS, 2004. ISBN: 0060531827 (paperback) (Grades 7–12)**
Matt Cruse, cabin boy on the luxury airship Aurora, feels more at home in the sky than on the earth. One night on watch, when he spies a damaged balloon, his fortunes take a turn to high adventure. Kate, the granddaughter of the deceased balloonist, engages his help to prove the existence of mysterious flying creatures described in her grandfather's journal. Sky pirates attack to rob the wealthy passengers, and extreme storms batter the Aurora, forcing a crash landing on an uncharted island. With hazardous situations, appealing heroes and heroines, evil villains, and even a little humor, *Airborn* is a satisfying read. Science and fantasy are expertly blended to make the reader a willing believer in this tale. Those who enjoy *Airborn* may wish to read its sequel, *Skybreaker.*
Awards: ALSC Notable Children's Book, BCCB Blue Ribbon, Beehive Award (Utah), Michael L. Printz Honor, Rhode Island Teen Book Award, *School Library Journal* Best Book, Thumbs Up Award (Michigan)
Related Subjects: Adventure, Balloons, Birds, Flight, Good vs. evil, Loss of parent, Pirates
Character Themes: Determination, Devotion, Friendship, Ingenuity, Self-image, Unselfishness

Paolini, Christopher, *Eragon.* **Alfred A. Knopf, 2003. ISBN: 0375826696 (paperback) (Grades 6–12)**
When farm boy Eragon finds a blue stone in the forest, he is more disappointed that he has been unsuccessful in hunting than pleased with his discovery. However, when the "stone" reveals itself to be a dragon's egg, with the hatchling breaking through, the young adventurer realizes that his life has been invaded. Dark powers compete to strip the young man of his prize or persuade him to join their side. When old Brom, the village storyteller, comes to Eragon's rescue, the two embark on a pilgrimage that may change the fate of the entire country. As Brom trains his protégé physically (at times, unmercifully), he is also teaching him valuable life lessons. Written when author Paolini was sixteen, this compelling story of courage, duty, demanding friendship, discipline, and dedication is a tribute to the talent of the writer, the integrity of Eragon, and the tenderness of a dragon named Saphira. This is the first book in *The Inheritance* series.
Awards: Gateway Award (Missouri), Nene Award (Hawaii), *New York Times* Best Seller, *Publishers Weekly* Best Seller, Rhode Island Teen Award, *USA Today* Best Seller, *Wall Street Journal* Best Seller, Young Reader's Choice Award (Pacific Northwest Library Association)
Related Subjects: Dragons, Good vs. evil
Character Themes: Cooperation, Courage, Friendship, Independence, Respect for authority

Pattou, Edith, *East.* **Magic Carpet Books/Harcourt, 2005. ISBN: 0152052216 (paperback) (Grades 7–12)**
Born into a large family, lively little Rose does not comprehend the extent to which her mother is controlled by superstition, nor how this reliance on fate will take her to the very door of death. When Rose's sister Sarah becomes ill and all remedies fail, help comes from a mysterious and frightening source, a white bear that speaks with a human voice. The solution offered by the night visitor, that Rose will leave with him, at first seems unthinkable to the family. However, the life of her sister hangs in the balance and Rose chooses to accept the adventure, allowing the huge silent creature to carry her far from home. Rose encounters mystery, magic, honor, deceit, and harrowing adventure, propelling her journey to a spellbinding conclusion. Based on the ancient fairy tale "East of the Sun and West of the Moon," this epic retelling will keep modern readers mesmerized.
Awards: Top Ten Best Book for Young Adults (YALSA), Junior Library Guild Selection, *School Library Journal* Best Book

Related Subjects: Folk literature, Siblings, Superstition
Character Themes: Cooperation, Courage, Determination, Hope, Loyalty

Rylant, Cynthia, *Gooseberry Park*. Illustrated by Arthur Howard. Harcourt Brace, 1995. ISBN: 0152322426 (hardcover) (Grades 4–6)
Four most unlikely friends, Murray the bat, Stumpy the squirrel, Gwendolyn the hermit crab, and Kona the chocolate lab, work together to ensure that Stumpy's new babies survive an ice storm. There are days of concern when Stumpy disappears, but all ends well. This is a story of courage, cooperation, survival, and some humor thrown in by a loquacious bat. Young readers learn that friends do not have to look alike, nor have homes alike or enjoy similar tastes to provide companionship, life lessons, and fun. Rylant has created a pleasant little novel with hidden messages that will benefit all who read it.
Awards: IRA Teachers' Choices
Related Subjects: Dogs, Pets, Squirrels
Character Themes: Compassion, Courage, Humor

Siegel, Robert, *Whalesong*. HarperCollins, 1981. ISBN: 0062507982 (paperback) (Grades 8–12)
Hruna, a humpback whale, narrates his journey from birth all the way through to the delight of becoming a father. With observations philosophical and mystical, he speaks with the soul of a poet and the voice of a threatened life-form. The first of the *Whalesong Trilogy*, this small novel holds appeal for young adults who are ecologically sensitive as well as those who take pleasure in the beauty of language.
Awards: Golden Archer Award (Wisconsin), Matson Award
Related Subjects: Ecology, Sea, Whales
Character Themes: Cooperation, Family unity, Respect

Spires, Elizabeth, *The Mouse of Amherst*. Illustrated by Claire A. Nivola. A Sunburst Book/Farrar, Straus & Giroux, 1999. ISBN: 0374454116 (paperback) (Grades 6–8)
Emmaline the mouse has found her way into the Dickinson residence in Amherst, Massachusetts. With her few possessions, a notebook being one, the diminutive narrator takes up residence in the wainscoting of mysterious Emily's room. Although the two never meet face to face, Emmaline becomes the inspiration and confidante of the posthumously famous Miss Dickinson. Delightful observations from the tiny, furry creature allow readers an intimate glimpse of the enigmatic poet. Of course, Dickinson's poems are sprinkled throughout the mouse-sized volume, complete with Emmaline's version of the object or occasion of their inspiration.

Awards: Children's Crown Award, *Publishers Weekly* Best Book of the Year
Related Subjects: Emily Dickinson, Mice, Poetry
Character Themes: Creativity, Imagination, Individuality

Steig, William (author and illustrator), *Dominic*. Farrar, Straus & Giroux, 1972. ISBN: 0374418268 (paperback) (Grades 4–8)
When Dominic the dog locks up his house, leaves a note for friends, and starts eagerly down the road to seek adventure, he has no idea just where his path will lead. Fighting off the wicked Doomsday Gang; befriending a wealthy, but dying pig; unintentionally earning great riches; and achieving hero status are only the highlights of this most distinctive canine escapade. This delightful read-aloud story painlessly and humorously introduces advanced vocabulary, deftly interwoven with a beguiling plot.
Awards: ALSC Notable Children's Book, Christopher Award, William Allen White Children's Book Award (Kansas)
Related Subjects: Adventure, Animal, Dogs
Character Themes: Compassion, Courage, Humor

White, John, *The Tower of Geburah*. Illustrated by Kinuka Kraft. Inter-Varsity Press, 1978. ISBN: 0877845603 (paperback) (Grades 6–10)
Wesley, Kurt, and Lisa disappear through the screen of a magical television from their uncle's house in Canada and reappear in the land of Anthropos, each for his or her own reasons. Lisa bravely sets out to aid imprisoned royalty, and her brothers follow to rescue their sister. Kurt is brimming with the desire for adventure, while cautious Wesley is sure that trouble lurks at every turn. Jinns, dwarfs, goblins, and talking wolves greet the children. Overriding all these creatures are the forces of good and evil led by the shepherd Gaal and the sorcerer Shagah. Forbidden doors and gates to open, delicious food and food that leaves one hungry, enticements and choices tailor-made for each character await the adventurers. This is the third in the *Archives of Anthropos* series, and readers will want all six.
Awards: Best Christian Children's Books 1942-1992
Related Subjects: Adventure, Family—Relationships, Good vs. evil, Quests, Siblings
Character Themes: Cooperation, Courage, Faithfulness, Leadership, Obedience, Trust

Winthrop, Elizabeth, *The Castle in the Attic*. Bantam Doubleday Dell Books for Young Readers, 1985. ISBN: 0440409411 (paperback) (Grades 4–7)
Ten-year-old William has been cared for by his babysitter/nanny, Mrs. Phillips, his entire life, while his parents are busy with their professions. Mrs.

Phillips spots William in his gymnastic routines, teaches him about gardening, reads him stories about King Arthur, and is simply his best friend. So, it is naturally a shock to William when Mrs. Phillips announces to the family that she is returning to her family home in England, now that William can take care of himself. However, William has other ideas about being "abandoned." When Mrs. Phillips attempts to soften the blow of her departure by giving her charge a castle that has been in her family for generations, she opens a door to enchantment that wields surprises for both nanny and child. This is the first in the series of Castle stories, and young readers will want to continue with the next as soon as the last page of this story is told.

Awards: California Young Readers Medal, Dorothy Canfield Fisher Children's Book Award (Vermont), IRA/CBC Children's Choices

Related Subjects: Castles, Fantasy, Restitution

Character Themes: Courage, Honor, Justice

CHAPTER FOUR

Historical Fiction

Through historical fiction, children can develop a sense of place in their family, their country, and the world. Historically based novels demonstrate the passing down of traditions, giving young readers an understanding of how their lives have been affected by the decisions and actions of others. Time period distinguishes historical fiction from all other works, for this genre is set in the years of generations past. The characters may be people who actually lived, or may simply be born in the writer's imagination and written into the context of the time period, but all are caught up in the historical events of the era in which they find themselves.

Whether historical novels show daily domestic events or are suspenseful thrillers or fast-paced adventure stories, setting is significant. No matter what the theme, well-written historical novels demonstrate a skillful blending of fact and fiction, information and imagination. Since accurate details of transportation, food, clothing, housing, and societal attitudes must fit the selected time and place, there are occasions when extensive description is required to accurately convey information to the reader. In this genre especially, the author is faced with the challenge of incorporating descriptions smoothly into the plot without interrupting the flow of the work, for above all, readers love a good story.

In order to encourage excellence in the genre of historical fiction, author Scott O'Dell established the Scott O'Dell Award in 1981. To win this award a work must be historically significant and potentially appealing to young readers as well as meet the usual literary criteria. In 1983, the state of Virginia established the Jefferson Cup award to honor titles of biography or historical fiction or nonfiction for young people. Both of these awards seek to encourage youth to become interested in the events of the past through timeless, compelling tales penned by talented writers.

Alder, Elizabeth, *The King's Shadow*. Farrar, Straus & Giroux, 1995. ISBN: 0374341826 (hardcover) (Grades 5–9)
When Evyn and his father are brutally attacked, his father is killed and Evyn's tongue is cut out. A few days later his uncle sells the mute boy as a slave to Lady Ealdgyth Swan Neck. Instead of leading to a life of servitude, his stay in Ealdgyth's household offers Evyn the opportunity to learn to read and write. These abilities make him useful to Earl Harold of Wessex, the future King of England. As Evyn travels with Harold, he chronicles the Saxon's many exploits up to his defeat at the Battle of Hastings. This is an inspiring account of turning disaster into personal victory.
Awards: ALA Best Book for Young Adults, Lone Star Reading List (Texas), Maine Student Book Award Master List
Related Subjects: Battle of Hastings, England, Harold Godwinson, Mutism, Orphans, Special needs—Physical disabilities, Wales
Character Themes: Loyalty, Overcoming adversity, Resilience

Anderson, Laurie Halse, *Fever, 1793*. Aladdin, 2002. ISBN: 0689848919 (paperback) (Grades 6–12)
When yellow fever invades Philadelphia in 1793, five thousand people die in a three-month period, including sixteen-year-old Mattie Cook's widowed mother. Mattie and her grandfather flee the city, but realize the disease is everywhere. Upon their return, they find that their servant Eliza has protected the family's coffeehouse while working with The Free African Society to nurse those who are ill. Though Mattie begins as a willful, self-centered young person, she develops strength and resourcefulness in the face of grave dangers. Anderson does an excellent job of drawing the reader into the drama of this devastating event while depicting eighteenth-century Philadelphia in rich historical detail.
Awards: ALA Best Book for Young Adults, IRA Teachers' Choices, Jefferson Cup Award (Virginia), Massachusetts Children's Book Award, Rebecca Caudill Young Reader's Book (Illinois), Sunshine State Young Readers Award (Florida)Award

Related Subjects: Death, Epidemics, Orphans, Cross-cultural relations, Yellow Fever

Character Themes: Family loyalty, Perseverance, Responsibility, Self-reliance

Armstrong, Jennifer, *Black-Eyed Susan.* **Illustrated by Emily Martindale. Dell Yearling, 1995. ISBN: 0697885560 (paperback) (Grades 4–7)**
Ten-year-old Susie loves the freedom of the Dakota Territory; she enjoys the sod house with its roof of loose dirt and blooming flowers. Her mother does not share Susie's joy, and has begun staying inside the little house, lacking the desire to step across the threshold. With increasing depression, the mother leaves more and more housework for her daughter. Neither father nor child knows what to do to lift their loved one's loneliness. One day, as they are returning from the nearby village, Susie and her dad encounter a large family of homesteaders moving farther west and offer hospitality for the night. The demands of guests, activities of the bustling family, and a special gift from one of the children act as rays of sunlight, piercing the walls of the dark sod house, and Susie's mother begins to approach life with a new spirit. This novel reflects the realities of prairie life on a level that will resonate with young readers, bringing life to history.

Awards: NCTE Notable Children's Trade Book

Related Subjects: 1800s, Family—Relationships, Midwest, Prairies, Sod houses

Character Themes: Independence, Joy, Love

Avi, *Crispin: The Cross of Lead.* **Clarion, 2002. ISBN: 0786808284 (hardcover) (Grades 4–9)**
Asta's thirteen-year-old son finds himself in great danger after the death of his mother. Declared a "wolf's head," or someone who can be killed on sight, for a crime he did not commit, the orphan must flee his village. Taking with him a lead cross that belonged to his mother, his only other possession is the discovery that his real name is Crispin. Fleeing across the English countryside, Crispin's fate becomes entwined with a huge juggler named Bear who forces the runaway into servitude while promising to protect him. He does, however, teach Crispin to think on his feet and in the end it is the boy who saves Bear while at the same time finding himself.

Awards: *New York Times* Best Seller, Newbery Medal

Related Subjects: 1300s, Adventure, England, Middle Ages

Character Themes: Courage, Friendship, Loyalty, Self-image

Avi, *The Secret School*. Scholastic, 2001. ISBN: 0439430062 (paperback) (Grades 3–6)
There is not a plentiful supply of teachers willing to live in remote western Colorado in the 1920s. So when Miss Fletcher returns to Iowa to care for her ailing mother, the school must shut down unless someone can be found to complete the term. Encouraged by her classmates, fourteen-year-old Ida takes on the task, hoping that no one will discover their plan. When the local school examiner pays a surprise visit, the secret is out and the children must prove the validity of their experiment by passing the exams to go on to the next grade.
Awards: IRA-CBC Children's Choices, Parent's Guide Children's Media Award
Related Subjects: Frontier and pioneer life, School, Teachers
Character Themes: Courage, Determination, Ingenuity

Bredsdorff, Bodil, *The Crow Girl*. Farrar, Straus & Giroux, 2004 (orig. 1993), reprinted from the Danish. ISBN: 0374312478 (hardcover) (Grades 6–12)
Living on an isolated cove in a remote area of Denmark, a young girl and her grandmother barely exist as they draw life from the sea and its deposits. With little of this world's goods, the two thrive on their ingenuity and an intuitive understanding of each other. Sensing death approaching, the grandmother leaves her beloved "Chick" with words of caution that guide the child through adventure, danger, survival, and finally to shared security with an unlikely assortment of friends. Each gem of wisdom, given during the grandmother's final days, surfaces to help Crow-Girl as she takes risks, helps others, and finally achieves the goal that pleases her and would have brought joy to her grandmother.
Awards: Mildred Batchelder Honor Award, Parents' Choice Silver Honor Award
Related Subjects: Cross-generational relationships, Denmark
Character Themes: Compassion, Courage, Sharing, Survival

Bunting, Eve, *Train to Somewhere*. Illustrated by Ronald Himler. Clarion Books, 1996. ISBN: 0395713250 (hardcover) (Grades 1–6)
From the mid-1850s to the late 1920s, nearly 100,000 children were rescued from poverty and homelessness by the Children's Aid Society and sent west by rail from New York City. As the trains stopped in small towns, farmers who needed another hand, women who wanted another household servant, and childless couples seeking their hearts' desire met and adopted the or-

phans. In this fictionalized account, Miss Randolph, the Aid representative, coaches the children in manners and grooming while easing their fears with gentle encouragement. At each station, one or more child is selected by a family. Finally, only Marianne is left. The last stop, a bittersweet moment, is captured in both text and illustration. Bunting and Himler have created a memorable child in Marianne and a compassionate counselor in Miss Randolph. Poignant and honest, this title offers rich ground for discussion in classrooms and among family members.

Awards: ALSC Notable Children's Book, *Booklist* Editors' Choice, Jefferson Cup Honor Award (Virginia)

Related Subjects: 1800s, 1900s, Adoption, Family—Nontraditional, Orphan Trains, Overcoming adversity, Railroads, Rejection

Character Themes: Acceptance, Hope

Burch, Robert, *Ida Early Comes Over the Mountain*. Avon, 1980. ISBN: 0380570912 (paperback) (Grades 3–6)

After the death of their mother, the Sutton children need someone to care for them. When free-spirited Ida Early shows up at the door asking for work, the family quickly chooses her over austere Aunt Earnestine. Ida is described as a gangly scarecrow wearing a baggy brown sweater, overalls, and clodhoppers. The housekeeping abilities she claims to have are questionable, but not her joyful spirit or the warmth she brings to this needy family. When their friends at school make fun of Ida, the Sutton children must decide where their loyalties lie.

Awards: ALSC Notable Children's Book, Boston Globe-Horn Book Award, William Allen White Children's Book Award (Kansas)

Related Subjects: 1930s, Appalachia, Death—Parent, Family—Single parent, Poverty, Siblings, The Great Depression

Character Themes: Humor, Loyalty, Self-acceptance

Choldenko, Gennifer, *Al Capone Does My Shirts*. Scholastic, 2004. ISBN: 0439692377 (paperback) (Grades 6–9)

Matthew Flanagan, known to family and friends as "Moose," has just moved to Alcatraz, where his father is employed as guard and electrician. Mr. Flanagan has taken both jobs and moved his family to this bleak twelve-acre rock so that his daughter, Natalie, can go to a school for special-needs children. The school, located just across the bay, is expensive, and seemingly the only hope that Natalie has of learning to cope with life. To assist with the cost of Natalie's school, Mrs. Flanagan has taken a job teaching music on the mainland, and Moose is left with the responsibility of caring for his teenage sister after school. On the island, Moose finds himself with a strange combination of friends, including Piper, the warden's conniving, dishonest, sometimes cruel daughter. Much adored by her father, Piper can wrangle almost any deal, and her scheme, which involves Moose, is not only illegal and complex, but could cost Mr. Flanagan his job. Moose's only outlet for being a normal boy is baseball, but that too, it seems, must be sacrificed for Natalie. This multilayered novel explores the stress and pathos of having a special-needs sibling, parents that are consumed with making life work, and peers of the opposite sex who are alternately unpredictable and compassionate. Although based on a fictional family, historical details are accurate, and the author has included notes and literature circle questions in this edition.

Awards: ALA Best Book for Young Adults, Garden State Teen Book Award (New Jersey), Iowa Teen Award, John and Patricia Beatty Award (California), Lone Star Reading List (Texas), Newbery Honor, Parents' Choice Silver Honor Award, Rebecca Caudill Young Readers Book Award (Illinois), Texas Bluebonnet Award

Related Subjects: 1930s, Autism, Baseball, Prison, Special needs—Siblings

Character Themes: Compassion, Friendship, Honesty, Responsibility

Cornelissen, Cornelia, *Soft Rain: A Story of the Cherokee Trail of Tears*. A Yearling Book, 1998. ISBN: 0440412420 (paperback) (Grades 4–7)
Soft Rain and her family are diligently preparing the soil for planting corn when white soldiers abruptly burst into their home and disrupt their lives. Her father and brother, Hawk Boy, are herded off with a different group than Soft Rain and her mother. The beloved Grandmother, who always told stories to keep history alive, is forced to stay in the cabin because she is old and ill. The family never sees her again. Through the long and painful trek from Georgia to Oklahoma, many of the Cherokee die, but in this story written for a younger audience, the family is reunited, and through the kindness of a white family, there is a relatively hopeful ending, with new crops to plant and school to attend. This little novel offers a great opportunity to share with elementary readers a shameful chapter in the history of America, and an occasion to honor the courage of those who survived.

Awards: CBC/NCSS Notable Children's Trade Book in Social Studies

Related Subjects: Ethnic cleansing, Native Americans—Cherokee, United States—History

Character Themes: Courage, Family love, Survival

Curtis, Christopher Paul, *Bud, Not Buddy.* **Delacorte Press, 1999. ISBN: 0385323069 (hardcover) (Grades 6–9)**
When Buddy's mother dies, he is placed in a succession of abusive foster homes until he decides to escape and look for Herman E. Calloway, the jazz musician that he believes to be his father. This humorous yet serious novel tackles issues of the Great Depression, the death of a parent, racism, homelessness, poverty, and foster care but still leaves the reader smiling. Curtis has packed the pages of this book with a cast of endearing, quirky characters including the spunky ten-year-old with childlike ways of thinking. Buddy's guide, which he has titled *Bud Caldwell's Rules and Things for Having a Funner Life and Making a Better Liar Out of Yourself*, is amusing and reveals how this precocious young boy has learned to deal with the problems he has encountered so early in life.
Awards: Coretta Scott King Award, Golden Kite Award, Land of Enchantment Award (New Mexico), Mitten Award (Michigan), Nene Award (Hawaii), Newbery Medal, Prairie Pasque Award (South Dakota), Young Reader's Choice (Pacific Northwest Library Association)
Related Subjects: Death of parent, Family—Foster, Father-son relationships, Foster care, Hoovervilles, The Great Depression
Character Themes: Determination, Humor

Cushman, Karen, *The Midwife's Apprentice.* **Clarion Books, 1995. ISBN: 0395692296 (hardcover) (Grades 5–9)**
Homeless, our heroine is found sleeping in a dung heap by Jane Sharp, the village midwife, who takes her in as an apprentice. Used to being called Brat by those who are chasing her, the young girl slowly gains respect for herself under Jane's tutelage and renames herself Alyce. Slowly Alyce blossoms as she discovers that she is not the ignorant, ugly creature people have called her in the past. Humor mixed with historical fact, fast-paced action, and a sprinkling of herbal remedies makes this a book to remember.
Awards: ALA Best Book for Young Adults, *Booklist* Editors' Choice, Horn Book Fanfare, Newbery Medal, Parents' Choice Gold Award, Young Reader's Choice (Pacific Northwest Library Association)
Related Subjects: Apprenticeship, Middle Ages, Midwives, Orphans, Survival
Character Themes: Compassion, Humor, Self-image

Dalgliesh, Alice, *The Courage of Sarah Noble.* **Simon & Schuster, 1991 (orig. 1954). ISBN: 0689715404 (paperback) (Grades 3–6)**
In 1707, eight-year-old Sarah Noble accompanies her father deep into the unsettled wilderness of Connecticut to build a new house for their family.

Facing unknown danger from wild animals and unfamiliar Indian tribes, they camp in a large cave that her father transforms into a comfortable shelter. While her father works, Sarah makes friends with the Indian children, teaching them English words and learning from them where to find delicious berries. When her father returns for the rest of the family, Sarah lives in the Indian village under the care of their friend "Tall John." In addition to encouraging courageous behavior, this saga based on a true story teaches that all persons should be treated with kindness and openness.

Awards: Lewis Carroll Shelf Award, Newbery Honor

Related Subjects: 1700s, Connecticut, Cross-cultural relations, Father-daughter relationships, Fear, Frontier and pioneer life, Native Americans

Character Themes: Courage, Faith, Friendship, Overcoming fear

Dowell, Frances O'Roary, *Dovey Coe*. Aladdin Paperbacks, 2001. ISBN: 0689846673 (paperback) (Grades 4–6)

Outspoken Dovey Coe loves the North Carolina mountains. A strong-minded twelve-year-old, she is very protective of her family, especially Amos, her deaf brother. Trouble begins when Parnell Caraway, the spoiled son of the town's wealthiest family, courts Dovey's beautiful sister Caroline. Publicly humiliated by Caroline's rejection, Parnell seeks revenge by brutally killing the Coes' dog. Attempting to intervene, Dovey becomes the object of the beating and is knocked unconscious. She comes to lying next to Parnell's dead body. Accused of murder, Dovey is dependent on the skill of a young, inexperienced court-appointed attorney to plead her case. Dovey is an engaging, inspiring heroine whose "mountain twang" lends authenticity to the story.

Awards: Edgar Award, Maud Hart Lovelace Book Award (Minnesota), Rebecca Caudill Young Readers Book Award (Illinois), William Allen White Children's Book Award (Kansas)

Related Subjects: Appalachia, Deafness, Mysteries, Siblings

Character Themes: Courage, Family loyalty, Self-respect

Eckert, Allan W., *Incident at Hawk's Hill*. Illustrated by John Schoenherr. Little, Brown & Co., 1971. ISBN: 0316208663 (hardcover) (Grades 4–9)

Six-year-old Ben is uncomfortable with people, but has an unusual affinity with animals. Wandering away from home one June day in 1870, he finds himself lost and stranded on the Canadian prairie in the middle of a thunderstorm. After finding shelter in a badger's tunnel, the young boy is accepted and cared for by the female badger for two full months. By the time

he is found by his older brother, Ben has adopted many badger ways and is reluctant to return home. Following after her adopted child, the mother badger meets with grave danger. This story is based on a true incident.
Awards: ALSC Notable Children's Book, George C. Stone Center for Children's Books Recognition of Merit (Ohio), Newbery Honor
Related Subjects: Badgers, Feral children, Survival
Character Themes: Compassion, Self-image

Fleischman, Paul, *Bull Run*. Woodcuts by David Frampton. Harper-Collins, 1993. ISBN: 006440588 (paperback) (Grades 6–12)
Through voices of fifteen fictional characters and one actual participant, the first battle of the Civil War is poignantly relived. Eight characters each, from both Union and Confederate positions—including men and women, black and white, soldier and civilian—speak from anticipation, through realization, and finally to resignation of what war is really like. Some are wounded, some are freed; all are changed. The format is adaptable for reader's theater with no narrative, just intimate and powerful dialogue. This little volume is one of Fleischman's most memorable additions to young adult literature.
Awards: ALA Best Book for Young Adults, ALSC Notable Children's Book, Horn Book Fanfare Honor, Scott O'Dell Award
Related Subjects: Civil War, United States—History
Character Themes: Courage, Perseverance, Survival

Griffin, Adele, *Hannah Divided*. Hyperion Paperbacks for Children, 2002. ISBN: 0786817275 (paperback) (Grades 7–12)
Thirteen-year-old Hannah Bennett is fascinated by math, in any form. She counts everything, and then takes the sum through further numerical processes. Hannah believes her lucky number is thirty-two, and whenever she thinks of anything related to thirty-two, she feels comforted. Numbers stimulate Hannah; they energize and drive her. Whenever the young math whiz is stressed, she copes by tapping out rhythms, or pacing a certain number of steps. In her small hometown of Chadds Ford, she is allowed her peculiarities. However, reading is another matter, and when Mrs. Sweet, from Philadelphia, arrives at her school to offer a scholarship to a needy student, Hannah is chosen. Selection means that she will have to leave her comfort zone and move into a house with Mrs. Sweet and other prodigies. The adjustment is difficult, but Hannah determines to use the love of math to shape her future. This is a story of courage, less than perfect circumstances, giftedness, and hope.
Awards: *Booklist* Editors' Choice, Georgia Children's Book Award

Related Subjects: 1930s, Math, Prodigy, Special needs, Obsessive-compulsive disorder
Character Themes: Determination, Individuality

Grimes, Nikki, *Talkin' About Bessie: The Story of Aviator Elizabeth Coleman*. Illustrated by E. B. Lewis. Scholastic, 2002. ISBN: 0439573424 (paperback) (Grades 3–8)
Elizabeth Coleman was a pioneer and adventurer in the field of aviation. The first licensed African-American female pilot, Bessie rose above many difficulties to achieve her success. Grimes uses the unusual technique of telling the story of Coleman's life through the voices of people who knew her. Beginning with her father, the free verse entries continue chronologically until her death in a tragic accident at the age of thirty-four. Full-page watercolor paintings accompany each eulogy.
Awards: ALSC Notable Children's Book, CBC/NCSS Notable Children's Trade Book in Social Studies, Coretta Scott King Award, Horn Book Fanfare, NCTE Notable Children's Book in the Language Arts
Related Subjects: African-Americans, Aviation, Prejudice, Women
Character Themes: Courage, Determination, Initiative

Gundisch, Karin, *How I Became an American*. Translated by James Skofield. Cricket Books, 2001. ISBN: 0812648757 (hardcover) (Grades 6–9)
This fictionalized account of a family emigrating from Austria-Hungary to Youngstown, Ohio, in 1902 is told from the viewpoint of ten-year-old John. Based on letters written by immigrants between 1902 and 1986, this narrative is filled with anecdotes of everyday life, which illustrate the gap between their old lifestyle and the new. Even the songs used by the shipping companies to entice people to emigrate are worked into the storyline. Though the family faces many difficulties, including the death of little sister Eliss, each member works hard and contributes to the family's budding prosperity.
Awards: ALSC Notable Children's Book, Mildred L. Batchelder Award
Related Subject: Death of child, Immigration
Character Themes: Family love

Harlow, Joan Hiatt, *Star in the Storm*. Margaret K. McElderry, 2000. ISBN: 0689829051 (hardcover) (Grades 4–8)
Because of greed and jealousy, all sheepherding dogs have been outlawed in the little coastal village where Maggie and her family live. However, Maggie's beloved pet, Sirius, a Newfoundland herding dog, is like a family member,

and the spunky young girl refuses to surrender her furry friend. The intelligence of Sirius is known across the village, but the power of the Rand family is also a force to be acknowledged and they believe that Sirius has killed one of their sheep. A lack of water, deadly illness, a glacier in the harbor, and finally a shipwreck plague the small village, revealing courage and forgiveness on the part of child, man, and beast in an exciting climax. In the afterword, Harlow includes the factual basis for her novel, as well as an introduction to its sequel, *Thunder from the Sea*.

Awards: ABA Book Sense Pick, ASPCA Henry Bergh Children's Book Award, Flicker Tale Children's Book Award Master List (North Dakota), IRA/CBC Children's Choices

Related Subjects: Dogs, Heroes, Newfoundland, Pets, Storms, Villages

Character Themes: Courage, Faith, Family love, Resourcefulness, Spunk

Henry, Marguerite, *Justin Morgan Had a Horse*. Drawings by Wesley Dennis. Scholastic, 1954. ISBN: 0590453122 (paperback) (Grades 6–8)

Young Joel Goss is invited by his schoolmaster, Justin Morgan, to walk with him from Randolph, Vermont, to Springfield, Massachusetts, to collect a debt. The young scholar has no hint of how his life is going to change. Joel is about to become a man, ready or not. Upon arriving at the destination, Mister Morgan has the staggering disappointment of discovering that the debtor cannot come forth with the cash. Instead, he offers a spirited colt, Ebenezer, and allows a runt, Little Bub, to follow along unbidden. Instantly, Joel and Little Bub bond in a way that only pet lovers can understand, and the boy begins to plan how he might own the undersized colt. Arriving back home, Joel is dealt a cruel blow when his father immediately binds him out as an apprentice for seven years, during which time Joel can own nothing but the clothes he is given by his master. Through many adventures and disappointments, Joel is finally reunited with the small workhorse, known by then as "Justin Morgan's" or the "Morgan" horse, just in time for a small moment of glory. Marguerite Henry breathes life and personality into both boy and horse in this true story of the American-bred Morgan.

Awards: Newbery Honor

Related Subjects: 1800s, Apprenticeship, Horses, Vermont

Character Themes: Determination, Diligence, Loyalty

Hesse, Karen, *Out of the Dust*. Scholastic, 1997. ISBN: 0590371258 (paperback) (Grades 5–8)

In sparse, conversational verse, Karen Hesse conveys the hopelessness and despair created by the constant dust storms that blew across Oklahoma in the

1930s, destroying crops, vehicles, and the hopes and dreams of those who farmed the land. Fourteen-year-old Billie Jo tells of her family's struggle to survive the harsh realities of daily life when sudden storms bury everything in drifts of gritty dust. Against this backdrop, the author creates a stoic, courageous young heroine who endures the pain of losing her mother in a terrible accident, as well as the ability to play her beloved piano. Although this tale abounds in sadness, it also ends in hope while conveying an understanding of the strength and importance of family love.

Awards: ALA Best Book for Young Adults, Jefferson Cup Honor Award, Maine Student Book Honor Award, Newbery Medal, Scott O'Dell Award, *School Library Journal* Best Book

Related Subjects: Death of parent, Dust Bowl, Family—Single parent, Father-daughter relationships, Grief, Oklahoma

Character Themes: Courage, Determination, Family loyalty

Hest, Amy, *When Jessie Came Across the Sea*. Illustrated by P. J. Lynch. Candlewick Press, 1997. ISBN: 0763600946 (hardcover) (Grades 2–5)
Living with her grandmother in a poor village in Eastern Europe, Jessie is surprised when given the opportunity to immigrate to America. Jessie goes, but vows to earn enough money for her grandmother to join her someday. The story of Jessie is the story of millions who came from Europe to America in the early 1900s. What sets this book apart is the picture-book format filled with the luminous illustrations of P. J. Lynch. Even primary children will be able to understand the struggles and the joys of this courageous young woman.

Awards: Kate Greenaway Medal (UK), Parents' Choice Gold Award

Related Subjects: Cross-generational relationships, Ellis Island, Grandparents, Immigration, Orphans

Character Themes: Courage, Diligence, Family love

Hill, Kirkpatrick, *The Year of Miss Agnes*. Scholastic, 2000. ISBN: 0439303435 (paperback) (Grades 4–7)
Told in first-person narrative by Fred, an enthusiastic student in the remote Alaskan village of Koyukuk, this is the story of one person who cares and makes a difference. Teachers come and teachers go, but few stay more than a year, and some don't survive that long in the tiny one-room school. When Miss Agnes arrives, the watchful villagers know that she is different. She wears slacks, so she must know the climate, and when she cleans out the teacher-house, she really whacks the rug, so she must be strong. What neither students nor their parents know is just how inventive and creative the

little Englishwoman can be, and how she will change scholastic progress. With her innovative approach, even the one hearing-impaired child is brought into the classroom for the first time. What will happen when her year is over? Anxious students anticipate the time of decision, as will eager readers.

Awards: Dorothy Canfield Fisher Children's Book Award (Vermont), Once Upon a World Children's Book Award, Rhode Island Children's Book Award, *School Library Journal* Best Book, Sunshine State Young Readers Award (Florida), William Allen White Children's Book Award (Kansas)
Related Subjects: Alaska, School Teachers, Villages
Character Themes: Discovery, Enthusiasm, Learning

Holm, Jennifer L., *Our Only May Amelia*. Scholastic, 1999. ISBN: 0439179106 (paperback) (Grades 4–8)
Growing up in the state of Washington in 1899, twelve-year-old May Amelia Jackson has seven older brothers and is not at all interested in being feminine. Much to her mother's disappointment, she is one hundred percent tomboy and loves doing everything her brothers do. Through May Amelia's adventures, readers glimpse life on the frontier including encounters with a cougar, a bear, and Chinook Indians. It takes a near tragedy to break down this spunky young girl's resistance to becoming a lady, but through these troubling events she begins to find her true identity.

Awards: CBC/NCSS Notable Children's Trade Book in Social Studies, Newbery Honor, Parents' Choice Silver Honor Award, Rhode Island Teen Book Award
Related Subjects: Family, Frontier and pioneer life, Self-concept, Siblings, Washington State
Character Themes: Family love, Humor, Self-respect

Holm, Jennifer L., *Penny from Heaven*. Random House Books for Young Readers, 2006. ISBN: 9780375836879 (hardcover) (Grades 6–8)
In the summer of 1953, eleven-year-old Penny Falucci enjoys spending the golden days listening to baseball games on the radio with Uncle Dominic and cheering on "Dem Bums," the Brooklyn Dodgers. Spoiled and adored by her deceased father's Italian family, Penny often finds herself defending each side of her heritage to the other while loving each for their individual quirks. Often wondering how her father died, Penny finds no one who will satisfy her curiosity until a tragedy brings both sides together across her hospital bed. Verbal explosions, there are. Loud accusations fly fast, but in the end Penny can accept her father's untimely death and she serves as a catalyst to bring

together those she loves. A memorable character, Penny will stay with readers long after the last page is turned. Writing from her own experience, Jennifer Holm shares her family portraits along with significant historical information about World War II in her author's notes at the conclusion of the book.

Awards: ALSC Notable Children's Book, Newbery Honor
Related Subjects: 1950s, Baseball, Family—Extended, Family—Single parent, Friendship, Italian-Americans, World War II
Character Themes: Coping, Family love

Hudson, Jan, *Sweetgrass*. Scholastic, 1991. ISBN: 0590434861 (paperback) (Grades 7–12)
Fifteen-year-old Sweetgrass is her father's favorite, and he is in no hurry for her to marry and leave the family tipi, even when all the other teenage girls are being promised. Hopeful that she will marry Eagle-Sun, the Blackfoot teen has no real clue as to her father's plans. Because of the workload imposed on her by her almost-mother, Bent-Over-Woman, and the teasing of Otter, her almost-brother, Sweetgrass longs to have her own tipi. However, she doubts the ability of Eagle-Sun to provide the number of horses that will please her father. At last Sweetgrass believes that all conditions are in her favor, and she is devastated when her father insists that she is not yet woman enough to marry. The deadly winter of 1837 brings with it the dreaded smallpox epidemic, changing both the tribe and Sweetgrass forever. However, with spring arrives hope. Told in first-person narrative, this small novel transports readers into the tipi, the wild strawberry fields, and the hearts of the Blackfoot tribe.

Awards: CLA Book of the Year for Children (Canada), Governor General's Award (Canada), *School Library Journal* Best Book
Related Subjects: 1830s, Epidemic, Native Americans—Blackfoot, Smallpox, United States—History
Character Themes: Love, Maturity, Responsibility

Ingold, Jeanette, *Airfield*. Puffin/Penguin Books, 1999. ISBN: 0141312165 (paperback) (Grades 8–12)
Fourteen-year-old Beatrice Donnough does not remember her mother. Since she can recall, Beatty, as she is known, has rotated living among her three aunts, while her uncommunicative father ferries passengers around the skies in a passenger plane. Beatty's favorite place to stay is with her Aunt Clo, only fifteen years her senior, who lives near the Muddy Springs Airport. Beatty also loves her uncle, Grif, who lets her hang around the airfield and help him with odd jobs. This summer, there is more stability to Beatty's life, since

Grif's job may be permanent at the Muddy Springs facility. To make her life even more interesting, Beatty meets Moss, a true teen of the thirties, on his own and working to send money home to his mom and houseful of younger brothers and sisters. As summer progresses, mysteries begin to unfold that have surrounded both of Beatty's parents, giving her a clearer picture of who she is, and who she wants to become. Adventure seems to seek out Moss and Beatty, as they each learn more about planes, flying, mechanics, the airfield, and each other. This is a rich sample of Ingold's realistic historical fiction transporting readers back to a time when life had its own set of challenges, as well as excitement.

Awards: New York Public Library Book for the Teen Age

Related Subjects: 1930s, Airplanes, Family, Father-daughter relationships, Gender roles

Character Themes: Determination, Perseverance

Ingold, Jeanette, *Hitch*. Harcourt Children's Books, 2005. ISBN: 0152047476 (paperback) (Grades 8–12)
Readers are time warped back to the 1930s as Moss Trawley discovers a place of his own in the Civilian Conservation Corps. Ingold fans met Moss in a previous novel, *Airfield*, and will be pleased that the warmhearted seventeen-year-old has found a place to belong. Still bound to his mother and younger siblings by feelings of being the responsible male, Moss needs employment and a secure future, which he finds in the Civilian Conservation Corps. Learning about protecting the environment and improved farming practices opens a door of opportunity for the capable young man. Moss also discovers his own hidden talents while developing camaraderie with other men. Readers watch Moss developing confidence, and even a sense of authority in this male-dominated environment. As the Corps works together, the men and boys overcome seemingly insurmountable odds with both nature and stubborn farmers, resulting in victory and maturity on both sides. Ingold whets readers' appetites for more 1930s fare as she writes about timeless lessons of compromise and the importance of teamwork. She deftly creates interest in a period of history that has been overlooked by most writers of historical fiction. Historically accurate, this novel will find its place in social studies classrooms, as well as on lists of favorites among adolescents.

Awards: Christopher Award, New York Public Library Book for the Teen Age, Society of School Librarians International Book Award, Tayshas Reading List (Texas)

Related Subjects: 1930s, Civilian Conservation Corps, Ecology

Character Themes: Leadership, Perseverance, Teamwork

Johnston, Julie, *Hero of Lesser Causes*. Puffin/Penguin, 1992. ISBN: 0140369988 (paperback) (Grades 7–10)
Keely and her brother Patrick are inseparable, and will dare each other to attempt the most hare-brained feats, even those involving heights, depths, and leeches. However, on a hot August afternoon, all that changes when Patrick is suddenly stricken with crippling polio. Although he survives the disease, he is left paralyzed, with his spirit suffering a major blow. Special nurses come and go; friends visit and get a cool and uncomfortable reception, and Patrick remains untouched behind his wall of bitterness and anger. However, Keely determines to make a difference and continues to press, push, cajole, and go to amazing lengths to get her brother to respond and return to life. With an iron will and innovative methods, a sister's love is finally rewarded. Keely will inspire readers of all ages.
Awards: ALSC Notable Children's Book, Governor General's Award (Canada), *School Library Journal* Best Book of the Year
Related Subjects: 1940s, Horses, Polio, Siblings, Special needs—Physical disabilities
Character Themes: Determination, Family love, Friendship, Ingenuity

Kinsey-Warnock, Natalie, *Lumber Camp Library*. Illustrated by James Bernardin. HarperCollins, 2002. ISBN: 0060293217 (hardcover) (Grades 3–7)
Ruby, her father's "little jewel," loves watching her father manage the most jumbled log jam while keeping the stubborn mass moving down the river. Pa even teaches Ruby some of these skills; however, more than anything, Pa wants Ruby to have an education. Once she begins to attend school, Ruby enthusiastically shares her knowledge by teaching her ten siblings, as well as her beloved father, in the evenings. Life becomes a logjam of its own when Pa drowns while rescuing a fellow logger, and the large Sawyer family must move into a tiny house in the nearby village. When Ruby befriends visually handicapped Mrs. Graham, exciting doors begin to open for the Sawyers. Happy surprises await readers in this heartwarming, realistic story of a little girl whose life, and the lives of those around her, are transformed through the power of books. This small novel and others of Kinsey-Warnock's stories are based on the experiences of seven generations of Vermonters.
Awards: Sunshine State Young Readers Award (Florida)
Related Subjects: 1900s, Blindness, Education, Libraries, Logging, Reading, Special needs— Physical disabilities, Vocations
Character Themes: Determination, Family love, Friendship, Love, Survival

Klages, Ellen, *The Green Glass Sea.* **Viking, 2006. ISBN: 0670061344 (paperback) (Grades 4–8)**
Ten-year-olds Suze Gordon and Dewey Kerrigan live in Los Alamos, New Mexico, a place that no one on the outside can know even exists. Perched high on a mesa and heavily guarded, primitive apartments, dormitories, and mud-rutted streets serve physicists, chemists, and technicians as they labor long hours on a secret project. Dinner conversation, when the parents arrive home in time to eat, cannot disclose the nature of the work, but all know that there is an earth-shattering mission in progress on "the gadget." Although Suze and Dewey are distinctly different, the intimacy of this unique community draws them together, and causes each to look at life through a broader lens. This is a novel of life and death, of cooperation and individuality, of sacrifice and immense accomplishment. Unique in its perspective, this novel will add a special zest to studies of World War II and the children who survived it.
Awards: Scott O'Dell Award
Related Subjects: Atomic bomb, Death—Parent, Friendship, Family—Nontraditional, Manhattan Project, New Mexico, Science, Special Needs—Physical disabilities, United States—History, World War II
Character Themes: Creativity, Imagination, Individuality, Sacrifice, Self-reliance, Spunk

LaFaye, A., *Worth.* **Simon & Schuster Books for Young Readers, 2004. ISBN: 0689857306 (hardcover) (Grades 5–8)**
Nathaniel's leg is crushed in the rush of getting one last load of hay into the barn before a storm destroys the crop. Burdened by the guilt of having put Nathaniel in danger as a result of his haste, Pa does not deal well with his only son's handicap, and most days, barely speaks to him. As harvest-time duties intensify, Pa sorely needs another farmhand. Nathaniel carries his own load of pain as he sees how much help his father needs around the farm—a need which Nathaniel will never again be able to fill. Into this milieu of love and bitterness comes city-bred John Worth, adopted from the Orphan Train. Seen as a godsend by Pa, an intruder by Ma, and a threat by Nathaniel, John exists on the bare perimeter of family life until malicious forces from the outside cause all members of the family to reexamine their values. Set at the time of the range wars, this well-crafted novel deftly places readers in a position to determine just what is of "worth."
Awards: *Booklist* Editors' Choice, Charlie May Simon Children's Book Award (Arkansas), Charlotte Award (New York), Louisiana Young Readers' Choice, Nebraska Book Award Honor, Scott O'Dell Award

Related Subjects: Farm life, Grief, Guilt, Orphan Trains, Orphans, Range wars, Special needs—Physical disabilities
Character Themes: Cooperation, Family loyalty, Love, Jealousy

Larson, Kirby, *Hattie Big Sky*. Delacorte Press, 2006. ISBN: 0385733135 (hardcover) (Grades 8–12)
Tired of being shifted from one relative to another after the death of her parents, sixteen-year-old Hattie Brooks is delighted to hear that Uncle Chester has left her the rights to his homestead claim in Vida, Montana. Knowing little of the rigors of homesteading, Hattie works her uncle's claim in the face of drought, blizzards, and back-breaking labor. With the help of neighbors like the Muellers, Leafie Purvis, and Rooster Jim she learns such diverse skills as stringing a fence and cooking edible biscuits. Much of the story is told through letters to Hattie's friend Charlie, who is fighting in Europe, and articles that she writes about homesteading for *The Arlington News*. Based on the author's family history, this is a story of courage, faith, and determination that will warm the heart.
Awards: Newbery Honor, *School Library Journal* Best Book of the Year
Related Subjects: Cross-cultural relations, Farm life, Homesteading, Montana, Orphans, Prairies, Survival, World War I
Character Themes: Courage, Friendship, Neighborliness, Perseverance, Resilience, Self-reliance

Lasky, Kathryn, *Dreams in the Golden Country: The Diary of Zipporah Feldman, a Jewish Immigrant Girl*. Scholastic, 1998. ISBN: 0590029738 (hardcover) (Grades 5–8)
The time is 1903; the place is Ellis Island. Jewish immigrants approach the New York harbor. Twelve-year-old Zipporah, or "Zippy," as she is known, writes in her diary of anticipation, fears, and above all her dreams of the unknown land. Having escaped persecution in Russia, the Feldman family embarks on a fresh life. With zest and humor, Zippy chronicles each startling discovery in her adopted country, often prefacing journal entries with "Guess what?" Each member of the Feldman family plays a significant role in Zippy's diary. As Papa, Mama, and sisters Miriam and Tova find futures that could unfold only in America, Zippy falls in love with drama, and chooses the Yiddish theater as her career. Since family life centers around religious observances, preparation and implementation of these celebrations are an integral part of Zippy's record. Kathryn Lasky writes with authority and charm, creating a memorable character in a fascinating setting.

Awards: Jefferson Cup recognition of entire *Dear America* series (Virginia)
Related Subjects: Immigration, Jews, Music, Religion, Theater
Character Themes: Adaptation, Courage, Family love, Humor, Religious faith

Levine, Gail Carson, *Dave at Night*. Scholastic, 1999. ISBN: 0439202086 (hardcover) (Grades 4–9)
After the death of his father, eleven-year-old Dave Caros is placed in a home for boys where cruelty is the rule. Sneaking off the grounds in the evening, Dave finds an escape from the dull life of the asylum through his friendship with Solly, a self-proclaimed fortune-teller. It is Solly who introduces him to the avant-garde world of musicians, painters, and writers who people the Harlem Renaissance, and it is Solly who helps to make life at the Hebrew Orphan Asylum livable for Dave and the other "elevens." Dave is a tough but winsome boy who discovers the value of true friendship in the face of great loss.
Award: ABA Book Sense Pick, ALSC Notable Children's Book, Newbery Honor, Young Hoosier Book Award (Indiana)
Related Subjects: African-Americans, Bullies, Harlem Renaissance, Jazz, Jews, Music, Orphans, The Great Depression
Character Themes: Friendship, Ingenuity, Talent

Lisle, Janet Taylor, *The Art of Keeping Cool*. Atheneum, 2000. ISBN: 0689837879 (hardcover) (Grades 7–10)
While his father is fighting the air war over Europe in World War II, Robert is battling to untangle the dark secrets surrounding his father's family at home. Confused and angered by the quick temper of his grandfather, Robert finds companionship with his artistic cousin Elliot. Together the boys establish a tenuous relationship with a German-born painter who is living as a recluse in the nearby woods. When suspicious circumstances stir violent prejudice in the town to a fever pitch, tragedy results. In this story, Lisle effectively shows the destructive power of war at home as well as on the battlefront.
Awards: Jefferson Cup Honor Award (Virginia), Rebecca Caudill Young Readers Book Award (Illinois), Scott O'Dell Award, Sunshine State Young Readers Award (Florida), Young Hoosier Book Award (Indiana)
Related Subjects: Family relationships, Prejudice, World War II
Character Themes: Friendship, Self-acceptance, Tolerance

McCaughrean, Geraldine, *The Kite Rider*. HarperCollins, 2001. ISBN: 0066238749 (hardcover) (Grades 5–9)
After his father's death, Haoyou becomes a kite rider in an effort to save his mother from a greedy uncle and an unfortunate second marriage. When

offered the opportunity by the Great Miao to travel with the Jade Circus, Haoyou entertains the crowds by soaring through the skies tied to a beautiful scarlet and gold kite. Haoyou's adventures traversing thirteenth-century China bring him fame and fortune, culminating in a command performance for Kublai Khan himself. Family duty, betrayal, and sacrifice fill the pages of this historical novel for young adults.

Awards: ALA Best Book for Young Adults, Angus Book Award (UK), Blue Peter Best Book to Keep (UK), Horn Book Fanfare, Nestlé Children's Book Prize (UK)

Related Subjects: China, Circus, Kites, Kublai Khan, Mongols

Character Themes: Courage, Family loyalty, Sacrifice, Self-image

McGraw, Eloise Jarvis, *The Golden Goblet*. Scholastic, 1961. ISBN: 0590445529 (paperback) (Grades 6–9)

When his father dies, Ranofer, the son of a famous goldsmith, has no place to go except to live with his half-brother Gebu. Hired out as a laborer, Ranofer still harbors dreams of becoming a master goldsmith, until he discovers that he has unwittingly been used to steal from his master. Beaten by wicked Gebu, he is forced to be an apprentice in his half-brother's stonecutting shop. Finding evidence that Gebu has indeed been stealing from a tomb in the City of the Dead, Ranofar and his two friends, Heqet and The Ancient One, determine to expose the plot and prove Gebu's nefarious ways.

Awards: Newbery Honor, William Allen White Children's Book Award Master List (Kansas)

Related Subjects: Abuse—Child, Egypt, Family—Relationships, Goldsmith trade, Orphans, Siblings

Character Themes: Courage, Friendship, Honesty, Loyalty

Meyer, Carolyn, *Gideon's People*. Gulliver Books/Harcourt Brace, 1996. ISBN: 0152003045 (paperback) (Grades 7–10)

This novel reveals the story of two cultures, Amish and Jewish, as reflected in the lives of two teens. On his first trip to help his peddler father deliver his wares to the Amish community, Isaac Litvak and the family horse, Goldie, are injured in an accident and taken in to heal by the Stolzfus family. While in recovery, Isaac learns about Amish religious beliefs and taboos while becoming friends with Annie and Gideon, two of the six Stolzfus children. Although Annie serves as his nurse, Gideon becomes his friend, and when the time comes for Isaac to return to his family, he is the means by which Gideon makes his escape from a life that is crushing him. This novel provides an intriguing juxtaposition of two young people on the brink of in-dependence and how each assesses his traditions and chooses to respond.

Awards: ABA Book Sense Pick, Colorado Blue Spruce Young Adult Book Award, Sydney Taylor Book Award, Young Hoosier Book Award (Indiana)

Related Subjects: Abuse—Physical, Amish, Family—Relationships, Father-son relationships, Heritage, Jews, Sibling loyalty

Character Themes: Independence, Loyalty, Religious faith, Spunk

Meyer, Carolyn, *Where the Broken Heart Still Beats: The Story of Cynthia Ann Parker.* **Harcourt Brace, 1992. ISBN: 0152006397 (paperback) (Grades 9–12)**

Cynthia Ann Parker was abducted from her family by Comanche Indians in 1836 in a raid where many of her family were killed. Twenty-five years later, Cynthia is recaptured by soldiers and returned to her white family to be "repatriated." During those twenty-five years in captivity, Cynthia had become accustomed to Indian ways and had married a Comanche chief. With continuing conflict between Indians and white settlers, Cynthia experiences little remorse for her "savage" ways and yearns to return to her Indian husband. Only young cousin Lucy shows a real desire to know her as a person and to alleviate her sorrow. This is a good title to use in a literature unit with *A Light in the Forest* or *Sing Down the Moon*.

Awards: ALA Best Book for Young Adults

Related Subjects: Native Americans—Comanche, Prejudice, Texas, Tolerance

Character Themes: Courage, Family loyalty, Survival

Park, Linda Sue, *A Single Shard.* **Clarion Books, 2002. ISBN: 0395978270 (hardcover) (Grades 4–8)**

In the twelfth century, Ch'ul'po is a small Korean town well known for its celadon pottery. Tree-ear lives there under a bridge, with the elderly and disabled Crane-man who has cared for Tree-ear and taught him how to survive on leftovers from the fields and the rubbish heaps. In addition, he has taught the boy courage, honesty, and the value of hard work. When Tree-ear accidentally destroys a piece of pottery created by a local master potter, he agrees to work off his debt—hoping at the same time to learn the potter's craft. When Min, the potter, has an opportunity to earn a royal commission, Tree-ear offers to make the long journey to deliver his work to the royal court at Songdo. On the way, he is attacked by robbers; the pottery is broken and the pieces are scattered. Determined to fulfill his obligation, Tree-ear continues the journey to deliver one small shard of what is left of Min's masterpiece.

Awards: Newbery Medal
Related Subjects: 1300s, Bibliotherapy, Cross-generational relationships, Korea, Orphans, Pottery
Character Themes: Ambition, Determination, Faithfulness, Integrity, Loyalty

Park, Linda Sue, *The Kite Fighters*. Clarion Books, 2002. ISBN: 0395940419 (hardcover) (Grades 3–6)
Competitive kite flying, a popular sport in medieval Korea, sets brother against brother in this tale that highlights Korean family traditions. Kee-sup, the elder, is talented in building and decorating these extraordinary kites, but Young-sup is better at making them respond to his wishes. When the young king of Korea requests the expertise of both brothers, in building and learning to fly a kite, family traditions are put to the test. The author catches the excitement of this ancient sport while highlighting the intense sibling rivalry between two brothers.
Awards: Arizona Young Readers Master List, California Young Readers Medal, Irma Simonton and James H. Black Award for Excellence in Children's Literature (Bank Street), Tayshas Reading List (Texas)
Related Subjects: Kites, Korea, Self-concept, Siblings
Character Themes: Determination, Loyalty, Respect

Paterson, Katherine, *Lyddie*. Puffin Books, 1992. ISBN: 0140349812 (paperback) (Grades 7–10)
When her father abandons his family and their failing Vermont farm, Lyddie and her brother Charles are hired out as servants. Wanting to escape the grinding labor of endless hours in a tavern, Lyddie strikes out for Lowell, Massachusetts, where she hears young girls can make a great deal of money working in the textile mills. Conditions in the mills are wretched, but Lyddie determines to make enough money to regain the family farm. A roommate introduces her to the delights of reading, and Lyddie realizes that a better future can be found through education.
Awards: ABA Book Sense Pick, ALA Best Book for Young Adults, ALSC Notable Children's Book, Jefferson Cup Honor Award (Virginia)
Related Subjects: Abolition, Child labor, Industrial Revolution, Labor reform, Textile mills, Women
Character Themes: Courage, Desire for education, Independence, Perseverance, Work ethic

Rabin, Staton, *Betsy and the Emperor*. Simon Pulse/Simon & Schuster, 2006. ISBN: 141691336X (paperback) (Grades 9–12)
When Napoleon Bonaparte is exiled to the island of St. Helena after his defeat by the British, he is housed, along with his retinue, at the expansive residence of the Balcombe family. Fourteen-year-old Betsy is drawn to the fallen emperor from his entrance, because he is brash, daring, and has a somewhat infamous reputation. The two play cards, eat together, argue, dance, and verbally bash each other, just for the sake of entertainment. In short, they become kindred spirits. When Napoleon is moved to a much more austere location, Betsy does all that is within her power to bring joy to his cheerless existence. This fascinating novel is based on the actual friendship of the military genius and a teenage girl who did much to brighten the last days of the would-be world conqueror.
Awards: ABA Book Sense Pick, New York Public Library Book for the Teen Age
Related Subjects: 1800s, Exile, Friendship, Napoleon
Character Themes: Audacity, Courage, Humor, Loyalty

Rinaldi, Ann, *In My Father's House*. Scholastic, 1993. ISBN: 0590447319 (paperback) (Grades 8–12)
From the first shots fired in the Civil War to the final surrender, the McLean family is at battle, sometimes on the field, always within the household. After the war begins on the lawn of the McLean property, "Daddy Will" McLean, stepfather to Oscie and Maria, decides to move his family to safety in the little village of Appomattox, Virginia. Hiding behind an emotional wall, Oscie, the oldest daughter, holds fierce loyalty to her deceased papa, and fights Will in every decision. Written from Oscie's point of view, this powerful story of a severed nation also reflects a divided family and the gray areas existing in both. Regardless of the side readers may choose in the War between the States, all will relate to the tug-of-war between adolescent and parent in this story. As always, Rinaldi supports her fiction with a listing of numerous factual resources. Her carefully researched description of the final surrender of Lee to Grant is visually stirring, as is her created description of the truce reached by Oscie and Will McLean.
Awards: ALA Best Book for Young Adults, Beehive Award (Utah)
Related Subjects: Civil War, Family, Stepfamilies
Character Themes: Courage, Loyalty

Rinaldi, Ann, A *Ride into Morning*. Gulliver/Harcourt Children's Books, 1991. ISBN: 0152006737 (paperback) (Grades 7–12)

Left with the responsibility of caring for her widowed and ailing mother as well as the guardianship of her teenage cousin, Temperance Wick finds freedom and release from duty only in breathtaking rides on her swift and sure-footed horse, Colonel. Encamped on the sprawling family farm is the Pennsylvania Line, a restless company of soldiers, some accompanied by their hungry wives and children. It is the families of soldiers who often come and beg at the kitchen door, unnerving the high-strung Tempe. Nearly at her breaking point, the barely adult patriot is blackmailed into promising a renegade soldier the loan of her adored Colonel as a stamp of authority to his cause of presenting grievances, while in reality, he is planning mutiny. Told from the viewpoint of the cousin, Mary Cooper, this story gives shape to the Revolutionary War legend of Tempe Wick, who reportedly kept her beloved horse in her house overnight, or longer, to keep him from being stolen by rebellious soldiers. As always, Rinaldi gives credentials to her story with abundant resources listed after the text. Having won numerous awards for her flawless historical fiction novels, the author states that this tale is one of her favorites.

Awards: New York Public Library Book for the Teen Age
Related Subjects: New Jersey, Revolutionary War, United States—History
Character Themes: Courage, Loyalty, Patriotism

Rivers, Francine, *The Last Sin Eater*. Tyndale House, 1998. ISBN: 0842335706 (paperback) (Grades 9–12)

Carrying the burden of guilt for a family tragedy, ten-year-old Cadi turns to the "sin-eater," a person designated by the members of the community to absolve them of their sins. Dissatisfied with the results of her efforts, Cadi seeks out a religious faith, which enables her to come to peace with her shame and reconcile with her family. Set in Appalachia in the 1850s, the story skillfully portrays the rugged, fierce independence of the Appalachian people through characters that are unique and believable. In *The Last Sin Eater*, Rivers has created a powerful modern parable based on historical practice.

Awards: Christian Book Award
Related Subjects: Appalachia, Death, Family—Relationships, Rejection, Superstition
Character Themes: Forgiveness, Friendship, Religious faith, Sacrifice

Ryan, Pam Munoz, *Esperanza Rising*. Scholastic, 2000. ISBN: 0439120411 (hardcover) (Grades 5–9)

As the daughter of a wealthy Mexican family, Esperanza lives a pampered life until her father is killed by bandits. After Papa's death, Esperanza and her mother flee to California with a faithful family of servants. In Mexico, they have been privileged landholders. In California, they face discrimination and hard labor, but also hope. While her mother works in the produce-packing sheds, Esperanza is expected to sweep floors and care for young children. Her mother's illness brings more challenges to the young Esperanza, who not only survives, but learns to find joy in serving, rather than being served.

Awards: Americas Award Honor Book, Jane Addams Children's Book Award, Jefferson Cup Honor Award (Virginia), Massachusetts Children's Book Award, Pura Belpré Award, Sunshine State Young Readers Award (Florida), Top Ten Best Book for Young Adults (YALSA)

Related Subjects: Death of parent, Immigration, Migrant labor, The Great Depression

Character Themes: Courage, Family loyalty, Hope, Humility

Strickland, Brad, *When Mack Came Back*. Penguin Putnam Inc., 2000. ISBN: 0803724985 (hardcover) (Grades 4–8)
Ben Painter leaves home to join the Allied forces without saying good-bye to his family, and his father refuses to forgive the abandonment. Consequently, there is much tension in the Painter household. When younger brother Maury happens upon an injured dog that looks much like the one Ben gave away, Mr. Painter refuses to believe that it is the same animal, and does not want it about. Besides, there is no extra money to pay a vet, and this dog definitely needs help. Kindhearted Maury loves the dog, and when he calls him "Mack," the name that Ben had given his dog, the weakened pup responds. The courageous and resourceful young man finds professional care for Mack and in the process makes a friend who will significantly impact his own life. This is a warmhearted story of a dog, a family at war within and without, and a bright young farm boy who loves Shakespeare.

Awards: Nutmeg Book Award (Connecticut), Young Hoosier Book Award (Indiana), Sunshine State Young Readers Award Reading List (Florida), William Allen White Children's Book Award (Kansas)

Related Subjects: Dogs, Farm life, World War II

Character Themes: Compassion, Determination, Ingenuity, Respect

Taylor, Mildred D., *The Land*. Phyllis Fogelman Books, 2001. ISBN: 0803719507 (hardcover) (Grades 8–12)
Born the son of a white plantation owner and a slave, Paul-Edward Logan and his sister Cassie are given many of the privileges that his white half-brothers enjoy. When Paul runs away as a teen, however, he begins to understand that society is not yet ready to give him that same respect. Determined to someday own land for himself, Paul perseveres against prejudice,

hardship, and betrayal to gain his impossible dream. Taylor presents the realities of post–Civil War society in the South without covering up the ugliness, yet without bitterness. Woven throughout is the thread of family love, strong friendship, and personal achievement. This compelling story, which is the prequel to Newbery winner *Roll of Thunder, Hear My Cry*, is based on actual events in the author's family.
Awards: Coretta Scott King Award
Related Subjects: African-Americans, Cross-cultural relations, Cross-generational relationships, Friendship, Siblings, Slavery
Character Themes: Courage, Determination, Independence, Ingenuity, Self-control, Work ethic

Tripp, Valerie, *Again, Josefina!* Illustrated by Jean-Paul Tibbles. Vignettes by Susan McAliley. Pleasant Company Publications, 2000. ISBN: 1584850329 (hardcover) (Grades 3–7)
When Josefina's father gives in to her pleas for piano lessons, taught by Tia Dolores, the nine-year-old is very excited because she loves music. However, Papa reminds Josefina that her chores cannot be neglected, and that daily practice is required so that her aunt is not wasting time in teaching her. Playing beautiful tunes as Tia Dolores does and practicing proper posture along with boring scales seem to be worlds apart, and the young would-be musician is quickly discouraged. Urged on by Papa's encouragement, her sisters' teasing, and the delighted response from a least-expected source, Josefina returns to practice again and again, with rewarding results. This volume is part of the *American Girls* series.
Awards: Akron Symphony Orchestra (Ohio)
Related Subjects: Family—Nontraditional, Mexican-Americans, Music
Character Themes: Diligence, Obedience, Patience

Tunnell, Michael O., *Mailing May*. Illustrated by Ted Rand. HarperTrophy, 2000. ISBN: 0064437248 (paperback) (Grades 1–3).
May's parents do not have the one dollar and fifty cent fee required to send her to visit her grandmother who lives in the Idaho mountains; in 1913, that is a whole day's pay. However, a creative solution offers itself through her Uncle Leonard, a postal railway clerk. Under her uncle's care, May is mailed to her grandmother for fifty-three cents. Warm and engaging illustrations enhance this true-to-life incident.
Awards: ALSC Notable Children's Book, CBC/NCSS Notable Children's Trade Book in Social Studies, Colorado Children's Book Award, IRA Teachers' Choices, Parents' Choice Gold Award

Related Subjects: 1900s, Cross-generational relationships, Postal service, Problem solving, Railroads
Character Themes: Family love, Ingenuity

White, Ruth, *Belle Prater's Boy*. Bantam Doubleday Dell Publishing Group, 1998. ISBN: 0440413729 (paperback) (Grades 4–8)
After his mother's disappearance in the middle of the night, twelve-year-old Woodrow comes to live with his grandparents in Coal Station, Virginia. Woodrow quickly becomes the center of interest as the whole town tries to figure out what happened to his mother, Belle. Despite his crossed eyes and hand-me-down clothes, Woodrow wins over his classmates with his witty stories and self-confident ways. Woodrow and his cousin Gypsy become fast friends and together they find resolution to their secret sorrows. In this Appalachian tale with a small-town atmosphere, White has created memorable characters who successfully face personal tragedy and find ways to overcome.
Awards: Boston Globe-Horn Book Honor Award, CBC/NCSS Notable Children's Trade Book in Social Studies, IRA Teachers' Choices, Newbery Honor
Related Subjects: Abandonment, Appalachia, Friendship, Loss of parent, Special needs—Physical disabilities
Character Themes: Courage, Family loyalty, Self-respect

White, Ruth, *Tadpole*. Farrar, Straus & Giroux, 2003. ISBN: 0374310025 (hardcover) (Grades 6–12)
After her husband deserts the family, Serilda works as a cook in the local hospital to support her family. The four daughters, Kentucky, Virginia, Georgia, and Carolina, named for all the states where their pa had been, mostly loll around the cabin wishing that life was different, and whining when their ma cannot buy things they desire. Cousin Winston Churchill Birch, better known as "Tadpole," arrives, and everything changes. With his zest for life and gift for music, the orphan boy brightens the home and lightens Aunt Serilda's workload with his willing hands and inventive spirit. Trouble arises when an abusive uncle, who has legal custody of Tad, arrives with the authority to take his nephew back to his spirit-deadening dwelling. The colloquial language may unnerve teachers and librarians, yet the spirit, camaraderie, and innocence of the 1950s rings across the hills and onto the pages of this warmhearted young adult novel. Tad inspires all who struggle with difficult circumstances, whether from loneliness, abuse, or poverty.
Awards: *School Library Journal* Best Book of the Year, William Allen White Children's Book Award Master List (Kansas)

Related Subjects: 1950s, Abuse—Child, Family—Single parent
Character Themes: Compassion, Individuality, Love, Survival, Talent

Wyatt, Leslie J., *Poor Is Just a Starting Place*. Holiday House, 2005. ISBN: 0823418847 (hardcover) (Grades 8–12)
Young Artie is tired of the Great Depression and the constant worry over food and other necessities. Her father is charming but somewhat irresponsible, and her mother is sickly and timid. There is always work to do on their farm and she and her brother Ballard seem to carry most of the responsibility for getting it done. Ballard will be happy to graduate from the eighth grade, but Artie dreams of going on to high school and escaping the hole of poverty in which her family is trapped. Relationships between family members are well drawn and Artie's growth in understanding life's challenges, realistic.
Awards: IRA Children's Book Award
Related Subjects: Father-daughter relationships, Kentucky, Poverty, The Great Depression
Character Themes: Ambition, Family loyalty, Perseverance

Yolen, Jane, *Girl in a Cage*. Philomel Books, 2002. ISBN: 0399236279 (hardcover) (Grades 6–10)
It is 1306, a year since William Wallace, perhaps known to readers as "Braveheart," was executed. Robert Bruce, the newly crowned king of Scotland, a fugitive, attempting to evade his enemy Edward I of England. To entice Bruce out of hiding, Edward Longshanks captures eleven-year-old Marjorie Bruce, daughter of Robert, and takes her to the town square in the English border town of Lanercost, where she is locked in a wooden cage. There she is left exposed to the rain, wind, and sun as well as the taunts of the villagers. Marjorie's first-person narration of her captivity is moving, and the way she deals with her imprisonment shows great ingenuity. Determined to make her father proud, Marjorie exhibits the qualities of a true princess and sways the villagers to her side.
Awards: ALA Best Books for Young Adults, Black-Eyed Susan Award (Maryland), Blue Hen Book Award (Delaware), Newbery Honor, Rhode Island Teen Book Award
Related Subjects: 1300s, England, Robert Bruce, Scotland
Character Themes: Courage, Determination, Loyalty, Patriotism, Spunk

CHAPTER FIVE

Nonfiction

The desire to learn is born in the hearts of all children and in their quest for knowledge; some prefer reading factual books to reading fiction. The test for excellence in nonfiction books is whether this information is presented in a way that creates a sense of awe and wonder in children, whetting their appetites for more information while satisfying their present curiosity. Although facts receive heavy emphasis in nonfiction, narrative is often used to carry along the interest of the child so that information is more easily absorbed. This is especially true for biographies, where young people can find inspiration to set and achieve goals for their own lives.

Illustration for children's books is an art form, and nowhere are graphics more important than in nonfiction books. In this genre, pictures convey a large percentage of the information given. With sixty to seventy percent of books in most libraries falling into the nonfiction genre, it is essential to establish guidelines for their selection. Accuracy and currency of data, clear structure, and adequate indexing are vital. These are some of the criteria used to judge books for the Orbis Pictus and the Robert F. Sibert awards, given yearly to promote and recognize outstanding nonfiction titles written for young people. As in all books for children, a clear, understandable writing style and age-appropriate vocabulary determine whether the child will be drawn into reading the volume or give up in frustration or boredom.

Anderson, M. T., *Handel, Who Knew What He Liked*. Illustrated by Kevin Hawkes. Candlewick Press, 2001. ISBN: 0763610461 (hardcover) (Grades 3–6)

Anderson and Hawkes have created a biography that is at once witty and irreverent yet respectful of this composer's immense talent. The events of Handel's life are condensed into a concise picture-book format but still capture the essence of his character and his accomplishments. Kevin Hawkes's ornate and sometimes humorous illustrations do much to portray the feel of the Baroque period. Side notes explain terms such as clavichord and oratorio, which may not be familiar to readers without a musical background. Anderson ends the tale with the struggles that led to what is perhaps Handel's greatest accomplishment, the composing of the *Messiah*.

Awards: ALSC Notable Children's Book, Boston Globe-Horn Book Honor Award, Parents' Choice Silver Honor Award

Related Subjects: Baroque, Biography, Composers, George Frideric Handel, Music, Self-concept

Character Themes: Creativity, Determination, Talent

Bernall, Misty, *She Said Yes*. Pocket Books/Simon & Schuster, 1999. ISBN: 0743400526 (paperback) (Grades 10–12)

On April 20, 1999, the world was shocked by the apparently unprovoked slaughter, by two students, of thirteen members of Columbine High School in Littleton, Colorado. This is the brief biography of one student, Cassie Bernall, told in first person by her mother. Misty Bernall is painfully honest about the personal struggles that both Cassie and her family had endured prior to the shootings, and the long-range effect of the courage displayed by her daughter during the murderous mayhem. Supported by numerous notes from Cassie's friends, her daughter's own introspective writings, and comments from her husband, son, and others, Bernall documents a dark day with rays of hope that readers can carry away to illuminate their own lives. If so, Cassie did not die in vain.

Awards: Christopher Award, *New York Times* Best Seller

Related Subjects: Bullies, Cassie Bernall, Colorado, Columbine High School, Family relationships, Grief, Martyrdom, School

Character Themes: Courage, Faithfulness, Friendship, Religious Faith

Borden, Louise, *The Journey That Saved Curious George: The True Wartime Escape of Margret and H. A. Rey*. Illustrated by Allan Drummond. Houghton Mifflin, 2005. ISBN: 0618339248 (hardcover) (Grades 5–12)

Although fans of the mischievous little monkey of this title number in the thousands, few may know the real story of how George came to be created, or how his authors saved his life from the Nazis. Replete with primary sources, this lively biography chronicles an exciting journey across the continents of South America, Europe, and finally North America. Born in Germany, the Reys first found success in Rio de Janeiro, where they also became fascinated with the antics of monkeys. However, when the two Jewish young people returned to Europe, they found themselves trapped in Paris, with Hitler's troops storming the gate. The rest of the story is a unique escapade of daring, hardship, and amazing success. Although the text is too difficult for George's youngest fans to read for themselves, adults will delight in sharing the story and will be amazed at the curious journey of H. A. and Margret Rey.

Awards: Parents' Choice Gold Award

Related Subjects: 1940s, Adventure, Authors, Biography, H. A. Rey, Margaret Rey, Paris, Survival, World War II

Character Themes: Courage, Creativity, Inventiveness, Resourcefulness

Bridges, Ruby, *Through My Eyes*. Edited by Margo Lundell. Scholastic Press, 1999. ISBN: 0590189239 (hardcover) (Grades 4–9)
In this volume, Ruby Bridges shares the experiences she had in 1960, braving the wrath of segregationists in New Orleans to successfully integrate a public school. The simple language used to portray the feelings of Ms. Bridges as a six-year-old child contrasts sharply with the sepia photographs, the newspaper excerpts, and the personal accounts of adults who played a part in this drama. Particularly poignant is the lack of bitterness shown by the author. This story goes beyond a recitation of facts and introduces readers to the emotional impact these events had on the lives of the participants. Included is a list of major events of the civil rights movement and an update on Ruby's successful life since 1960.

Awards: Carter G. Woodson Award (NCSS), Flora Stieglitz Straus Award, Great Lakes Book Award (Michigan), Jane Addams Children's Book Award, Jefferson Cup Award (Virginia), Once Upon a World Children's Book Award, Orbis Pictus Award, Parents' Choice Gold Award

Related Subjects: 1960s, African-Americans, Civil rights, Cross-cultural relations, Integration—School, New Orleans, Prejudice

Character Themes: Courage, Determination, Sacrifice

Carlson, Laurie, *Boss of the Plains: The Hat that Won the West*. Illustrated by Holly Meade. Dorling Kindersley Publishing, 1998. ISBN: 0789426579 (paperback) (Grades 4–6)
Growing up, John Batterson Stetson may have been working in his father's hatmaking shop, but his heart was in the adventurous Wild West. When

John was old enough to strike out on his own, go west he did, but adventure came in an unexpected guise. After creating a waterproof tent for his friends, he used the skills he had learned in his father's shop to create a large protective hat—unlike any seen before. Almost immediately, a cowboy bought the invention right off John's head for more than twice the price that would have been paid back East. Thus began the career of the Stetson, a commodity that became a necessity of cowboys, gamblers, and ranchers of the western plains. Author and artist collaborate to create this engaging vignette of the now world-famous "Boss of the Plains."

Awards: Charlotte Zolotow Honor Award, Irma Simonton and James H. Black Award for Excellence in Children's Literature (Bank Street), Jefferson Cup Honor Award (Virginia), *Parent's Guide* Award, *Working Mother* Best Book

Related Subjects: Hats, John Batterson Stetson, The West, United States—History

Character Themes: Creativity, Diligence, Ingenuity

Ehlert, Lois, *Feathers for Lunch.* **Scholastic, 1998. ISBN: 0590224255 (paperback) (Grades K–4)**

This little picture book just brims with drama. Ehlert's amazing sense of pacing, design, and color engages young readers or listeners in the suspenseful prowl of a cat in search of "something wild," or more specifically, birds, for his meal. Stealthily, he approaches ten different species of birds, which Ehlert has skillfully placed in proper habitats, and for which she has written out their calls. Not to worry; the cat has been "belled," and catches only feathers for lunch. As young readers are breathlessly awaiting the fate of each feathered friend, they are also painlessly learning facts. The book concludes with "The Lunch That Got Away" page, listing size, food, home, and area of each escapee. What a great idea!

Awards: Humane Society of Greater Akron (Ohio), Kentucky Bluegrass Award, IRA Teachers' Choices, Redbook Children's Picture Book Award

Related Subjects: Birds, Cats, Habitats, Nature, Science

Character Themes: Humor, Survival

Freedman, Russell, *Kids at Work: Lewis Hine and the Crusade against Child Labor.* **Scholastic, 1994. ISBN: 0590543342 (hardcover) (Grades 5–12)**

In this excellent photo essay, Freedman documents the efforts of photographer Lewis Hine to bring attention to the horrors of child labor in America in the early 1900s. The photos of somber children working in cotton mills and coal mines speak eloquently of the long hours and appalling conditions under which these young people were forced to work. Freedman's commentary explains Hine's work as an investigative photographer, his connections with the national Child Labor committee, and his crusade for improved labor laws. Readers are introduced not only to an important aspect of American history, but are shown how one person's talents can improve society.

Awards: Garden State Teen Book Award (New Jersey), Jane Addams Children's Book Award, Orbis Pictus Honor Award
Related Subjects: 1900s, Child labor, Photography, Social reform
Character Themes: Compassion, Courage, Dedication

Giovanni, Nikki, *Rosa*. Illustrated by Bryan Collier. Henry Holt & Co., 2005. ISBN: 0805071067 (hardcover) (Grades 2–4)
Narrative and illustration are inseparable in this award-winning portrayal of the bravery shown by Rosa Parks. Refusing to give up her seat on the bus to a white man made her a central figure in the civil rights movement of the 1960s. A quiet woman who became tired of the inequality of always putting white people first, Rosa demonstrated strength and dignity by insisting on being treated as an equal human being. Her consequent arrest provided a rallying point for those who joined in her cry for freedom. A double-page foldout shows the resolve of many individuals who refused to ride the buses of Montgomery, Alabama, for nearly a year, pressing for the Supreme Court to intervene. The vibrant collage and watercolor illustrations add drama to Giovanni's straightforward text.

Awards: ALSC Notable Children's Book, Caldecott Honor, Coretta Scott King Award, Parents' Choice Gold Award
Related Subjects: 1960s, African-Americans, Civil rights, Cross-cultural relations, Integration, Prejudice, Rosa Parks
Character Themes: Cooperation, Courage, Integrity, Self-acceptance

Greenfield, Eloise, and Lessie Jones Little, *Childtimes: A Three-Generation Memoir*. Illustrated by Jerry Pinkney. Thomas Y. Crowell, 1979. ISBN: 0690038747 (hardcover) (Grades 5–12)
Through the voices of her grandmother, her mother, and herself, Greenfield shares wonderful stories of three generations of her family. Faced with situations that would have discouraged many, this family met life's challenges with courage and mutual respect. Told from a child's point of view, small, everyday events hold center stage. Difficulties are described, but not dwelt on. The qualities that shine through these pages are the family love and loyalty carried from one generation to the next. In addition to black-and-white

illustrations by Jerry Pinkney, photographs from the author's family albums introduce the reader to Greenfield's ancestors.

Awards: Boston Globe-Horn Book Honor Award, Carter G. Woodson Award (NCSS), CBC/NCSS Notable Children's Trade Book in Social Studies, Library of Congress Notable Children's Book

Related Subjects: African-Americans, Cross-cultural relations, Cross-generational relationships, Family—Relationships, Heritage

Character Themes: Courage, Family love, Loyalty, Steadfastness

Hoose, Phillip, *The Race to Save the Lord God Bird*. Melanie Kroupa Books/Farrar, Straus & Giroux, 2004. ISBN: 0374361738 (hardcover) (Grades 6–12)

Although the title of this work reflects the urgency of rescuing a specific species, the impact of the content extends far beyond a single beleaguered bird. Readers learn of the birth of the Audubon Society and the scholarly work of Roger Tory Peterson, while developing empathy for the ivory-billed woodpecker. Interest in the distinctive appearance, call, and diet of the unique bird predates the Civil War and extends to contemporary avian enthusiasts in the United States and Cuba. Documented battles between fashion, big business, and nature create page-turning text, informing the audience of issues confronting naturalists and the wildlife they attempt to defend. Sidebars of fascinating information and authentic photographs chronicle this noteworthy race for survival.

Awards: ALA Best Book for Young Adults, ALSC Notable Children's Book, Irma Simonton and James H. Black Award for Excellence in Children's Literature (Bank Street), Lupine Award (Maine), NCTE Notable Children's Book in Language Arts Honor, Orbis Pictus Award

Related Subjects: Audubon Society, Birds—Ivory-billed woodpecker, Ecology, Ecosystems, Endangered species, Roger Tory Peterson

Character Themes: Compassion, Determination, Knowledge

Houston, Gloria, *My Great-Aunt Arizona*. Illustrated by Susan Condie Lamb. HarperTrophy, 1992. ISBN: 0064433749 (paperback) (Grades 1–3)

Born in a log cabin in the Blue Ridge Mountains, Arizona grew flowers, caught tadpoles in the creek with her brother, and helped her father tap the maple trees. She loved to read, sing, and square dance, but all the while she dreamed of faraway places. When the opportunity came, Arizona went to live with her Aunt Suzie to learn to be a teacher. She never did visit all the places she envisioned, but she returned to Henson Creek to teach generations of children about numbers and words and faraway places they would someday visit.

Awards: ALSC Notable Children's Book, CBC/NCSS Notable Children's Trade Book in Social Studies, IRA Teachers' Choices, NCTE Notable Children's Book in Language Arts

Related Subjects: Appalachia, Blue Ridge Mountains, Family—Extended, Frontier and pioneer life, School, Teachers

Character Themes: Dedication, Enthusiasm, Learning, Sharing

Jenkins, Steve (author and illustrator), *The Top of the World: Climbing Mount Everest*. Houghton Mifflin, 1999. ISBN: 0395942187 (hardcover) (Grades 3–6)

Sitting on the border between Tibet and Nepal, Mount Everest has captured the imagination of mountain climbers for decades, but many never reach its summit. Steve Jenkins addresses some of the factors that make this particular mountain so challenging in his unusual picture book packed with practical information about weather conditions and technical detail regarding necessary equipment. The stunning collage illustrations, created with highly textured papers, portray both the drama and the danger of the mountain-climbing experience. Designed more to impart information than to tell a story, this book nevertheless succeeds in conveying the mystique surrounding this majestic mountain.

Awards: Boston Globe-Horn Book Award, Orbis Pictus Award, Robert F. Sibert Informational Book Medal

Related Subjects: Adventure, Mount Everest, Mountain climbing, Nepal, Tibet

Character Themes: Boldness, Courage, Perseverance

Kerley, Barbara, *The Dinosaurs of Waterhouse Hawkins*. Illustrated by Brian Selznick. Scholastic, 2001. ISBN: 043945137X (hardcover) (Grades 3–6)

Born with a love for drawing animals, Waterhouse Hawkins found his true passion in creating the first life-sized replicas of dinosaurs. In partnership with scientist Richard Owen, he compared fossil remains to living animals to imagine how the gigantic creatures must have appeared. With flamboyant style, he courted those who could provide opportunities for him to educate the public about these amazing creatures. Receiving a commission from Queen Victoria, he completed models for the Crystal Palace in London, many of which still stand today. In America, his efforts to establish a display in Central Park were destroyed by corrupt politicians, but he found better success at Princeton University and the Smithsonian Institution in Washington,

D.C. Thanks to this one man, the fascinating world of dinosaurs was made real.
Awards: ABA Book Sense Pick, Caldecott Honor, Garden State Children's Book Award (New Jersey), Great Lakes Books Award (Michigan), Orbis Pictus Award
Related Subjects: Dinosaurs, Fossils, Sculpting, Waterhouse Hawkins
Character Themes: Determination, Devotion, Imagination

Kerley, Barbara, *Walt Whitman: Words for America.* Illustrated by Brian Selznick. Scholastic Press, 2004. ISBN: 0439357918 (hardcover) (Grades 4–6)
Walt Whitman's poetry celebrated America and its people and was a departure from the carefully metered poems that people were accustomed to reading in the 1800s. When his first edition of *Leaves of Grass* was published, many loved its fresh spirit while others ridiculed his style. Nevertheless, Whitman persevered to become one of America's best-loved poets. Large plentiful illustrations fill the pages of this story of his life, but the subject matter and text make it a book for older readers. Excerpts of his poems are included, with at least half of the pages highlighting his visits to soldiers wounded in the battles of the Civil War. *Drum-Taps*, published after peace was secured, was a tribute to the warriors of this bloody conflict, and helped the nation to recover from the pain surrounding the war. In their award-winning tribute, Kerley and Selznick have created a special book about an extraordinary man.
Awards: Robert F. Sibert Informational Book Honor Medal
Related Subjects: 1800s, Biography, Civil War, Medicine, Poetry, Walt Whitman
Character Themes: Compassion, Dedication, Perseverance, Talent

Krensky, Stephen, *George Washington: The Man Who Would Not Be King.* Scholastic, 1991. ISBN: 0590437305 (paperback) (Grades 5–9)
Beginning with his birth in 1732, Krensky has created a biography of George Washington that is highly readable as well as historically significant. The author places Washington in the context of the extraordinary events of his time while showing the important part he played in the development of this country. Krensky portrays Washington as a man who repeatedly set aside his own interests and desires to serve a budding nation. Krensky's list of biographies about other famous Americans includes such names as Paul Revere, Christopher Columbus, Davy Crockett, and Nellie Bly.
Awards: IRA Children's Choices

Related Subjects: George Washington, Government, Revolutionary War—
United States
Character Themes: Dedication, Determination, Steadfastness, Unselfishness

Krull, Kathleen, *Wilma Unlimited*. Illustrated by David Diaz. Harcourt Brace, 1999. ISBN: 0152020985 (hardcover) (Grades 2–6)
Wilma Rudolph was a very unlikely person to become a three-time winner of Olympic gold medals. Only four pounds at birth, this nineteenth child of a loving and supportive family was encouraged in her dreams of achievement. Around five years of age, this brave young lady contracted polio, which left her with a twisted leg. Not willing to let this terrible illness stop her, Wilma worked hard at exercising the weakened limbs until she first learned to walk with a steel brace and finally without it. By 1960 the hard work of this budding athlete had taken her to Rome, Italy, as a member of the United States Olympic team. The bold illustrations of David Diaz are the perfect accompaniment to the story of this outstanding woman.
Awards: ALSC Notable Children's Book, *Booklist* Editors' Choice, Jane Addams Children's Book Award, Parents' Choice Gold Award
Related Subjects: African-Americans, Heroes, Polio, Running, Track and field, Wilma Rudolph
Character Themes: Courage, Determination, Family loyalty

Lasky, Kathryn, *The Man Who Made Time Travel*. Illustrated by Kevin Hawkes. Farrar, Straus & Giroux, 2003. ISBN: 0374347883 (hardcover) (Grades 2–5)
In 1714, loss of life on the sea prompted the British government to offer £20,000 to the person who could create a way to accurately determine a ship's east-west position on the ocean. Clockmaker John Harrison was audacious enough to counter the prevailing scientific opinion that the only way to accomplish this was through mapping the heavens. He persevered until he was able to create a small timepiece, now called a chronometer, which altered navigation forever. Illustrations by Kevin Hawkes should have great appeal to children.
Awards: ALSC Notable Children's Book, Orbis Pictus Honor Award
Related Subjects: Chronometer, Clockmakers, Invention, John Harrison, Longitude, Sea, Technology
Character Themes: Determination, Ingenuity

Locker, Thomas (writer and illustrator), *John Muir: America's Naturalist*. Fulcrum Publishing, 2003. ISBN: 1555913938 (hardcover) (Grades 4–12)
Locker, an award-winning illustrator in his own right, pays tribute to one of the pioneers of American ecology, Scotsman John Muir. With sparse

biographical text and accompanying quotes by the subject, Locker shares the wisdom and passion of the unique explorer, who valued equally company with wildlife and President Teddy Roosevelt. Muir's love of the environment is reflected in his reverence for nature and his lack of patience with those who spoil it. Muir's efforts at preservation resulted in the formation of the Sierra Club, which continues actively to preserve the environment. Locker's magnificent paintings pair perfectly in mood and grandeur with the text. This is a volume that should be shared across generations, and the illustrations offer beauty for many moments of pleasant contemplation.

Awards: California Department of Education Recommended Reading List
Related Subjects: Alaska, California, Camping, Conservation, Ecology, John Muir, Nature, National Parks—Yosemite, Outdoor Life, Seasons, Sequoias, Sierra Club, Trees
Character Themes: Conservation, Contemplation, Respect, Solitude—Love of

Macaulay, David (author and illustrator), *Castle*. Houghton Mifflin, 1977. ISBN: 0395257840 (hardcover) (Grades 6–12)
Although the British Lord Kevin and the Welch town of Aberwyvern are fictitious, young readers easily become caught up in the lives of both. Beginning with nothing but workers, thatched houses, and raw materials, Macaulay engages his audience in the creation of a huge castle, the surrounding village, and a medieval town that later surrounds both. Pen-and-ink illustrations of the landmass, a diagram of the floor plan of the castle, laborers, and their tools make concrete the abstract vocabulary of the time so far removed from contemporary readers. By giving characters names, and even including the dog belonging to Master James, the author time-warps the twenty-first-century reader to the exact spot so realistically that he can almost hear the ring of the hammer.

Awards: Caldecott Honor
Related Subjects: 1200s, England, Architecture, Castles, Wales
Character Themes: Cooperation, Craftsmanship, Diligence

McKissack, Patricia, and Frederick McKissack, *Christmas in the Big House, Christmas in the Quarters*. Illustrated by John Thompson. Scholastic, 1994. ISBN: 0590430270 (hardcover) (Grades 4–6)
In this picture book for older readers, the McKissacks have crafted a historically accurate picture of Christmas as celebrated on a Southern plantation shortly before the Civil War. Alternating chapters clearly delineate the stark differences between the celebration in the plantation house and that in the

slave quarters. Pictures of slaves being invited into the "big house" for part of the festivities are contrasted with the daughter's request for her own personal slave, and the flight of a slave father on the Underground Railroad. Throughout the book, information is given in a straightforward manner without sentimentality or sensationalism. Rhymes, recipes, and extensive notes add richness and authenticity to the text. Thompson's beautiful, realistic illustrations add depth and emotional strength.

Awards: Coretta Scott King Award, Orbis Pictus Award

Related Subjects: 1800s, African-Americans, Christmas, Cross-cultural relations, Family, Holidays, Plantations, Slavery, Underground Railroad

Character Themes: Coping, Resolve, Survival

McKissack, Patricia, and Fredrick McKissack. *Sojourner Truth: Ain't I a Woman?* **Scholastic, 1992. ISBN: 0590446908 (hardcover) (Grades 8–12)**

Born into slavery in New York State in the late 1700s, Isabella Van Wagener remained in bondage for the first twenty-eight years of her life. A large woman, Belle worked hard and faithfully for the families who owned her. In 1826, with the help of the Quakers, Belle obtained her freedom. As the emancipation movement increased in fervor, this former slave changed her name to Sojourner Truth and began to speak to groups in the North and the Midwest. An eloquent spokeswoman, she gained national and international fame for her efforts to advance the cause of those who still suffered. Before her death at age eighty-six, she had met with three presidents, traveled thousands of miles, and advanced the causes of emancipation for blacks and suffrage for women. This documentation of her exemplary life is both readable and inspiring. Photos enrich the text.

Awards: Boston-Globe Horn Book Award, Coretta Scott King Honor Award

Related Subjects: African-Americans, Civil rights, Cross-cultural relations, Heroes, Prejudice, Slavery, Sojourner Truth, Suffrage, Women

Character Themes: Boldness, Courage, Dignity, Persistence, Sacrifice, Self-expression

McLimans, David (author and illustrator), *Gone Wild: An Endangered Animal Alphabet.* **Walker & Company, 2006. ISBN: 0802795641 (hardcover) (Grades 5–12)**

In this unique alphabet book, David McLimans has halted, at least on paper, the extinction of twenty-six birds, beasts and insects. From the Chinese alligator to Grevy's zebra, from the huge black rhinoceros to the tiny St. Helena earwig, each species is in some state of passing from the earth. A fact box on

each page discloses class, habitat, range, threats, and status of endangerment. Stark black-ink drawings on bright white pages impress readers with the value of each life-form. Annotations describing each subject conclude the book, creating a desire in readers to continue with further research. Although difficult to place on a reading level, this picture book will find a home in science and art classes across grade levels, with its quickly absorbed facts and stylized drawings.
Awards: Caldecott Honor, *New York Times* Best Illustrated Children's Book Award
Related Subjects: Animals, Art, Endangered Species
Character Themes: Activism, Respect for nature, Survival

Meigs, Cornelia, *Invincible Louisa*. Scholastic, 1933. ISBN: 059043439X (paperback) (Grades 8–12)
Although she is best known for her novels, Louisa May Alcott was also a nanny, teacher, nurse, seamstress, traveling companion, and general guardian of her family before fame discovered her. Throughout her life, Louisa found solace in writing in her journals, but being shy, she lacked the confidence to throw herself totally into writing. She believed that her first loyalty lay with her father, mother, and three sisters, and they were always in need. Diligently, she worked to support, encourage, and provide financial assistance for her family. After Louisa's grueling experience as a Union nurse, she was left so weak that for the first time in her life, someone else had the responsibility of taking care of her. In her midthirties, while still regaining her strength, a wise publisher suggested that she "write a book for girls." Louisa did not think that she could, considering herself to be less than feminine in many respects. However, with her usual enthusiasm, she tried. *Little Women* was an immediate success, and from that point, Ms. Alcott was able to care for her family in the way that she had always hoped. This is a well-told story of an American icon with intimate glimpses of the family that offered inspiration for Alcott's most enduring and endearing work.
Awards: Newbery Medal
Related Subjects: Authors, Civil War—Union, Louisa May Alcott, Transcendentalism, Women, Writers
Character Themes: Compassion, Creativity, Diligence, Family love, Strength, Talent

Mochizuki, Ken, *Passage to Freedom: The Sugihara Story*. Illustrated by Dom Lee. Lee & Low Books, 1997. ISBN: 1880000490 (hardcover) (Grades 3–6)
In 1940, many Jewish refugees seeking to flee the Nazi threat in Poland camped outside the Japanese consulate seeking visas. When his government

refused to grant their wish, Sugihara was faced with the decision to obey his government or follow his conscience. Unable to refuse their pleas, Sugihara ignored the policy of his government and worked to save close to 10,000 Jewish lives. Sepia-toned illustrations convey the intense emotions of those who lived these events.

Awards: ALSC Notable Children's Book, IRA Teachers' Choices, NCTE Notable Children's Book in Language Arts, Parents' Choice Gold Award

Related Subjects: Chiune Sugihara, Diplomats, Holocaust, Jews, Nazis, Poland, Prejudice, World War II

Character Themes: Compassion, Courage, Initiative, Unselfishness

Murphy, Jim, *An American Plague: The True and Terrifying Story of the Yellow Fever Epidemic of 1793*. Clarion Books, 2003. ISBN: 0395776082 (hardcover) (Grades 6–12)

Jim Murphy paints a clear picture of the confusion and chaos brought about by the epidemic of yellow fever that hit Philadelphia in the summer of 1793. With little but supposition and guesswork, those doctors who were brave enough to remain struggled valiantly to stem the daily death toll. Most residents who had the means fled the city, but thousands died. Since Philadelphia was the temporary capital of young America, George Washington and members of Congress had to leave, effectively shutting down the government. Murphy highlights the heroic work of Dr. Benjamin Rush and the Free African Society and their ministrations to the sick. Illustrations from the time period are used and thirteen pages of source material are listed at the back of the book for those who desire information for further study.

Awards: ALSC Notable Children's Book, National Book Award Finalist, Newbery Honor, Robert F. Sibert Informational Book Medal, *School Library Journal* Best Book

Related Subjects: Benjamin Rush, Epidemics, Fear, Free African Society, Government, Medicine, Philadelphia, Social issues, Yellow fever

Character Themes: Courage, Faithfulness, Overcoming fear, Survival

Murphy, Jim, *Blizzard*. Scholastic, 2000. ISBN: 0590673092 (hardcover) (Grades 4–12)

With personal anecdotes, photos, and sepia-toned prints, Jim Murphy tells the story of the blizzard of 1888 and the devastation it wrought in people's lives up and down the east coast. From street people to politicians, Murphy's historical narrative shows how no one was untouched by the storm's fury. Going beyond the immediate event, the author details the long-lasting reform that resulted as citizens demanded improvements from their city governments.

Underground wiring, underground transportation systems, and reliable snow removal were implemented to prevent such disaster from happening again.
Awards: Jefferson Cup Award (Virginia)
Related Subjects: Blizzards, Natural disasters, Social reform, Storms, Survival, Weather
Character Themes: Courage, Sacrifice

Murphy, Jim, *The Great Fire*. Scholastic, 1995. ISBN: 0590472666 (paperback) (Grades 4–12)
Using the stories of actual survivors of the great Chicago fire of 1871, Jim Murphy places the reader in the middle of this terrible disaster, which left over 100,000 people homeless. Debunking the popular belief that the inferno was caused by Mrs. O'Leary's cow, he demonstrates how a variety of factors led to its spread. Photos, engravings, and newspaper clippings adorn the pages while maps scattered throughout the text show the track of the burning. Murphy gives a fascinating account of an unforgettable historic event.
Awards: ALA Best Book for Young Adults, Boston Globe-Horn Book Honor Award, CBC/NCSS Notable Children's Trade Book in Social Studies, Jefferson Cup Award (Virginia), Newbery Honor
Related Subjects: Chicago, Fear, Fire
Character Themes: Coping, Generosity, Ingenuity

Myers, Laurie, *Lewis and Clark and Me: A Dog's Tale*. Illustrated by Michael Dooling. Scholastic, 2002. ISBN: 0439474841 (paperback) (Grades 3–6)
In the early 1800s, when Thomas Jefferson engaged Meriwether Lewis to investigate the westernmost regions of the United States, Lewis purchased Seaman, a Newfoundland dog, to accompany the expedition. This account of their adventures is told from the viewpoint of the dog on a level that even young children can understand. Excerpts from Lewis's diary are interspersed throughout the narration. Excellent, detailed artwork raises the book above the commonplace.
Awards: Great Lakes Book Award (Michigan), IRA Teachers' Choices, Pennsylvania Young Reader's Choice, Texas Bluebonnet Award
Related Subjects: 1800s, Dogs, Explorers, Lewis and Clark expedition, Meriwether Lewis
Character Themes: Courage, Inquisitiveness, Loyalty, Survival

Nagda, Ann Whitehead, and Cindy Bickel, *Tiger Math: Learning to Graph from a Baby Tiger*. Scholastic, 2000. ISBN: 0439264294 (paperback) (Grades 3–6)
Orphaned when just a few weeks old, T. J., a Siberian tiger born at the Denver Zoo, must be fed by hand. Cared for by the veterinary staff, his progress is carefully charted by the doctors. The story of T. J.'s growth is told using easily understood graphs and charts. Picture graphs and pie charts show how many tigers are left in the wild. Bar and line graphs are used to measure the tiger's growth in pounds as he matures. This innovative approach to teaching math successfully accomplishes the added purpose of emphasizing the need for saving the habitat needed to sustain the tiger population around the world.
Awards: Colorado Children's Book Award, Great Lakes Book Award (Michigan), NSTA Outstanding Science Trade Book for Children, Utah Children's Informational Book Award
Related Subjects: Animals, Graphing, Mathematics, Tigers, Veterinarians, Zoos
Character Themes: Dedication, Survival

Nelson, Marilyn, *Carver: A Life in Poems*. Front Street, 2001. ISBN: 1886910537 (hardcover) (6–12)
This highly readable book portrays the life of a man who overcame enormous odds while contributing greatly to the wealth of scientific knowledge. Through these poems, the reader feels the powerful presence of a life grounded in a deep religious faith and driven by a passion for learning. Portrayed is a man concerned about the welfare of those around him who exemplified the qualities of determination, unselfishness, and ingenuity. The combination of the author's poetic skill and the excellence of the life being celebrated create a powerful reading experience that will touch the life of all who venture into its pages. One poem contains strong language and violent action.
Awards: ALA Best Book for Young Adults, Boston Globe-Horn Book Award, Coretta Scott King Award, Flora Stieglitz Straus Award, Newbery Honor, William Allen White Children's Book Award (Kansas)
Related Subjects: Agriculture, Art, Cross-cultural relations, George Washington Carver, Invention, Science
Character Themes: Determination, Faith, Forgiveness, Genius, Humility, Inventiveness, Loyalty, Religious faith, Unselfishness

North, Sterling, *Rascal*. Puffin/Penguin, 1963. ISBN: 0140344454 (paperback) (Grades 4–8)
In May 1918, when the whole world seemed to be at war, eleven-year-old Sterling North unearthed and adopted a furry child of the wilds that he later immortalized in this wonderfully personal autobiography. Rascal, as the tiny raccoon was called, became a family member, eating from a high chair and consuming with relish the same diet as humans. Having lost his mother and gained the confidence of his somewhat casual father, Sterling is allowed a lifestyle reminiscent of Tom Sawyer, except that he is not an orphan, and his father really does care about what happens to him and to his many pets. Chapter titles are organized by the months of Rascal's life from his discovery in May to the realistic conclusion the following April. Much natural history of birds, fish, and other wild creatures as well as wonder at the exceptional intelligence of raccoons are woven seamlessly into this unforgettable narrative. Any child who loves animals and has, or desires to have, a pet will enjoy this timeless story.
Awards: Newbery Honor, Young Reader's Choice Award (Pacific Northwest Library Association), William Allen White Children's Book Award (Kansas)
Related Subjects: 1900s, Family—Single parent, Nature, Pets, Raccoons, World War I
Character Themes: Humor, Ingenuity, Responsibility

Pinkney, Andrea Davis, *Duke Ellington: The Piano Prince and His Orchestra*. Illustrated by Brian Pinkney. Hyperion Books for Children, 1998. ISBN: 0786801786 (hardcover) (Grades 3–6)
With words that are music themselves, Andrea Pinkney tells the story of the man considered by many to be one of the greatest jazz musicians who has ever lived. Just like Ellington's music, the text of this energetic picture book dances off the page right into the readers minds. Brilliant colors flow from the instruments of the musicians in Brian Pinkney's vibrant illustrations, perfectly demonstrating the joyful exuberance created by this master musician and his band. This is an excellent introduction to jazz music and a fitting tribute to the life of an important African-American.
Awards: Caldecott Honor, Coretta Scott King Award
Related Subjects: African-Americans, Duke Ellington, Jazz, Music
Character Themes: Creativity, Self-expression

Rappaport, Doreen, *Martin's Big Words: The Life of Dr. Martin Luther King, Jr.* Illustrated by Bryan Collier. Hyperion Books for Children, 2001. ISBN: 0786807148 (hardcover) (Grades 1–4)
The illustrations carry great emotional weight in this picture book about Martin Luther King Jr. From the lifelike portrait on the front cover to the

bold title on the back, the influence of this great man is conveyed to the reader. Most two-page spreads contain a short historical narrative followed by a quote from his speeches next to an illustration done in collage and water-color. Rappaport has kept her text spare and powerful. The quotations from King's own words have been carefully and effectively chosen. This is an excellent choice to use with very young children.

Awards: Caldecott Honor, Coretta Scott King Honor Award, Great Lakes Book Award (Michigan), Jane Addams Children's Book Award, Orbis Pictus Award
Related Subjects: African-Americans, Civil Rights, Cross-cultural relations, Dr. Martin Luther King Jr., Heroes, Intergration, Martyrdom
Character Themes: Courage, Determination, Love

Rubin, Susan Goldman, *Margaret Bourke-White: Her Pictures Were Her Life*. Photographs by Margaret Bourke-White. Harry N. Abrams, 1999. ISBN: 0810943816 (hardcover) (Grades 8–12)
Choosing descriptors for this daring pioneer in photography is difficult, because she blazed the trail, especially for women, on multiple frontiers. At twenty-three, Margaret wrote in her journal, "I want to become famous and I want to become wealthy." She achieved both goals, through the vehicle of photojournalism. No jungle was too dangerous, no height too lofty, no celebrity too intimidating for Bourke-White to tackle. Reptiles fascinated her, skyscrapers and airplanes beckoned to her, meeting renowned figures challenged her. This slice-of-life autobiography from the pre– and post–World War II eras is generously illustrated with the indomitable photographer's most famous shots, ranging from victims of apartheid in South Africa to an up close and personal view of Lady Liberty in the New York harbor. Anyone interested in photojournalism, the advance of women's issues, or American icons will enjoy this volume.

Awards: ALA Best Book for Young Adults, Jefferson Cup Honor Award (Virginia), Tayshas Reading List (Texas)
Related Subjects: Aviation, Biography, Journalism, Margaret Bourke-White, Photography, Photojournalism
Character Themes: Ambition, Courage, Determination, Motivation

Rumford, James (author and illustrator), *Sequoyah: The Cherokee Man Who Gave His People Writing*. Translated by Anna Sixkiller Huckaby. Houghton Mifflin, 2004. ISBN: 0618369473 (hardcover) (Grades 4–9)
In the early 1800s, Sequoyah realized that the strength of his people would be greatly enhanced if the Cherokee language could be captured in writing. Persisting against much opposition by members of his tribe, he developed a

syllabary of eighty-four symbols that could be easily learned. Using these signs, the Cherokee nation published newspapers and books that they took with them when they were forced to move west in the 1830s. *The Phoenix*, the first newspaper printed in Cherokee, is still being printed today.

Awards: Parents' Choice Gold Award, Robert F. Sibert Informational Book Award

Related Subjects: Language, Native Americans—Cherokee, Sequoyah

Character Themes: Diligence, Genius, Perseverance

Ryan, Pam Munoz, *When Marian Sang: The True Recital of Marian Anderson, the Voice of the Century*. Illustrated by Brian Selznick. Scholastic, 2002. ISBN: 0439269679 (hardcover) (Grades 1–4)

In the face of obstacles continually placed before her because of racism, Marian Anderson persevered to become known as one of the greatest voices of our century. Rejected by American music schools, she received training in France and eventually was invited to sing before kings, queens, and presidents. In 1939 more than 75,000 people made up the integrated crowd that attended her triumphant concert on the steps of the Lincoln Memorial. Marian was the first African-American vocalist to be invited to sing at the Metropolitan Opera House. Lyrics from the songs for which she is most famous are sprinkled throughout this simple, yet elegant text. The sepia-toned illustrations beautifully convey the quiet dignity that characterized the life of this heroic woman. Older readers can find a more complete biography in the award-winning book *The Voice that Challenged a Nation*, by Russell Freedman.

Awards: ALSC Notable Children's Book, Black-Eyed Susan Award (Maryland), Jefferson Cup Honor (Virginia), Mitten Honor Award (Michigan), Orbis Pictus Award, Parents' Choice Gold Medal, Robert F. Sibert Informational Book Honor Award

Related Subjects: African-Americans, Heroes, Marian Anderson, Music, Prejudice, Self-expression

Character Themes: Courage, Dignity, Perseverance, Talent

Stanley, Diane (author and illustrator), *Peter the Great*. HarperCollins, 1986. ISBN: 068816708X (hardcover) (Grades 4–8)

As the tsar of Russia, Peter was accustomed to getting what he wanted, and what he wanted most of all was a modern Russia modeled after the countries of Western Europe. In his search for information he became the first tsar to ever travel to the West. When he returned, he brought with him inventions, over eight hundred specialists in all fields, and most of all ideas of how to change his country. His determination and his desire to see changes made immediately caused hardship for many but also brought great progress in a short amount of time. Stanley's painted illustrations show great detail in architecture and clothing. This would be an excellent companion to the study of world history.

Awards: ALSC Notable Children's Book, *Booklist* Editors' Choice, CBC/NCSS Notable Children's Trade Book in Social Studies, Golden Kite Honor Award, Orbis Pictus Award
Related Subjects: 1600s, Peter I, the Great, Emperor of Russia, Russia, Tsars
Character Themes: Boldness, Curiosity, Inventiveness, Leadership

Thimmesh, Catherine, *Team Moon: How 400,000 People Landed Apollo 11 on the Moon.* **Houghton Mifflin, 2006. ISBN: 0618507574 (hardcover) (Grades 6–12)**
Thimmesh gives a different perspective on the Apollo 11 space flight that landed American astronauts on the moon, by highlighting people who worked behind the scenes. From project engineers, to photographers, to seamstresses who created the space suits, thousands of individuals are shown to be a part of the team that achieved this historic accomplishment. Crammed with photographs and quotations arranged on black background, these pages convey to the reader the excitement and pride each person felt in carrying out his or her piece of the mission.

Awards: ALA Best Book for Young Adults, Golden Kite Award, NSTA Outstanding Science Trade Book for Children, Orbis Pictus Honor Award, Robert F. Sibert Informational Book Award
Related Subjects: Apollo 11, Explorers, Moon, Space travel
Character Themes: Cooperation, Dedication

Tunis, Edwin (author and illustrator), *Frontier Living.* **Thomas Y. Crowell, 1961. ISBN: 0690010648 (hardcover) (Grades 6–12)**
For the person who desires to know what life was truly like on the American frontier, this is the book to read. Illustrations and descriptions of homes, clothing, food, tools, and transportation are clearly given. From the east coast to the western plains, frontiersmen, ranchers, mountain men, and farmers are introduced along with their lifestyles. Detailed cutaway sketches reconstruct machines that were built and used. Maps delineate the territories covered. Flintlock guns, Conestoga wagons, branding irons, and sod houses are just a few of the drawings included. All is not technical, however, for the author interjects humor and the broad range of human emotions experienced by those who dared to face the hardships of pioneering.

Awards: Newbery Honor

Related Subjects: Exploring, Frontier and pioneer life, Homesteading, Survival, Transportation
Character Themes: Determination, Fortitude, Ingenuity

Walker, Barbara M., *The Little House Cookbook: Frontier Goods from Laura Ingalls Wilder's Classic Stories.* **Illustrations by Garth Williams. Harper & Row, 1979. ISBN: 0060264187 (hardcover) (Grades 4–9)**
Walker has created much more than a cookbook in this volume. In addition to giving the ingredients and directions for preparing each dish, she provides the context of the story in which the food appears. Also included is historical background about how the food was obtained. Chapters are divided by the origin of the food, such as the country store, the woods, tilled fields, gardens and orchards, or the barnyard. Black-and-white illustrations by Garth Williams enhance the work.
Awards: ALSC Notable Children's Book, CBC/NCSS Notable Children's Book in Social Studies, Library of Congress Children's Book of the Year
Related Subjects: Cooking, Food, Frontier and pioneer life, Rural life
Character Themes: Cooperation, Family love, Inventiveness, Work ethic

Warren, Andrea, *Surviving Hitler: A Boy in the Nazi Death Camps.* **Pictures from the U.S. Holocaust Memorial Museum. HarperCollins, 2001. ISBN: 0688174973 (hardcover) (Grades 6–12)**
Surviving Hitler narrates the true experiences of a young Jewish boy forced into the Nazi concentration camps of World War II. Through small daily events, the author conveys the horror of the camps with a minimum of nightmarish detail. Torn from his family, Jack Mandelbaum survived with the hope of being reunited with those he loved. His courage, determination, and the friendship he showed to others enabled him to live when others died. Pictures from the archives of the U.S. Holocaust Memorial Museum increase the effectiveness of the narrative.
Awards: ALSC Notable Children's Book, Rebecca Caudill Young Readers Book Award, Robert F. Sibert Informational Book Honor Medal, William Allen White Children's Book Award (Kansas)
Related Subjects: Holocaust, Jack Mandelbaum, Persecution, World War II
Character Themes: Courage, Determination, Forgiveness, Ingenuity, Survival

Wells, Rosemary, *Mary on Horseback: Three Mountain Stories.* **Illustrated by Peter McCarty. Scholastic, 1988. ISBN: 0439207304 (paperback) (Grades 3–6)**

The poverty-stricken Kentucky Mountains had no medical services until the pioneering Mary Breckenridge established the Frontier Nursing Service in the 1920s. Through the eyes of three whose lives were changed by her care, the reader is shown the harsh realities of mountain life and the hope that Mary and her nurses brought to the backwoods. These stories are powerful in their simplicity while remaining true to historical fact. Illustrations are based on photographs taken by Marvin Breckinridge Patterson for the Frontier Nursing Service.

Awards: Christopher Award, Horn Book Fanfare, Jefferson Cup Honor Award, *School Library Journal* Best Book, *Smithsonian Magazine* Notable Book for Children.

Related Subjects: 1920s, Appalachia, Frontier Nursing Service, Heroes, Mary Breckenridge, Medicine, Nursing

Character Themes: Determination, Ingenuity, Unselfishness

Wells, Rosemary, and Tom Wells, *The House in the Mail*. Illustrated by Dan Andreasen. Viking, 2002. ISBN: 0670035459 (hardcover) (Grades 2–5)

In 1927 it was possible to order a house and all the supplies necessary to build it from a catalog, shipped to the location of one's choice. For the Cartwright family this was an exciting event. No more would Emily and her brother Homer have to sleep in their grandparents' attic. This wonderful new house would also have the modern conveniences of electricity and running water. Told in the voice of young Emily, this picture book gives children a visual image of everyday life in America in the early 1900s.

Awards: Virginia Young Readers' Award

Related Subjects: 1920s, Homebuilding, United States—History

Character Themes: Family love, Resourcefulness, Teamwork

Wick, Walter (author and photographer), *A Drop of Water: A Book of Science and Wonder*. Scholastic, 1997. ISBN: 0590221973 (hardcover) (Grades 3–6)

Walter Wick has created a book that can be enjoyed on several levels. Foremost it presents clear, straightforward explanations of how water responds to various environmental conditions. This is done through text that is easily understood, accompanied by carefully staged photographs. What sets this book apart, however, is the beauty of the images created by the author. As the title suggests, the illustrations go beyond scientific fact, creating a sense of wonder about the beauty of the world. This title should appeal to those interested in science, art, and photography.

Awards: Beehive Award, (Utah), Horn Book Fanfare, Orbis Pictus Award, Robert F. Sibert Informational Book Award
Related Subjects: Photography, Science, Water
Character Themes: Curiosity, Wonder

CHAPTER SIX

Picture Books

None would question the value of early exposure to the world of story, and picture books meet this important need. With improved printing methods, every artistic appetite can be tempted by the various media and techniques currently used. From pen-and ink-drawings to paper collage and interactive pop-ups, from cartoon images to pictures that capture the style of old-world artists, picture books cut across lines of taste, subject, and philosophy. To honor and encourage excellence in illustration, the American Library Association gives the Caldecott Award, one of the most prestigious awards that an illustrator of children's books can receive.

These books encourage prereading skills like predication and sequencing, as well as more sophisticated devices such as irony and understatement. Wordless books entertain while educating prereaders in basic concepts of reading and mathematics. By definition, picture books contain an appropriate balance of text and illustration, complementing each other to form a union that is as pleasing to the eye as to the ear. Though the content leans heavily on visual portrayal, a well-developed plot is as essential to a picture book as to any other genre. Successful picture books often touch on serious matters with humor and tenderness, but whatever the subject, the story must deal with an issue that has meaning to its audience. Picture books provide the perfect vehicle to encourage children in discovering new worlds and to planting in them a lifelong love of the world of literacy.

Adler, David, *The Babe and I*. Illustrated by Terry Widener. Gulliver Books/Harcourt Brace, 1999. ISBN: 0152013784 (paperback) (Grades K–3)
Shocked to see his father selling apples on the street when he is supposed to be going to the office each day, a young boy takes his friend's advice and gets a job as a "newsie." Stationing themselves outside Yankee Stadium, the boys use the exploits of the great Babe Ruth to entice readers to buy their papers. When "The Babe" himself buys a paper from the boy, the youngster feels a real partnership with the star. Eventually, father and son come to an unspoken understanding that they also are a team working to help the family survive the Great Depression. Widener's bold illustrations prove effective for the subject.
Awards: California Young Readers Medal, Jefferson Cup Honor Award (Virginia), Nutmeg Award (Connecticut), Rhode Island Children's Book Award
Related Subjects: Athletes, Babe Ruth, Baseball, Family, Great Depression, "Newsies"
Character Themes: Cooperation, Family loyalty, Friendship

Baker, Keith (author and illustrator), *Big Fat Hen*. Harcourt Brace, 1994. ISBN: 0152002944 (paperback) (Grades K–2)
This illustrator has updated an old nursery rhyme with bold, colorful graphics. With a henhouse as the backdrop, each page shows mother hen and her chicks bringing life to the rhythmic lines of poetry. Illustrations take center stage with no more than three words on each page. Young children will love the bright colors and humorous pictures while learning rhyming and counting skills.
Awards: ABA Book Sense Pick, Golden Kite Award, Parents' Choice Gold Award
Related Subjects: Animals, Chickens, Counting, Farm life, Nursery rhymes
Character Themes: Cleverness, Humor

Baker, Olaf, *Where the Buffaloes Begin*. Illustrated by Stephen Gammell. Troll Associates, 1981. ISBN: 0140505601 (paperback) (Grades 3–6)
Stephen Gammell perfectly captures the dreamlike quality of Olaf Baker's tale of the young Indian brave named Little Wolf and his search for the lake where his people say the buffalo begin. Captivated by thoughts of the buffalo, Little Wolf slips out of the village very early in the morning to seek out these great beasts. Overcome with passion at the sight of the vast herd, his fiery cry begins a stampede that endangers his life, but saves the lives of those in his village. Words and pictures provide poetry for the eyes as well as the ears in this timeless story.

Awards: Boston Globe-Horn Book Award, Caldecott Honor
Related Subjects: Buffalo, Native Americans, Prairies
Character Themes: Courage, Fearlessness, Initiative

Berenstain, Stan, and Jan Berenstain (authors and illustrators), *Inside, Outside, Upside Down*. Random House, 1968. ISBN: 0394911423 (paperback) (Grades K–1)
Young children are introduced to basic concepts of space in this book for early readers. Simple graphic illustrations reinforce the concepts of being inside, and outside, and upside down. Repetition reinforces learning while humor makes the experience enjoyable. This is only one of a series of books for the younger set created by this husband-and-wife team.
Awards: Boston Globe-Horn Book Award, British Book Centre Honor Book
Related Subjects: Concept Book, Easy Reading
Character Themes: Humor, Inquisitiveness, Understanding

Birtha, Becky, *Grandmama's Pride*. Illustrated by Colin Bootman. Albert Whitman & Company, 2005. ISBN: 080753028X (hardcover) (Grades 1–3)
Since she does not yet know how to read, Sarah believes that her grandmother doesn't want them drinking from the public water fountain because the iced tea she has at home is better. She thinks that her grandmother walks to town for the exercise, not because she is too proud to sit in the back of the bus where people of color are forced to sit. When Sarah learns to read, however, it becomes clear why there are four different bathrooms instead of two in the bus station and why they never eat at the public grill in the five-and-ten. Soon, however, she begins to hear of places like Montgomery, Alabama, and to see words in the newspaper like "Boycott" and "Civil rights." The next time Sarah and her sister visit their grandmother, they ride in the front seat of the bus and sit down at the lunch counter at the rest stop. Things have changed because grandmother and others like her have held their ground.
Awards: Golden Kite Award
Related Subjects: 1950s, African-Americans, Civil rights—Segregation, Cross-cultural relations, Cross-generational relationships, Grandparents
Character Themes: Dignity, Family love, Pride

Bloom, Suzanne (author and illustrator), *A Splendid Friend, Indeed*. Boyds Mill Press, 2005. ISBN: 1590782860 (hardcover) (Grades PreK–1)
Bear and Goose are polar opposites. Goose wants to talk while Bear wants to read. Goose gets between Bear and his book and wants to read aloud. Bear

wants to think; Goose wants to ask questions. What can keep these pals from blowing apart? The precious solution arises from an open heart, and their friendship is made even stronger. Bright full-page illustrations make this a perfect read-aloud, and the lesson in patience, tolerance, and eventual bonding will speak to all children. Spare text makes this a natural source for group discussion, and humorous expressions provide joy for the prereader who simply wants to take pleasure in "reading" the pictures.

Awards: Theodore Seuss Geisel Award
Related Subjects: Friendship
Character Themes: Acceptance, Humor, Tolerance

Brett, Jan (author and illustrator), *Daisy Comes Home*. Scholastic, 2002. ISBN: 0439388465 (paperback) (Grades K–2)
Mei Mei did her best to keep all of her chickens happy but did not realize that the other hens were picking on Daisy, the smallest of the brood. One day, when she is chased out of the henhouse, Daisy's basket is swept down the river in a rainstorm. Encountering more danger than she ever did in Mei Mei's care, Daisy learns that she can defend herself against those that are larger and more aggressive. Rescued by her owner and returned to the safety of the farm, Daisy is no longer afraid of the other hens. Jan Brett's signature border designs expand elements of the storyline.

Award: Chicago Public Library Best Book for Children, Volunteer State Book Award (Tennessee)
Related Subjects: Bullies, Chickens, China
Character Themes: Boldness, Cleverness, Resourcefulness

Brett, Jan (author and illustrator), *The Hat*. Scholastic, 1997. ISBN: 0590282077 (hardcover) (Grades K–3)
Illustrations play an integral part in the telling of this winter tale set in Scandinavia. When a little hedgehog becomes stuck inside a sock that has blown off the clothesline, the other animals of the farm and woods make fun of him. Turning the situation to his advantage, "Hedgie" convinces the other animals that they, too, need a hat to wear. Soon all the clothes that were placed on the line to air have found new owners. Cameo vignettes fill the borders with plots and subplots to augment this engaging story. Brett's detailed illustrations are sure to please.

Awards: ABA Book Sense Pick, Bill Martin Jr. Picture Book Award (Kansas)
Related Subjects: Animals, Hats, Scandinavia, Winter
Character Themes: Cleverness, Humor

Briggs, Raymond (author and illustrator), *The Snowman*. **Random House, 1978. ISBN: 0394839730 (hardcover) (Grades K–2)**
What child has not imagined that the snowman he created could really come to life? This is a delightful wordless book that will verify that dream. When the household is asleep, a young boy slips outside and is greeted by the snowman he created earlier in the day. Together they enjoy many lively adventures, each showing the other wonders he has never seen. Soft, misty illustrations provide the perfect background for these whimsical experiences. Over 175 pictures tell a story that even a preschooler can read.
Awards: Boston Globe-Horn Book Award, IRA Children's Choices, Kate Greenaway Medal (UK)
Related Subjects: Seasons, Snow, Storyboarding, Winter, Wordless books
Character Themes: Creativity, Friendship

Bunting, Eve, *Dandelions*. **Illustrated by Greg Shed. Harcourt Brace, 1995. ISBN: 0153075368 (paperback) (Grades 1–3)**
When Zoe's family moves by covered wagon to Nebraska, her mother has difficulty adjusting to the miles of flat prairie surrounding their sod house. Neighbors are three miles away and the nearest town is a full day's ride. To her mother, the wide-open space is endless and monotonous. Hoping to lighten her mother's near depression, Zoe digs up a patch of dandelions to plant on the roof of their soddy to make it stand out brightly from the surrounding landscape. The soft gauche-on-canvas paintings in yellow and orange tones emphasize the vast expanse of this sun-drenched land.
Awards: ABA Book Sense Pick, CBC/NCSS Notable Children's Trade Book in Social Studies, IRA Teachers' Choices, Jefferson Cup Honor Award (Virginia)
Related Subjects: Family, Frontier and pioneer life, Loneliness, Midwest, Nebraska, Prairies, Sod houses
Character Themes: Family love, Resourcefulness, Sacrifice

Bunting, Eve, *Smoky Night*. **Illustrated by David Diaz. Harcourt, 1994. ISBN: 0152699546 (hardcover) (Grades 1–3)**
Bunting approaches a subject many children's authors avoid in *Smoky Night*. When their city erupts in a night of racial rioting, David and his mother must find their way to a nearby neighborhood shelter. Forced together with neighbors they have previously avoided, families find ways of cooperating with each other to achieve a common purpose of survival. The mixture of acrylic paintings mounted on heavily textured collage backgrounds created with found objects are a powerful reflection of the emotions experienced by those

involved. Told from a child's point of view, the emphasis is placed on the strong sense of community that can come out of disaster.
Awards: ABA Book Sense Pick, Caldecott Medal, ALSC Notable Children's Book, *School Library Journal* Best Book of the Year
Related Subjects: African-Americans, Cross-cultural relations, Diversity, Korean-Americans, Prejudice, Survival
Character Themes: Cooperation, Kindness, Neighborliness, Overcoming fear

Capucilli, Alyssa Satin, *Biscuit Goes to School*. Illustrated by Pat Schories. HarperTrophy, 2002. ISBN: 0064436160 (paperback) (Grades K–2)
When Biscuit's pal boards the bus for school, the adventurous little puppy is determined to go as well. Crossing the pond and the park, Biscuit locates an open door in the hall of education and makes himself right at home. Exploring the gym, the cafeteria, and the library, the furry interloper is suddenly discovered by his young owner, who is horrified that her pet is trespassing. However, Biscuit will not remain confined, and finally makes his way right into the classroom, where the teacher welcomes his new student and all ends happily. A part of the "I Can Read Book" series, this slim volume is a great introduction to Biscuit, and is certain to encourage beginning readers to want to learn more about the winsome little pup.
Awards: Garden State Children's Book Award (New Jersey)
Related Subjects: Adventure, Dogs, Easy Reading, Exploring, School
Character Themes: Acceptance, Independence

Cherry, Lynn (author and illustrator), *The Great Kapok Tree*. Harcourt, 1990. ISBN: 0152005207 (hardcover) (Grades 1–4)
Lynne Cherry explains the disappearance of the world's rain forests in terms that children can understand. Her lovely pictures and simple text parade before the reader the great variety of animals whose habitats are slowly being destroyed. Snakes, tree frogs, birds, monkeys, and even a jaguar describe the effects that cutting down the great Kapok tree will have on their supply of food and air.
Awards: Charlotte Award (New York), Iowa Children's Choice Award, IRA Teachers' Choices, NSTA Outstanding Science Trade Book for Children
Related Subjects: Ecology, Jungles, Rain forests, Trees—Kapok
Character Themes: Responsibility

Cooney, Barbara (author and illustrator), *Miss Rumphius*. Viking Press, 1982. ISBN: 0670479586 (hardcover) (Grades K–4)
Sitting on her grandfather's knee, Alice listened to his stories of faraway places. Enthralled with his tales, she vowed that she would one day travel the

world and then return to live by the sea as her grandparents had done. At her grandfather's urging she added one more goal to her list. She resolved to someday make the world a more beautiful place. Eventually she followed her dream, visiting many wonderful places until an injury to her back forced her to return. Inspired by the beauty of the lupines that she had planted in her garden by the sea, she began to spread their seeds through the fields and along the lanes where she lived. The next spring the fruit of her labor bloomed in glorious color, fulfilling her promise to leave beauty as her inheritance. Today the International Reading Association gives the Miss Rumphius Award to teachers who make the world a more beautiful place.
Awards: National Book Award
Related Subjects: Adventure, Flowers, Self-expression, Travel, Women
Character Themes: Beauty, Generosity, Joy

Cronin, Doreen, *Click, Clack, Moo: Cows That Type*. Illustrated by Betsy Lewin. Scholastic, 2000. ISBN: 0439216486 (paperback) (Grades K–2)
When the cows find an old typewriter in the barn, they begin to type out their demands for better conditions to Farmer Brown. Adamant at first that their demands are unfounded, the farmer refuses to capitulate. However, he is unable to stand against a coalition of cows and chickens refusing to produce both milk and eggs. When Farmer Brown gives in, peace is restored until the ducks take over the old typing machine.
Awards: Bill Martin Jr. Picture Book Award (Kansas), Buckaroo Book Award (Wyoming), Caldecott Honor, IRA/CBC Children's Choices, Irma Simonton and James H. Black Award for Excellence in Children's Literature (Bank Street)
Related Subjects: Animals, Cows, Farm life
Character Themes: Cooperation, Humor, Inventiveness

Dillon, Leo, and Diane Dillon (authors and illustrators), *Rap a Tap Tap: Here's Bojangles—Think of That*. Blue Sky Press, 2002. ISBN: 0590478834 (hardcover) (Grades K–4)
Using the same beat that Mr. Bojangles himself, Bill Robinson, expressed through tap, the Dillons take readers on a rhythmic romp down city streets. Illustrations reproduce the movements of the dancing legend so well that readers can almost hear the clicking of steel on concrete and wood. Robinson's friendliness, fame, and generosity are portrayed in rhyming text accompanied by amazing collage. This tribute will serve as an introduction for contemporary readers to the entertainment personality that made audiences smile and tap a toe themselves during the Great Depression and beyond. As stated in the text and the afterword, "He talked with his feet," and his style

has never been duplicated. An important book to add to any collection, this volume is a delight to read and to share.

Awards: Coretta Scott King Honor Award, Parents' Choice Gold Award
Related Subjects: African-Americans, Bill Robinson, Dance, Music, Poetry, Rhythm
Character Themes: Friendliness, Joy, Talent

Duke, Kate (author and illustrator), *Aunt Isabel Tells a Good One*. Puffin Unicorn Books, 1992. ISBN: 0140505342 (paperback) (Grades 3–9)
When Penelope mouse asks for a bedtime story, Aunt Isabel uses the opportunity to teach the little mouse the elements that make up a good tale. Eliciting contributions from young Penelope, Isabel begins with a When and a Where and adds a Problem and Villains and a little Danger. What results is a delightful story-within-a-story that delivers two enchanting adventures for the price of one. Wonderfully engaging illustrations enhance the telling with decorations in the borders and sidebar vignettes.

Awards: IRA Children's Choices
Related Subjects: Mice, Storytelling, Writers
Character Themes: Creativity, Humor, Imagination

Frasier, Debra (author and illustrator), *Miss Alaineus: A Vocabulary Disaster*. Harcourt, 2000. ISBN: 0152021639 (hardcover) (Grades 3–5)
Young Sage, staying at home with a cold, misunderstands one of the vocabulary words given to her for homework over the phone. Not able to find the meaning for this strange new word, Sage makes up her own. When the class is sent into gales of laughter at her imaginative definition, Sage is mortified. Several days later she turns her embarrassment into triumph at the Annual Vocabulary Parade when she appears dressed as Miss Alaineus, Queen of all Miscellaneous Things. A border of sentences Sage writes for another assignment describes her feelings as the story unfolds. Words are defined in the text and a hidden word game appears on the end papers.

Awards: IRA Children's Choices, IRA Teachers' Choices
Related Subjects: Language Arts, Spelling, Vocabulary
Character Themes: Imagination, Self-expression

Freymann, Saxton, and Joost Elffers, *How Are You Peeling? Foods with Moods*. Arthur A. Levine Books, 1999. ISBN: 0439104319 (hardcover) (Grades K–2)
Using fruits and vegetables, the author and illustrator have created pages expressing all kinds of emotions that children may feel. Peppers, onions, mel-

ons, lemons, and tomatoes are transformed into faces with black-eyed peas as eyes. Confusion, amusement, frustration, shyness, and sadness are all conveyed through these animated foods positioned in front of vibrant, colorful backgrounds. The rhyming text guides the reader to identify the emotions portrayed and what situations may cause them. This is an excellent book to use in leading children to talk about their emotions. It can help them realize that they are not alone in what they experience.

Awards: *New York Times* Best Illustrated Children's Book
Related Subjects: Emotions, Food, Rhyming
Character Themes: Creativity, Humor, Self-expression

Henkes, Kevin (author and illustrator), *Chrysanthemum*. HarperTrophy, 1996. ISBN: 0688147321 (paperback) (K–2)

Chrysanthemum loves her unusual name until she goes to school and becomes the target of teasing, especially by the mean-spirited Victoria. Her parents attempt to reassure Chrysanthemum and give her much love and encouragement, only to have her self-esteem torn apart again the next day. It is the kind and insightful music teacher, whose name happens to be Delphinium, who is able to turn the tide and make flower names a distinction to be treasured.

Awards: ALSC Notable Children's Book, Horn Book Fanfare Honor List, *School Library Journal* Best Book of the Year
Related Subjects: Names, School, Self-concept
Character Themes: Family love, Kindness, Self-respect

Henkes, Kevin (author and illustrator), *Kitten's First Full Moon*. Greenwillow Books/HarperCollins, 2004. ISBN: 0060588284 (hardcover) (Grades K–3)

Kitten's perception of her first full moon is limited by the tiny thing's lack of experience. Believing the big white round light to be a gigantic bowl of milk, Kitten attempts to reach the favorite dish by jumping, climbing, and diving, without success. However, satisfaction is finally achieved right on her own doorstep. Young audiences will delight in being smarter than the little feline, while giggling at her expressive face as she doggedly pursues her goal. Kevin Henkes' skill at character development with sparse text and spare line is a tribute to his already acclaimed talent. This simple book is quickly read, but remembered long after, with a smile.

Awards: ALSC Notable Children's Book, Caldecott Medal, *School Library Journal* Best Book
Related Subjects: Animals, Cats
Character Themes: Determination, Humor

Hill, Eric (author and illustrator), *Spot's First Walk.* **G. P. Putnam's Sons, 1981. ISBN: 0399244824 (board book) (Grades PreK–1)**
Spot, the puppy, is about to go out on his first adventure alone. His mother warns him about getting lost, and sends him on his way. With tail-wagging enthusiasm, the little explorer visits many places within his boundaries, meeting animal and insect friends along the way. Each new discovery is hidden from young readers by a flap, increasing the anticipation and giving opportunity for prediction and interaction. Large, primary-sized type invites beginning readers to sight-read, and the board-book format encourages ownership by even the smallest hands. Having read this volume, young fans of Spot will want to read or hear all of the books in this charming series. The gentle stories that tell of family and adventure are great read-alouds that will become I-can-read favorites.
Awards: Humane Society of Greater Akron (Ohio)
Related Subjects: Animals, Dogs, Easy reading
Character Themes: Independence, Joy

Hoban, Russell, *Bedtime for Frances.* **Illustrated by Garth Williams. HarperCollins, 1960. ISBN: 006027106X (hardback) (Grades K–3)**
When the endearing little badger Frances is lovingly put to bed at seven o'-clock, Father and Mother settle down to watch television and relax a bit, but Frances is not sleepy. One more kiss, a glass of water, her original song-to-get-sleepy, a scary thing in the corner, a shared piece of cake, tooth brushing, and billowing curtains all provide occasions for revisiting her parents. Finally, her patient father, surprised out of his sleep by Frances standing by his bed, delivers an ultimatum that his lively little daughter understands. Making a wise choice, Frances discovers that she is sleepy, and the badger household settles down for the night. This cozy little volume is a part of the *Frances* series that has delighted young readers for generations.
Awards: ALSC Notable Children's Book
Related Subjects: Animals, Badgers, Bedtime, Fear
Character Themes: Family love, Humor, Patience

Jenkins, Steve, *What Do You Do With a Tail Like This?* **Illustrated by Robin Page. Houghton Mifflin, 2003. ISBN: 0618256288 (hardcover) (Grades K–2)**
The author and illustrator of this ingenious book have created an excellent tool for introducing children to the similarities and differences of various species in the animal kingdom. Using cut-paper illustrations, Page illustrates double page spreads with noses, ears, mouths, and tails while Jenkins asks

how these different body parts might be used for the animal's benefit. While young readers can practice the skill of prediction, older children will be encouraged to carefully observe the animal's characteristics in detail. Thirty creatures are featured with additional information about each animal given on four pages at the back of the book.

Awards: Caldecott Honor, *Child Magazine* Best Books of the Year, Garden State Children's Book Award (New Jersey)
Related Subjects: Animals, Nature, Science
Character Themes: Survival

Johnson, Angela, *When I Am Old with You*. Illustrated by David Soman. Orchard Books, 1990. ISBN: 0531058840 (paperback) (Grades K–2)
Any child who has spent quality time with a grandparent will identify with this winsome picture book in which an African-American child dreams of the things he will do with his grandfather when he grows old with him. Images of sitting in dual rocking chairs telling stories, going fishing, roasting corn over a big fire, and taking long walks are beautifully represented by Soman's watercolors. These are universal pictures of a loving and nurturing relationship between generations.

Awards: ALSC Notable Children's Book, CBC/NCSS Notable Children's Book in Social Studies, Coretta Scott King Honor Book
Related Subjects: African-Americans, Cross-generational relationships, Family—Relationships, Grandparents
Character Themes: Family love, Friendship

Keats, Ezra Jack (author and illustrator), *Goggles*. Macmillan Company, 1998 (orig. 1969). ISBN: 0140564403 (hardcover) (Grades K–3)
When Peter finds a pair of lens-less motorcycle glasses near his special hideout, he shares the treasure with his friend Archie and his loyal dachshund, Willie. Engrossed in pretend adventures, the two boys do not see older and larger fellows coming to steal their fun. When Peter bravely attempts to face down the bullies, he loses the glasses, but Willie rushes to a creative and humorous rescue. In the end, Peter, Archie, and Willie get the last laugh, and the bullies get nothing but disappointment for their pains. Keats's individual style is at its best with well-chosen collage pieces and adorable happy faces reveling in their success.

Awards: Caldecott Honor
Related Subjects: African-Americans, Bullies, Dogs, Friendship, Pets, Urban life
Character Themes: Courage, Creativity, Spunk

Kellogg, Steven (author and illustrator), *Pinkerton, Behave!* Dial Press, 1979. ISBN: 0803765738 (hardcover) (Grades PreK–3)
When Pinkerton the Great Dane first becomes a family member, Mother reads a book about dog training while demonstrating unsuccessfully to her watchful daughter how obedience should be achieved from the new pet. Following disastrous (but hilarious) results, Mother, Daughter, and Pinkerton attend doggy school, hoping to accomplish compliance from the pony-sized charmer. When the defeated and frazzled instructor vociferously dismisses Pinkerton and his family from her school, the three slink away with exhaustion and chagrin. However, with characteristic humor, Kellogg redeems the lovable canine by using Pinkerton's strengths to achieve victory. This lively account will bring laughs from dog owners and children who long for a personality-filled pet such as Pinkerton. Kellogg's signature illustrations enhance the joy of the sparse text.
Awards: Georgia Children's Book Award, Humane Society of Greater Akron (Ohio), Junior Library Guild Selection
Related Subjects: Dogs, Mother-daughter relationships
Character Themes: Humor, Obedience

Lehman, Barbara (author and illustrator), *The Red Book.* Houghton Mifflin, 2004. ISBN: 0618428588 (hardcover) (Grades K–3)
The old proverb that states "A picture is worth a thousand words" reflects the essence of this intriguing wordless book. A little girl walking to school in a city that is wrapped in winter finds a red book partially submerged in the snow. Concentration in the classroom becomes difficult with a new book in her bag, so she peeks and discovers a lone boy walking on the sand at his island home far away. Discovering a red book, almost hidden in the sand, the boy also investigates, and the two worlds meet, enchantingly. Vivid, imaginative illustrations, with no text, offer young readers or those who struggle with the skill of reading equal pleasure with adults or avid bibliophiles.
Awards: Caldecott Honor
Related Subjects: Books, Reading, Wordless book
Character Themes: Curiosity, Imagination

Lester, Helen, *Hooway for Wodney Wat.* Illustrated by Lynn M. Munsinger. Houghton Mifflin, 2002. ISBN: 061821612X (paperback) (Grades 1–3)
Any child who has ever faced a schoolyard bully will cheer for Rodney Rat. Teased by his classmates for not being able to pronounce the letter "R," Rodney routinely hides his head in his jacket. When big, mean Camilla Capy-

bara joins the class, however, everyone is intimidated. Chosen as leader in a game of Simon Says, Rodney unwittingly outsmarts Camilla and becomes the class hero. This little rodent reminds children that their defects can, in fact, be turned to strengths. The spare illustrations are a perfect complement to this laugh-out-loud story.

Awards: ALSC Notable Children's Book, Arkansas Diamond Primary Book Award, Blue Hen Book Award (Delaware), Buckaroo Book Award (Wyoming), North Carolina Children's Book Award, Parents' Choice Gold Award, *School Library Journal* Best Books of the Year, Beehive Award (Utah)
Related Subjects: Bullies, Rats, Special needs—Speech defects
Character Themes: Courage, Self-acceptance

Lester, Helen, *Tacky the Penguin*. Illustrated by Lynn Munsinger. Sandpiper/Houghton Mifflin, 1988. ISBN: 0395562333 (paperback) (Grades K–3)
Although Tacky lives with companions Goodly, Lovely, Angel, Neatly, and Perfect, he is not fazed by their obvious character qualities. Instead, the young individualist wears flowered camp shirts, cannot march in a line, sings his own brand of off-key music, and pounds everyone on the back in gregarious greeting. Tolerated for his offbeat behavior, Tacky stumbles blithely through his arctic life, until one life-changing day when hunters arrive with weapons and tools to steal any penguins they can catch. Goodly, Lovely, Angel, Neatly, and Perfect hide behind the nearest ice formation, while Tacky heads off the invaders with resounding slaps on the back, bumbling marches, and earsplitting song. Completely befuddled by the bizarre behavior of what they assume to be a typical resident, the intruders run for a saner society, and the community is saved. Lauded for his bravery, the humble little outcast becomes a hero.

Awards: California Young Readers Award, Colorado Children's Book Award, Golden Sower Award (Nebraska), Humane Society of Greater Akron (Ohio)
Related Subjects: Animals, Antarctica, Penguins
Character Themes: Courage, Humor, Individuality

Lewis, Rose, *I Love You Like Crazy Cakes*. Illustrated by Jane Dyer. Little, Brown & Co., 2000. ISBN: 0316525766 (board book) (Grades Toddler–Kindergarten)
Based on the real-life experience of Massachusetts television producer Lewis, this picture book is a must-have for adoptive parents. In simple text and

tender illustrations, Lewis and Dyer unfold the story of a little girl in an orphanage in China, and the single lady in the United States whose life is incomplete without a baby. In tender words Lewis chronicles the first moments with her daughter with such love that any adopted child will feel more secure just hearing and seeing the union of mother and baby. A great gift for any nursery, this board-book edition is sturdy and will be enjoyed by all little ones who are loved like crazy cakes.

Awards: ABA Book Sense Pick, Children's Gallery Award
Related Subjects: Adoption, China, Family—Single parent, Mother-daughter relationships
Character Themes: Love, Self-acceptance

Lobel, Arnold (author and illustrator), *Mouse Tales*. Harper & Row, 1972. ISBN: 0060239417 (hardcover) (Grades K–3)
At bedtime, seven little mouse brothers beg for a story. Papa Mouse agrees to tell not one, but seven stories, and the fun begins. The seven stories are a mix of adventure, humor, and fantasy, blended with family joys and sorrows. By the end of the tales, Papa asks if anyone is awake, and when he hears no answer, he bids a loving "good night, my boys" and moves quietly to the fireplace to sip a cozy cup of tea alone with Mama Mouse. This little volume serves as a read-aloud for the parent who wants to calm a weary child, or as an easily mastered chapter book for the beginning reader.

Awards: Horn Book Fanfare, Irma Simonton and James H. Black Award for Excellence in Children's Literature (Bank Street), Library of Congress Children's Book Award
Related Subjects: Bedtime, Easy reading
Character Themes: Family, Love, Humor

Lorbiecki, Marybeth, *Sister Anne's Hands*. Illustrated by K. Wendy Popp. Puffin Books, 1998. ISBN: 0140565345 (paperback) (Grades 1–3)
When school opens, second-grader Anna Zabrocky is surprised at the color of her teacher's hands. She has never seen skin that dark. Though some parents pull their children from the class, Anna responds to the kindness and excitement for learning that her teacher conveys. The soft, luminous illustrations complement the story beautifully.

Awards: Grand Canyon Young Readers Award (Arizona), Show Me Readers Award Nominee (Missouri)
Related Subjects: Cross-cultural relations, Prejudice, School, Teachers
Character Themes: Courage, Tolerance

Martin, Bill, Jr., *Panda Bear, Panda Bear, What Do You See?* **Illustrated by Eric Carle. Henry Holt & Co., 2003. ISBN: 0805017585 (hardcover) (Grades PreK–3)**

Already beloved for *Brown Bear, Brown Bear, What Do You See?*, author Martin teams with illustration legend Carle to present the serious topic of endangered species to young readers in a style that is both vivid and entertaining. Each of the eight animals, birds, beasts, and sea creatures, look ahead to the next character and finally to the child who can make a difference in whether or not they continue to exist. The message is not heavy handed, and the text is simple enough so that even youthful prereaders can participate in sharing the text and yet absorb the message with enthusiasm.

Awards: IRA Children's Choices, *New York Times* Best Seller

Related Subjects: Animals, Bears—Pandas, Endangered Species

Character Themes: Compassion, Initiative

Martin, Jacqueline Briggs, *Snowflake Bentley.* **Illustrated by Mary Azarian. Houghton Mifflin, 1998. ISBN: 0395861624 (hardcover) (Grades K–3)**

Wilson Bentley was passionate about studying all forms of moisture from a very young age, but his special interest was snowflakes. By the age of fifteen he was drawing the snow crystals he saw through an old microscope. At sixteen, with the help of a camera equipped with its own microscope that his parents gave him, Willie was finally able to capture the beauty of these flakes for everyone to see. Although many laughed at his interest, Willie won the respect of the scientific world and became known as the "Snowflake Man." The hand-colored woodcuts lend an old-fashioned feel to the work.

Awards: Caldecott Medal, Lupine Award (Maine)

Related Subjects: Nature, Science, Snow, Wilson Bentley, Winter

Character Themes: Appreciation of nature, Determination, Ingenuity, Inquisitiveness, Perseverance

McCloskey, Robert (author and illustrator), *One Morning in Maine.* **Penguin Books, 1952. ISBN: 0670526274 (hardcover) (Grades K–3)**

Readers who first met Sal in her debut title, *Blueberries for Sal*, will be happy to revisit her island home in Maine and discover that she is growing up. The chubby-cheeked preschooler is now old enough to lose her first tooth, which offers one adventure for the morning. The other adventure is that Sal and baby sister Jane are going to have the treat of crossing the water with their dad to shop at Buck's Island. Inimitable young Sal announces to all birds, sea life, and mankind that she has a loose tooth, and Jane tags along, creating her own form of entertainment. Although Sal suffers one disappointment, congenial friends in the village of their destination more than grant her secret wish. Windblown black-and-white illustrations of each adventure complete this pleasant excursion in coastal family life.

Awards: Caldecott Medal
Related Subjects: Adventure, Coastal life, Family, Maine
Character Themes: Friendliness, Generosity, Joy

Noble, Trinka Hakes, *Meanwhile Back at the Ranch.* **Illustrated by Tony Ross. Dial Books for Young Readers, 1987. ISBN: 0800370338 (hardcover) (Grades 2–5)**
Rancher Hicks drives his truck eighty-four miles to the town of Sleepy Gulch, because nothing ever happens on his ranch. The most exciting event he witnesses is a turtle crossing the road, which the entire town turns out to see. Meanwhile, back at the ranch, Elna, his wife, enjoys quite a different day. The cat has kittens, the dog has puppies, an unexpected inheritance arrives in the mail, the pig delivers piglets, and Elna strikes oil while digging for potatoes, all before Rancher Hicks has even had his lunch in town. As the afternoon progresses, events in Elna's life escalate. However, when her beloved returns, she greets him with a warm welcome, and loving appreciation for his turtle story. Only then does Rancher Hicks realize what he has missed at the ranch. Tony Ross's illustrations provide the perfect visual humor for the dry wit of Noble's text.

Awards: Grand Canyon Young Reader Award (Arizona)
Related Subjects: Ranching, The West, Villages
Character Themes: Humor, Sharing

Numeroff, Laura Joffe, *If You Give a Mouse a Cookie.* **Illustrated by Felicia Bond. A Laura Geringer Book/HarperCollins, 1985. ISBN: 0060245867 (hardcover) (Grades K–3)**
An unknown but experienced narrator speculates to the reading audience about the demands that would be made if the tiny rodent in question should come to call. Charming illustrations reveal a hospitable little boy graciously meeting the desires of his guest through a cookie, milk, napkin, mirror, nail scissors, broom, mop, mouse-sized bed with blanket and pillow, bedtime story, crayons, paper, pen, tape, and back to milk and cookies. The story is such a delight to read that young readers will happily memorize the sequence without even realizing that they are strengthening their reading skills.

Awards: Buckeye Children's Book Award (Ohio), Colorado Children's Book Award, Emphasis on Reading Winners (Alabama), Georgia Children's Book Award
Related Subjects: Mice, Sequencing
Character Themes: Humor, Sharing

Parish, Peggy, *Amelia Bedelia and the Baby.* **Illustrated by Lynn Sweat. Avon Books, 1982. ISBN: 038057067X (paperback) (Grades K–3)**
Amelia Bedelia has blessed generations with chuckles, and this story carries on the tradition. When Mrs. Rogers lends her bumbling maid to a friend to babysit, the results are slapstick at best, but the baby is kept happy most of the time, and all are satisfied in the end. Always the literalist, Amelia plays with the baby toys herself, wears the bib, and lets the baby eat catsup and strawberries and generally make a mess. When the parents arrive home, although the mother is aghast at the chaos, the baby loves her new sitter, and both parents find the strawberry tarts that Amelia has made quite tasty. Young readers love having the inside knowledge that the adult, Amelia, apparently does not, and will giggle in anticipation of her actions. This series is a great way to introduce the beginning reader to the pure fun of the printed page.
Awards: IRA Children's Choices
Related Subjects: Babysitting
Character Themes: Humor

Pfister, Marcus (author and illustrator), *The Rainbow Fish.* **Translated by J. Alison James. North-South Books, 1992. ISBN: 1558580093 (hardcover) (Grades PreK–3)**
With his uniquely beautiful shimmering scales, Rainbow Fish is the most spectacular little fish in the sea. However, when other fish want him to join their games, his vanity causes him to ignore their overtures of friendship and swim away by himself. One day, a would-be playmate approaches Rainbow Fish and asks if he might have just a single shiny scale. He is denied, and from that day forward it is Rainbow Fish who is ignored. In time, his values change, and all ends happily. This is a simple story of sharing, with a moral that the youngest readers cannot miss. Shimmering scales decorate each spread and will hold little listeners' attention to the very last page.
Awards: ABBY, Christopher Award, Florida Children's Book Award, IRA/CBC Children's Choices, North Carolina Children's Book Award
Related Subjects: Fish, Friendship, Pride, Sea
Character Themes: Cooperation, Generosity, Sharing

Pinkney, Jerry (author and illustrator), *Noah's Ark.* **SeaStar Books, 2002. ISBN: 1587172011 (hardcover) (Grades K–2)**
Jerry Pinkney's beautiful illustrations portray the drama and the power of the story of Noah and the ark that God instructed him to build. Detailed drawings show the structure of the enormous boat and portray the hard labor involved in preparing it for its cargo of people and animals. Much time can be spent poring over the intricate pictures of animal pairs gathering to enter their doors. Those who are looking for an accurate and attractive rendition of this biblical story would do well to consider Pinkney's exquisite edition.
Awards: ALSC Notable Book, Caldecott Honor
Related Subjects: Animals, Nature—Forces of, Noah's Ark
Character Themes: Courage, Family loyalty, Perseverance, Religious faith, Trust

Polacco, Patricia (author and illustrator), *Mrs. Katz and Tush.* **Dell, 1992. ISBN: 0440409365 (paperback) (Grades 2–4)**
Mrs. Katz, a lonely Jewish widow, lives in the same building as Larnel's African-American family. When Larnel brings a kitten to Mrs. Katz, she agrees to take it only if he will stop by to help take care of the little animal. He learns to love the cat, but he also loves the kugel Mrs. Katz bakes and the stories she tells about the old country. When Tush, the cat, disappears one day, it is Larnel's father who finds it and brings it back. Steadily, the two become the best of friends and the young boy begins to realize that their ancestors suffered similar times of slavery and prejudice. The author's signature illustrations add depth and delight to the telling of this engaging tale.
Awards: Jane Addams Children's Honor Book
Related Subjects: African-Americans, Cats, Cross-cultural relations, Cross-generational relationships, Jews, Prejudice
Character Themes: Ethnic pride, Friendship, Joy, Neighborliness, Respect for elders

Polacco, Patricia (author and illustrator), *Thank You Mr. Falker.* **Philomel, 1998. ISBN: 0399231668 (paperback) (Grades 3–8)**
Trisha is so excited about starting school because she wants to read! But in first grade, second grade, third grade, and fourth grade, she just can't make those squiggly lines and marks on the page make any sense. She feels different and alone, and the other children make fun of her. It isn't until fifth grade that Trisha discovers why the process is so hard for her to understand. Thanks to her new teacher, Mr. Falker, she learns that she has a reading problem that he can help her overcome. Based on her own experience, Polacco

has crafted a story that will resonate with everyone who has ever struggled with something that others have found easy to do.

Awards: Boston Area Educators Award for Social Responsibility, Keystone to Reading Book Award (Pennsylvania), Emphasis on Reading Winner (Alabama), Parents' Choice Silver Honor Award, Rhode Island Children's Book Award

Related Subjects: Dyslexia, Learning disabilities, Reading, Self-concept

Character themes: Acceptance, Compassion, Determination, Patience

Rathmann, Peggy (author and illustrator), *Officer Buckle and Gloria.* **Putnam Juvenile, 1995. ISBN: 0399226168 (hardcover) (Grades K–3)**

In *Officer Buckle and Gloria*, Rathmann cleverly serves up safety tips in a way that will make children laugh as they learn. Though Officer Buckle has a passion for teaching children to be safe, his lessons put the students to sleep, until the new police dog Gloria joins his presentations. As Gloria mimes the tips behind the unsuspecting officer's back, the students are suddenly enthralled. When Officer Buckle finds that the students' interest is in his dog and not his lessons, he is hurt and stops going to the schools. Gloria, however, does not fare well on her own and the two realize that the best safety tip of all is to "stick with your buddy."

Awards: Caldecott Medal, Golden Archer Award (Wisconsin), Humane Society of Greater Akron (Ohio), North Carolina Children's Book Award, Wisconsin Children's Choice

Related Subjects: Dogs, Police, Safety, School

Character Themes: Cooperation, Friendship, Humor

Recorvits, Helen, *My Name Is Yoon.* **Illustrated by Gabi Swiatkowska. Farrar, Straus & Giroux, 2003. ISBN: 0374351147 (hardcover) (Grades K–2)**

Moving to the United States from Korea is a difficult adjustment for Yoon to make. When her father asks her to write her name in English, she resists, stating that it looks happier when written in her native language. At school, when her teacher introduces the word "cat," she decides that she wants to be a cat to hide in a corner. When the word "bird" is taught, she is a bird flying away back to Korea. When another little girl gives Yoon a cupcake, she thinks that if she were a cupcake everyone would like her. Finally, she is comfortable enough to be herself and to claim her own name Yoon, which means Shining Wisdom. Illustrator Gabi Swiatkowska gives full expression to Yoon's emotions and imagination.

Awards: Ezra Jack Keats New Illustrator Award, Georgia Children's Book Award, Monarch Award (Illinois)

Related Subjects: Cross-cultural relations, Immigration, Korean-Americans, Language, Names, School
Character Themes: Adaptation, Family unity, Self-image

Sabuda, Robert (author and illustrator), *America the Beautiful.* **Simon & Schuster, 2004. ISBN: 0689847440 (hardcover) (Grades K–12)**
Sabuda's unprecedented craftsmanship in the field of pop-up books has created a stunning tribute to America in his re-creation of this title song. From the Golden Gate Bridge to the fields of waving grain in the Midwest to the Statue of Liberty in New York's harbor, each page offers a feast of carefully designed details to delight the eye. A miniature booklet on the final page highlights various patriotic symbols, including the Twin Towers. Though designed for children, there is no age limit to those who will enjoy this feat of paper engineering.
Awards: New York Public Library 100 Titles for Reading and Sharing, Oppenheim Toy Portfolio Platinum Award
Related Subjects: America, Art, Craftsmanship, Music
Character Themes: Cleverness, Craftsmanship, Patriotism

Schur, Maxine Rose, *The Peddler's Gift.* **Illustrated by Kimberly Bulcken Root. Dial Books for Young Readers, 1999. ISBN: 0803719787 (hardcover) (Grades K–3)**
Shimon the peddler spoke so few words that the children of Korovenko thought he was a simpleton and called him Shnook. In truth, nothing he did seemed to come out right. On one particular visit, when a dreidel fell under the table, Leibush reasoned that the peddler would never know it was gone. He would just borrow it until the peddler's next visit. When his conscience will not let him rest, Leibush rushes to return the toy and discovers that Shnook is not a fool after all. Lovely illustrations augment the story.
Awards: Smithsonian Notable Book of the Century, Sydney Taylor Book Award
Related Subjects: Dreidels, Jews, Peddlers, Russia
Character Themes: Forgiveness, Honesty, Kindness, Respect, Wisdom

Shannon, George, *White Is for Blueberry.* **Illustrated by Laura Dronzek. Greenwillow Books/HarperCollins, 2005. ISBN: 006029275X (hardcover) (Grades PreK–2)**
Shannon and Dronzek view ten common objects in nature with both artistic and scientific eyes. The audience peeks inside, outside, through shadows and sunset for a look at the commonplace with a fresh view. Youthful readers will

wonder how a crow can be pink; a poppy, black; a sweet potato, brown; snow, purple; or a sky, orange. Full-page illustrations in bold colors with large type make this volume one to be enjoyed by groups as well as individuals. Teachers, librarians, or parents may choose to enliven read-aloud time by asking, "How can this be?" while youthful scientists make predictions. This colorful volume will find a home in both science and art classes with topics of seasons, cold and heat, stages of life, plants, and animals.
Awards: ALSC Notable Book
Related Subjects: Colors, Life cycles, Nature, Seasons
Character Themes: Appreciation of nature, Wonder

Sidman, Joyce, *Song of the Water Boatman and Other Pond Poems*. Illustrated by Beckie Prange. Houghton Mifflin, 2005. ISBN: 0608135472 (hardcover) (Grades 4–12)
Unique in its combination of nonfiction and poetry, this multifaceted picture book splashes across the fields of both art and science. Author Sidman has juxtaposed some rather amazing facts with poetry that speaks to all ages. Illustrator Prange takes the reader to the pond's edge and beyond for an intimate view of each aquatic form. Her woodcuts in muted earth and water tones are the perfect complement to the text. Each spread offers both poetry and scientific details about pond flora and fauna, decorated with the artist's interpretation of not only the subject, but its personality, as well. From the familiar wood duck and the heron, known as "queen of the pond," to the rarely seen water bear, the aquatic environment plays host to plants, insects, and animals that are equally intriguing. This is one volume of poetry that appeals to both sides of the brain.
Awards: Caldecott Honor
Related Subjects: Art, Nature, Pond life, Science, Seasons
Character Themes: Discovery, Wonder

Simont, Marc (author and illustrator), *The Stray Dog*. Scholastic, 2001. ISBN: 0439385911 (paperback) (Grades K–2)
As they are enjoying a picnic in the park, a family is joined by a stray dog that stays to entertain the children all day. The children want to take him home, but their parents are afraid he may belong to someone else. All the following week, thoughts of the little dog preoccupy each member of the family until they decide to return to the park to see if he might still be there. As they begin their lunch, the little dog streaks by with the dogcatcher in hot pursuit. The children convince the dogcatcher that he is indeed their dog and joyfully take him home. The author uses few words and simple but expressive pictures to tell this delightful tale.

Awards: Caldecott Honor ALSC Notable Book, Boston Globe-Horn Book Honor, Parents' Choice, *School Library Journal* Best Book
Related Subjects: Dogs, Family
Character Themes: Compassion, Determination, Ingenuity

Smucker, Anna Egan, *No Star Nights*. Illustrated by Steve Johnson. Alfred A. Knopf, 1989. ISBN: 0679867244 (paperback) (Grades 4–6)
The author takes a nostalgic look at life in a steel town in the mid-1900s, when the mills were going strong. Memories of nights when the sky glowed red from the furnaces and days when the smokestacks billowed rust-colored clouds flow through the pages. But not every remembrance had to do with the mills. There were games of dodgeball, and Fourth of July parades, and trips to see the Pittsburgh Pirates play ball. Although the slag hills are now covered with grass and many families have moved away, the memories of a vibrant childhood linger. The lovely illustrations effectively portray the tone of the prose.
Awards: ALSC Notable Book, IRA Children's Book Award
Related Subjects: Childhood, Steel mills, West Virginia
Character Themes: Families, Work ethic

Soto, Gary, *Chato's Kitchen*. Illustrated by Susan Guevara. Scholastic, 1995. ISBN: 0590897489 (paperback) (Grades 2–4)
This is a cat-and-mouse tale with a Latin twist. Chato and his cool friend Novio Boy think they are going to enjoy mice for dinner until the mice turn the tables on their plans by bringing with them their friend Chorizo, a low-riding dachshund. Set in the barrio, Soto peppers his wonderfully funny dialogue throughout with Spanish terms. A glossary is included on the front pages. Susan Guevara's brightly colored illustrations are humorous depictions of urban life in Los Angeles.
Awards: Americas Award Honorable Mention, Pura Belpré Award, Tomás Rivera Mexican-American Children's Book Award
Related Subjects: Cats, Hispanic-Americans, Mice, Trickster tales
Character Themes: Cooperation, Ingenuity

St. George, Judith, *So You Want to Be President*. Illustrated by David Small. Philomel Books, 2000. ISBN: 0399234071 (hardcover) (Grades 3–6)
Judith St. George has written a history of the men who have filled this powerful position in America that is fun, as well as reflective. Presenting trivia, such as how many presidents were named James, how many were born in log cabins, and how many went to college (nine did not), she succeeds in

demonstrating the great diversity of men who have achieved this high office. Amusing anecdotes display the humanity of these great men and add interest to the telling. David Small's hilarious cartoon-style illustrations emphasize the lighthearted tone. Despite the humorous approach, the author succeeds in conveying to her readers that the office of the President is one of great responsibility to which anyone can aspire.

Awards: Caldecott Medal, Mitten Honor Award (Michigan)
Related Subjects: Government, Presidents, United States—History
Character Themes: Courage, Dedication, Humor, Patriotism, Sacrifice

Steig, William (author and illustrator), *Brave Irene.* **Farrar, Straus & Giroux, 1986. ISBN: 0374309477 (hardcover) (Grades 3–6)**
When Mrs. Bobbin the dressmaker falls ill, she is unable to deliver the ball gown she has sewn for the duchess. Unwilling for her mother's creation not to reach its intended patron, young Irene determines to make the delivery herself. With snow coming down fiercely, Irene finds herself in a contest with the wind, which seems determined to foil her plans. Undaunted, she overcomes one challenge after another to put the gown in the hands of the duchess. Winsome illustrations and clever, humorous dialogue should make young Irene a favorite with adults as well as children.

Awards: *Booklist* Editors' Choice, Horn Book Fanfare, *New York Times* Best Illustrated Children's Book Award
Related Subjects: Mother-daughter relationships, Storms—Snow
Character Themes: Courage, Determination, Family love

Stewart, Sarah, *The Gardener.* **Illustrated by David Small. Farrar, Straus & Giroux, 1997. ISBN: 0374325170 (hardcover) (Grades 3–6)**
It is the time of the Great Depression when ten-year-old Lydia Grace is sent to the city to help in her uncle's bakery. Lydia is a resilient, optimistic child and quickly makes it her goal to coax a smile from her kind but rather dour uncle. Lydia works hard to learn the routines of the bakery and puts in long hours helping with the chores, but slowly, one bloom at a time, she begins to transform her surroundings. This story, told entirely through the letters that Lydia writes back home, is genuine and touching. It speaks volumes about the impact that one small individual can make on the lives of those around her.

Awards: ABA Book Sense Pick, Caldecott Honor Award, Literature from the Garden List
Related Subjects: Family, Gardening, Great Depression, Letter writing
Character Themes: Kindness, Overcoming adversity, Overcoming fears, Thoughtfulness, Work ethic

Updike, John, A *Child's Calendar*. Illustrated by Trina Schart Hyman. A Holiday House Book, 1999 (orig. 1965). ISBN: 0823414450 (hardback) (Grades K–3)
A Pulitzer Prize–winning author and a Caldecott-winning illustrator coordinate nicely to produce poems and pictures that take children and their adults through the year. Updike's poems are titled by the twelve months; Hyman's illustrations incorporate seasonal and holiday themes. Although this is a reissuing of a timeless book, Hyman's illustrations of multicultural friendships and a biracial family give a fresh feel with each turn of the page.
Awards: Caldecott Honor
Related subjects: Family—Biracial, Holidays, Seasons
Character themes: Family love, Friendship

Weatherford, Carole Boston, *Moses: When Harriet Tubman Led Her People to Freedom*. Illustrated by Kadir Nelson. Hyperion Books for Children, 2006. ISBN: 0786851759 (hardcover) (Grades 4–12)
Weatherford and Nelson have created a masterpiece of sparse prose, prayer, and sweeping illustration. This oversized picture book chronicles the amazing life of Harriet Tubman, slave in the South, free woman at last in Philadelphia. Using the metaphor of Moses freeing the Israelite nation from the clutches of a mighty lord, the author depicts Harriet in dialogue with her Lord as he leads her to safety with the mandate to return and help others escape the horrors of slavery. Readers become eavesdroppers as Harriet seeks direction from the Almighty. Although the story is a fictionalized account of the amazing work of this conductor on the Underground Railroad, a historical record given at the end of the work attests to the fact that she returned south nineteen times and led to freedom more than three hundred people, never losing a soul. Perhaps if readers knew all, the book is not fictionalized after all.
Awards: Coretta Scott King, Caldecott Honor
Related Subjects: 1800s, Harriet Tubman, Heroes, Prayer, Slavery, Underground Railroad
Character Themes: Audacity, Courage, Creativity, Perseverance, Religious faith, Unselfishness

Wiesner, David (author and illustrator), *Flotsam*. Clarion, 2006. ISBN: 0618194576 (hardcover) (Grades K–3)
Once again David Wiesner stretches the imagination of his readers. In a wordless book full of fantastical sea creatures, a young boy finds a camera that washes up on the beach. When the film is developed he finds pictures of

starfish islands, blowfish balloons sailing above the waves, and shell cities riding on the backs of sea turtles. Perhaps most importantly, he finds a picture of the children who have, through the ages, found the camera and recorded their images. Wiesner has taken an ordinary day at the beach and made it a truly extraordinary adventure.

Awards: *Booklist* Editors' Choice, Caldecott Medal, Horn Book Fanfare, *New York Times* Best Seller

Related Subjects: Photography, Science, Sea, Wordless books

Character Themes: Curiosity, Imagination

Wiesner, David (author and illustrator), *Sector 7.* **Clarion Books, 1999. ISBN: 0395746566 (hardcover) (Grades K–3)**

On a field trip to the Empire State Building, a young boy makes friends with a mischievous cloud. This new friend takes him to a floating cloud factory resembling Grand Central Station, where clouds are created according to blueprints drawn by uniformed adults. Seeing that the clouds are unhappy with the unimaginative shapes they have been given, the young boy alters the blueprints to give the clouds fantastic shapes of sea life. Although the boy is quickly sent back to his class by the unhappy grownups, the clouds have taken on their new shapes and make the Manhattan skies much more interesting to behold.

Awards: Caldecott Honor, Horn Book Fanfare, *School Library Journal* Best Book of the Year

Related Subjects: Art, Clouds, Dreams, Friendship, Weather, Wordless books

Character Themes: Humor, Imagination

Weitzman, Jacqueline Preiss, *You Can't Take a Balloon Into the Museum of FineArts.* **Illustrated by Robin Glasser. Dial, 2002. ISBN: 0803725706 (hardcover) (Grades 2–6)**

Two young children approaching the Museum of Fine Arts in Boston with their grandparents realize that the balloon one of the girls is holding cannot be taken with them into the building. Remaining outside to keep the balloon, Grandma loses it from her grasp. What follows is a madcap race past the major tourist sights of Boston as Grandma gathers more and more help in her efforts to retrieve the floating toy. The scenes created at each landmark seem to mirror the pieces of art being viewed by the children in the museum. Hidden within the illustrations of this humorous wordless book are drawings of famous Boston citizens, both present and past.

Awards: ALSC Notable, ABA Pick of the Lists, New York Public Library 100 Titles for Reading and Sharing

Related Subjects: Art, Balloons, Boston, Museum of Fine Arts, Wordless books
Character Themes: Cooperation, Discovery, Humor

Wiles, Deborah, *Freedom Summer*. Illustrated by Jerome Lagarrigue. Atheneum Books for Young Readers, 2001. ISBN: 0689830165 (hardcover) (Grades K–3)
Joe and John are friends who have grown up and played together. In particular, they love the swimming spot they created by damming up the creek with rocks and sticks. Then, in 1964, a law is passed forbidding segregation. Excited, they run to the city pool, knowing they can swim there together for the first time. Sadly, they discover that it is being filled with cement in protest against the law. Unfortunately, they realize that people's hearts take more than a written law to make them change. Not willing to allow their friendship to be affected, they stop at the store on the way home and with determination enter it together. Stunning illustrations convey the effects of racial division in a form that even young children can understand.
Awards: Coretta Scott King, Ezra Jack Keats Award, Once Upon a World Children's Book Award, CBC\NCSS Notable Book in Social Studies
Related Subjects: 1960s, African-Americans, Civil rights Cross-cultural relations, Friendship
Character Themes: Courage, Loyalty

Wojciechowski, Susan, *The Christmas Miracle of Jonathan Toomey*. Illustrated by P. J. Lynch. Candlewick Press, 1995. ISBN: 1564023206 (hardcover) (Grades 2–6)
Although he is the best woodcarver for many miles, Jonathan Toomey seems to take no joy in his skill or in life. No one knows of the loss he suffered with the death of his wife and child, and so with little sympathy, neighbors call him Mr. Gloomy. When the widow McDowell and her young son Thomas ask him to carve a crèche to replace one they have lost, a relationship develops between Jonathan and the boy, and a slow transformation begins in Jonathan's heart. It is difficult to choose a favorite aspect of this picture book for older readers—the graceful text or the lovely illustrations.
Awards: ALSC Notable Book, Carolyn W. Field Award (Pennsylvania), Parents' Choice Silver Honor, IRA Teachers' Choices, Kate Greenaway Medal (UK), Christopher Award
Related Subjects: Christmas, Friendship, Grief, Redemption, Woodcarving
Character Themes: Inquisitiveness, Persistence

Woodson, Jacqueline, *Show Way.* **Illustrated by Hudson Talbott. G. P. Putnam's Sons, 2005. ISBN: 0399237496 (hardcover) (Grades 3–6)**
In poetry format, Woodson pays tribute to the strong, courageous women in her family who led their daughters toward freedom and self-sufficiency. Passing down the art of quilt making from generation to generation, these women used this particular art form to tell the story of their path from emancipation to independence. Using various artistic methods, Talbott has created extraordinary, emotionally moving illustrations filled with historical information. Introducing nine generations of maternal family members, this author and illustrator have created an excellent family history in picture-book form.
Awards: ALA Best Book for Young Adults, Newbery Honor, New York Public Library 100 Titles for Reading and Sharing
Related Subjects: African-Americans, Cross-generational relationships, Heritage, Quilting, Slavery, Underground Railroad
Character Themes: Courage, Creativity, Family love, Inventiveness

CHAPTER SEVEN

Poetry

Defining poetry is not an easy task. Some say that it expresses the essence or core of life; others would disagree and claim that poetic thoughts embody an ethereal quality that defies the boundaries of definition. All would agree that poetry captures a thought, concept, act, or scene in an economy of words, leaving readers with a fresh view or deeper insight.

Writers of poetry for children have a daunting task in taking the abstract and making it concrete for an audience not yet on the developmental level of adult readers. They may be introducing a new art form to a young audience familiar only with Mother Goose rhymes. Their task is to go an aesthetic step further, touching a more sensitive part of the young reader's psyche. However, some wordsmiths, such as Jack Prelutsky, craft poems with humor, even slapstick, and have succeeded admirably in creating a love for their particular wares and amassing a huge readership.

Formats for sharing poetry with children vary from general selections brought together between two covers, to themed collections focusing on one topic, to single poems accompanied by enlightening illustrations. Some volumes are designed to be read aloud to a child, while others are simple enough to tempt youthful audiences to enjoy them alone.

Awards for poetry include the Claudia Lewis Award, the Myra Cohn Livingston Award, the Lee Bennett Hopkins Poetry Award, and others. With the advent of technology, aspiring young writers of poetry have the option of seeing their original creations online, and can enjoy the amateur works of others at such sites as www.poetry.com. However, before the thrill of writing comes the joy of reading, hearing, and sharing, so it is essential to share quality verse with young readers as soon and as often as possible. With the wealth of books available, there is something to please every taste.

Abeel, Samantha, *Reach for the Moon*. Illustrated by Charles R. Murphy. Pfeifer-Hamilton Publishers, 1993. ISBN: 1570250138 (hardcover) (Grades 9–12)

In eighth grade, Samantha Abeel was finally recognized as learning disabled after years of disheartening struggle with math, and was placed in a special education class. She triumphantly reports that it was the best thing that ever happened to her. In sixth grade, Samantha had begun to experiment with creative writing, and in seventh, her mother and her English teacher gave the budding young author the freedom to revel in something that she could do well. By ninth grade, the Abeel family had decided that her message needed to be shared with the world. The results of Samantha's talents and the farsightedness of her mother and teacher are presented to the world in the pages of this beautiful poetry book. Murphy, a friend of the family, was already known internationally for his hauntingly lovely watercolors, and willingly allowed his paintings to serve as inspiration. This first work is not about learning disabilities, but about creativity. However, Samantha has included advice to parents who think their child might have a learning disability, addresses of helpful organizations, and a touching tribute to her teacher, Mrs. Williams.

Awards: Margot Marek Award
Related Subjects: Art, Learning disabilities, Nature
Character Themes: Creativity, Self-expression

Adoff, Arnold (editor), *I Am the Darker Brother: An Anthology of Modern Poems by African Americans*. Illustrated by Benny Andrews. Simon & Schuster Books for Young Readers, 1997. ISBN: 0689812418 (hardcover) (Grades 10–12)

In 1968, Arnold Adoff published a collection of poetry written by black writers that has stayed in print for over thirty years. This expanded edition includes titles by twenty-one new poets, strengthening its power and usefulness. Poets include such highly respected names as Langston Hughes, James Weldon Johnson, Paul Laurence Dunbar, Maya Angelou, and Gwendolyn Brooks. This volume was designed to be used with young readers but does not avoid the difficult issues of racial conflict and injustice. Heroes such as Rosa Parks and Frederick Douglass are honored and children are encouraged to have pride in their identity. Fifteen pages of author biographies and nine pages of notes explain terms used in the poems.

Awards: ALSC Notable Children's Book, Child Study Association of America—Children's Book of the Year Citation

Related Subjects: Civil rights relationships, Cross-cultural

Character Themes: Courage, Ethnic pride, Self-acceptance

Adoff, Arnold, *Sports Pages*. Illustrated by Steve Kuzma. J. B. Lippincott, 1986. ISBN: 0397321023 (hardcover) (Grades 7–12)

From the angst of the football player completing a less than successful play, to the rhythm of the gymnast working out on the parallel bars, to the rush the basketball player feels when putting the ball through the hoop, Adoff covers the sacrifice and success of those enthusiastic about their sport. Thirty-seven poems take the reader to the field, the track, and the gym, exploring the joys and heartaches of the athlete striving for excellence in his or her chosen event. Well known for his contributions to literature for children and adolescents, Adoff has once again provided a volume that should appeal to young and old alike.

Awards: Child Study Association of America—Children's Book of the Year Citation

Related Subjects: Athletes, Basketball, Football, Gymnastics, Horse racing, Skating, Tennis, Track and field, Wrestling

Character Themes: Competition, Cooperation, Dedication, Sacrifice

Carlson, Lori M. (editor), *Cool Salsa: Bilingual Poems on Growing Up Latino in the United States*. Henry Holt & Co., 1994. ISBN: 0805031359 (hardcover) (Grades 8–12)

Contemporary Latino poets give voice to the difficulties of being torn between two cultures in the thirty-six works assembled in *Cool Salsa*. They express the frustration of maintaining their personal identity while blending into the lifestyle of the United States. These poets are true storytellers, enabling the reader to taste, hear, and see the Latino culture. Broad subject areas include school days, the home, hard times, and the future. Some poems appear in English and in Spanish translation. Others are a mix of both languages. A glossary of Spanish terms is included, arranged under individual poem titles. Short biographical notes about each poet add to the value of the work.

Awards: Americas Award, Parents' Choice Noteworthy Product, Outstanding Books for the College Bound: Poetry (YALSA)

Related Subjects: Bilingual, Food, Hispanic/Americans, Prejudice, Self-concept

Character Themes: Ethnic pride, Family love, Self-acceptance

Creech, Sharon, *Love That Dog*. Scholastic, 1993. ISBN: 0439569869 (paperback) (Grades 6-8)
Written completely in blank verse, this unique little volume demonstrates how a seed of appreciation, planted for the love of poetry, can grow into full-fledged passion. Jack, a student in Miss Stretchberry's class, does not want to write poetry because it is something that girls do. Through the introduction of works by William Carlos Williams, Robert Frost, Valerie Worth, S. C. Rigg, and triumphantly, Walter Dean Myers, Jack comes to appreciate style. He also learns that imitation is the sincerest form of responding to inspiration, and that poetry really does mirror life. Literature circle questions and four activities add special interest for teachers, parents, or ambitious readers.
Awards: Claudia Lewis Award, Great Stone Face Award (New Hampshire), Humane Society of Greater Akron (Ohio), Land of Enchantment Award (New Mexico), Maine Student Book Award, Volunteer State Book Award (Tennessee)
Related Subjects: Dogs, Walter Dean Myers
Character Themes: Creativity, Enthusiasm, Humor, Originality

Crist-Evans, Craig, *Moon Over Tennessee: A Boy's Civil War Journal*. Wood engravings by Bonnie Christensen. Houghton Mifflin, 1999. ISBN: 0395912083 (hardcover) (Grades 6–12)
Moon Over Tennessee tells the story of a thirteen-year-old boy and his father, who travel from Tennessee to Virginia so the father can join in the efforts of the Confederate army. Too young to fight, the boy goes along to care for the horses and perform other chores around camp. Father and son arrive in time to be a part of the bloody battle of Gettysburg. Although he is writing only as an observer, the young boy finds himself in the midst of this ferocious battle, which has tragic results for his family. Told in a simple, candid style, this journal has great emotional impact, showing the personal cost that families pay for war. Christensen's wood engravings are the perfect companion to the powerful images created by these verses.
Awards: Lee Bennett Hopkins Poetry Award
Related Subjects: Civil War, Gettysburg, Grief, Journals, Soldiers, U.S. History, War
Character Themes: Courage, Loyalty, Responsibility

Dunning, Stephen, Edward Lueders, and Hugh Smith (compilers), *Reflections on a Gift of Watermelon Pickle . . . and Other Modern Verse*. Lee & Shepard Company, 1967. ISBN: 0673033635 (hardcover) (Grades 6–12)
Wanting to encourage young people to read, these editors compiled an anthology of poems with the stated purpose of reaching the adolescent.

Whether penned by new poets or well-known names like Langston Hughes, Dorothy Parker, Eve Merriam, or Robert Frost, titles are clear and straightforward without classical references that may obscure understanding. Poems featuring animals, family, modern society, personal success or failure, and ecology all find a place in this work. Black-and-white photos strengthen the impact of the verse.

Awards: ALA Best Book for Young Adults, Horn Book Fanfare, Lewis Carroll Shelf Award, Outstanding Books for the College Bound: Poetry

Related Subjects: Animals, Ecology, Family, Nature, Social issues, Sorrow

Character Themes: Appreciation of nature, Humor, Joy, Self-acceptance

Ehlert, Lois (author and illustrator), *Waiting for Wings*. Harcourt, 2001. ISBN: 0152026088 (hardcover) (Grades K–3)

Using half pages to heighten anticipation for the event of metamorphosis, artist and author Ehlert holds her young audience in suspense until just the right time. Each stage of the life cycle is celebrated with vivid color and verse. Brilliant hues of magenta, orange, yellow, and green blossoms herald the birth of the Buckeye, Painted Lady, Monarch, and Tiger Swallowtail butterflies. Five pages of information about the insects, host plants, and even the procedure for growing a butterfly garden complete this unique volume of art, poetry, and intriguing facts.

Awards: Monarch Award (Illinois)

Related Subjects: Butterflies, Life cycles, Science

Character Themes: Beauty, Discovery, Patience, Wonder

Florian, Douglas (author and illustrator), *Beast Feast*. Harcourt Brace, 1994. ISBN: 0152951784 (hardcover) (Grades K–4)

Twenty-one birds, insects, mammals, and reptiles from land and sea are invited to serve as subjects for this banquet of fun and frivolity. From the walrus who is "walrusty" to the baby kangaroo who lives in a "kangaroom," humor, wordplay, and a unique perspective provide the recipe for the theme. Illustrations encourage young readers to try their hands at drawing the cast of characters. Children will laugh; parents, teachers, and librarians will smile; and fun will jump off the pages for all who read this book together. No adult can read this book silently without intermittently saying, "Let me read you this one." Definitely a welcome addition to the poetry shelves—only it will not stay on the shelves.

Awards: ALSC Notable Children's Book, Lee Bennett Hopkins Award, NCTE Notable Children's Book in Language Arts

Related Subjects: Animals, Art, Science

Character Themes: Creativity, Humor

Florian, Douglas (author and illustrator), *Insectlopedia.* **Harcourt Brace, 1998. ISBN: 0152013067 (hardcover) (Grades 4–8)**
The twenty-one insect and spider poems creep, fly, buzz, and bite in a manner that scientist, artist, and creative writer will enjoy. From the silent inchworm to the chirping cricket, a symphony of life emerges. From the near-invisibility of the walking stick to the color-splashed monarch butterfly, nature's preservation of life can be seen. Humor melds with factual information as Florian wraps both in a variety of poetic forms. Illustrations face each verse and support the theme in colorful coordination. This title is one that librarians will want to share with art, science, and language arts teachers. Young readers will be inspired to write and draw their own thoughts about these little-appreciated citizens of field, pond, and tree.
Awards: Beehive Award (Utah), IRA Children's Choices
Related Subjects: Insects, Science, Spiders
Character Themes: Creativity, Humor

George, Kristine O'Connell, *Hummingbird Nest: A Journal of Poems.* **Illustrated by Barry Moser. Harcourt, 2004. ISBN: 0152023259 (hardcover) (Grades K–12)**
Surprised by the intrusion of a whizzing jewel of a bird while having breakfast on the patio, author Kristine O'Connell and her daughters discover a tiny nest ready for hummingbird eggs. The O'Connell ladies follow with amazing intimacy the progress of their winged wonder through her nesting cycle. Privileged readers have the quiet pleasure of sharing each step through the tender paintings of renowned illustrator Barry Moser. Poems chronicle the progression from egg, firstborn, second baby, feeding, and finally flight. There is a feeling of loss, yet wonder at being able to witness life so small, yet so vibrant at arm's length. This thin volume will be a cherished edition for verse, subject, and paintings.
Awards: Children's Literature Assembly Notable Children's Books in the Language Arts, Flora Stieglitz Straus Award, Myra Cohn Livingston Award
Related Subjects: Birds—Hummingbirds, Nature
Character Themes: Observation, Wonder

Glenn, Mel, *Class Dismissed II: More High School Poems.* **Photographs by Michael J. Bernstein. Clarion, 1986. ISBN: 0899194435 (hardcover) (Grades 10–12)**
This volume is the third in a unique series by Glenn and Bernstein. Teachers as well as public and secondary school librarians may want to own all three, since few writers have the capacity for realism that Glenn expresses

through the lives of these fictitious teens. Glenn writes with created names, while Bernstein puts faces to the names with photographs that could be "Craig Blanchard" or "Miguel DeVega." Concerns are tackled that will resonate with most of the audience. Although published in the 1980s, and some obvious style changes in pop culture have occurred since that time, issues remain timeless, and Glenn's voice makes vulnerable the teen audience he introduces. Parents, counselors, and librarians, as well as teachers, will benefit from reading the minds of these adolescents who are struggling to be heard, though often silent to those who care the most.

Awards: Christopher Award

Related Subjects: Coming of age, Communication, Diversity, Family, Peers, School, Self-concept

Character Themes: Maturity, Resilience, Self-control, Self-image

Gordon, Ruth (compiler), *Pierced by a Ray of Sun: Poems about the Times We Feel Alone.* HarperCollins Children's Books, 1995. ISBN: 0060236140 (hardcover) (Grades 8–12)

What person has not felt lonely or alienated from others or even from themselves? Addressing this universal emotion, Ruth Gordon pulls together contributions from all over the world. Though originally written in tongues other than English, American readers can enjoy these works through the efforts of gifted translators. Some of the themes addressed include AIDS, teen pregnancy, having to stand alone against those who disagree, and the trauma of losing a limb. Read in one sitting, these offerings might prove a little depressing, but used in conjunction with a specific need, they can offer a ray of sun to those experiencing a difficult time in their lives.

Awards: Outstanding Book for the College Bound: Poetry (YALSA)

Related Subjects: AIDS, Death, Loneliness, Special needs—Physical disabilities, Teen pregnancy

Character Themes: Courage, Perseverance

Greenfield, Eloise, *Night on Neighborhood Street.* Illustrated by Jan Spivey Gilchrist. Dial Books for Young Readers, 1991. ISBN: 0803707770 (hardcover) (Grades 2–4)

Family ties run deep in these poems when the Robinsons gather for games and reading together, when Karen lets her older sister fill in for mama, and when Nerissa tells jokes to cheer her parents. Whether it is expressing the desire for one more hug before going to bed, singing songs of praise in church, or showing the strength to say no to the man selling drugs, the characters that people these verses celebrate life and community. The soft illustrations and expressive verse are a happy combination in this picture book.

Awards: Coretta Scott King Award
Related Subjects: African-Americans, Emotions, Family—Relationships
Character Themes: Family love, Unselfishness

Grimes, Nikki, *What Is Goodbye?* Illustrated by Raul Colón. Hyperion Books for Children, 2004. ISBN: 0786807784 (hardcover) (Grades 4–12)
Jessie and Jerilyn react differently when the death of their older brother Jaron shatters their lives. Each struggles to deal with the sorrow and finds relief through varied forms of expression. Although the verse is written in the young voices of brother and sister, the pain of the parents is reflected in the lives of their children. Nikki Grimes captures the essence of grief in a way that speaks to children in this collection of sensitive poems. The surreal illustrations, colored in subdued tones, effectively follow the narrative in this family's journey from anguish to wholeness.
Awards: Parents' Choice Silver Honor Award, Tayshas Reading List (Texas), William Allen White Children's Book Award (Kansas)
Related Subjects: Death, Grief, Siblings
Character Themes: Courage, Family love

Holbrook, Sara, *Walking on the Boundaries of Change: Poems of Transition*. Boyds Mills Press, 1998. ISBN: 1563977370 (paperback) (Grades 6–12)
Holbrook's ability to get inside the thoughts and emotions of adolescents is uncanny. She treats her subjects with dignity and respect, while expressing with humor and compassion the angst of surviving the roller-coaster years. Although Holbrook's specialty is middle school, older readers can surely find themselves in her intimate lines. Relationships, peer influence, and self-concept are dominating themes, although parents and teachers come in for their share of the spotlight, as well. Often the last line of her blank verse is the clincher, and that feature itself will hook even those who are not fans of poetry. The official homepage, www.saraholbrook.com, lists Holbrook as "Poet, Author, Speaker, Educator," so her audience should not be surprised that she speaks to each profession at some point.
Awards: Parents' Choice Award
Related Subjects: Parents, Peers, School, Self-concept
Character Themes: Cooperation, Creativity, Independence, Individuality, Self-acceptance

Hopkins, Lee Bennett, *Been to Yesterdays: Poems of a Life*. Illustrated by Charlene Rendeiro. Wordsong/Boyds Mills Press, 1995. ISBN: 1563974673 (hardcover) (Grades 6–10)

Expressing his feelings in verses that contain no more than five words on each line, Lee Bennett Hopkins describes one tumultuous year in his life. Beginning with the picture of a family that seems to be perfect, Hopkins shows a relationship being torn apart by bitter, angry words until the end result is divorce. Single-parent struggles and the specter of alcoholism are added to the death of a grandmother whose love had previously been the author's sustaining power. Surprisingly, the last verses do not voice hopelessness but a prayer for strength and the author's decision to become a writer. These short lines carry a large emotional impact and may prove helpful to young people going through similar situations.

Awards: Christopher Award, Golden Kite Honor Award, *School Library Journal* Best Book of the Year

Related Subjects: Alcoholism, Death, Divorce, Family—Relationships, Family—Single parent, Writers

Character Themes: Coping, Resolve, Self-reliance

Hopkins, Lee Bennett (compiler), *Hand in Hand: An American History through Poetry*. Illustrated by Peter M. Fiore. Simon & Schuster, 1994. ISBN: 067173315X (hardcover) (Grades 6–12)

Seventy-five poems have been chosen by Hopkins to tell the story of America's history. From the arrival of the Pilgrims in 1620 to the space flights of the twentieth century, these poems re-create the adventure of discovering, settling, and creating the identity of this great land. Familiar titles such as "Paul Revere's Ride," "O Captain! My Captain," and "I Hear America Singing" appear alongside contributions by previously unpublished writers. Poems are arranged in chronological order with the chapter titles indicating the time periods represented. Peter M. Fiore's soft watercolor illustrations offer the perfect backdrop for these excellent verses.

Awards: CBC/NCSS Notable Children's Trade Book in Social Studies, New York Public Library 100 Books for Reading and Sharing

Related Subjects: America, Civil War, Great Depression, Revolutionary War—United States, the West, War

Character Themes: Courage, Loyalty, Patriotism

Janeczko, Paul B., *Stone Bench in an Empty Park.* **Photographs by Henri Silberman. Orchard Books, 2000. ISBN: 0531302598 (hardcover) (Grades 6–12)**

Entries in this volume, which use the Japanese form of poetry called haiku, explore the beauty found in everyday life. Unlike those works that praise the glory of the wild, these poems display an appreciation for urban life. Silberman's black-and-white photographs are thought-provoking and effectively portray the essence of each verse. Contributors such as Jane Yolen, Nikki Grimes, and Myra Cohn Livingston are names that are well known to those who share literature with children and young adults. An additional feature is the inclusion of an explanation of the poetical form of haiku found in the introduction to the book.

Awards: ALSC Notable Children's Book
Related Subjects: Haiku, Nature, Photography, Urban life
Character Themes: Appreciation of nature

Kennedy, X. J., and Dorothy M. Kennedy (compilers), *Talking like the Rain: A First Book of Poems.* **Illustrated by Jane Dyer. Little, Brown & Company, 1992. ISBN: 0316488895 (hardcover) (Grades K–6)**

More than 100 poems grouped by chapters such as Play; Families; Birds, Bugs, and Beasts; Calendars and Clocks; and six other topics are compiled by the Kennedy teacher/writer husband-and-wife team. Poems spring from such familiar pens as the classic authors Robert Louis Stevenson and Edward Lear to contemporary writers Jack Prelutsky and Eve Merriam, with something for every taste bridging the gap. Although the title may indicate an audience just learning about poetry, there is much for the older child, as well. Jane Dyer's realistically whimsical art is the perfect complement for every page.

Awards: ALSC Notable Children's Book, Kentucky Bluegrass Award
Related Subjects: Birds, Family, Fun, Time, Weather
Character Themes: Beauty, Humor, Knowledge, Wonder

Mannis, Celeste Davidson, *One Leaf Rides the Wind.* **Illustrated by Susan Kathleen Hartung. Viking, 2002. ISBN: 0670035254 (hardcover) (Grades K–3)**

Engaging illustrations of a young girl meandering through the garden immediately attract readers to this little volume. The verses do not disappoint, but introduce young children to the delights of a Japanese garden in easily understood haiku. As well as serving as a counting book, this work introduces various aspects of ancient Japanese culture in the pictures and in additional text at the bottom of the page.

Awards: IRA Children's Book Award, Parents' Choice Silver Honor Award, Junior Library Guild Selection
Related Subjects: Counting, Diversity, Haiku, Japan—Gardens
Character Themes: Appreciation of nature, Curiosity, Discovery

Mora, Pat, *My Own True Name: New and Selected Poems for Young Adults, 1984-1999*. Arte Publico Press, 2000. ISBN: 1558852921 (paperback) (Grades 10–12)
Poems in this small volume address the difficulty of finding one's identity when loyalties are split between two cultures. Born of Mexican-American parents, the author has experienced a rich double heritage, but has also faced the pain of cultural rejection. Her poems joyously celebrate the things that make the Mexican culture special, such as the food and the resilient beauty of women whose skin is tanned by the sun. They also give expression to the simmering poison of prejudice and its effects on a people. Written over a period of fifteen years, this anthology is rich in lessons of survival and determination.
Awards: New York Public Library Book for the Teen Age, Tomás Rivera Mexican-American Children's Literature Finalist
Related Subjects: Loneliness, Mexican-Americans, Prejudice, Rejection, Self-concept, Survival
Character Themes: Courage, Determination, Ethnic pride

Moss, Lloyd, *Zin! Zin! Zin! A Violin*. Illustrated by Marjorie Priceman. Simon & Schuster Books for Young Readers, 1995. ISBN: 0671882392 (hardcover) (Grades K–3)
Lloyd Moss has created an exuberant introduction to the instruments of the classical orchestra. One at a time the instruments are described in rhyming words that sweep and soar across the pages like the music they represent. At the same time, counting concepts and the names of various musical groups are painlessly integrated into the verse. The brightly colored illustrations are as lyrical as the verse, full of joy and humor. Words and pictures blend perfectly to portray the character of the instrument described. The playful cats, dog, and mouse give readers another element to follow through the book. This work definitely deserves an encore.
Awards: Akron Symphony Orchestra Award (Ohio), Caldecott Honor
Related Subjects: Counting, Music, Orchestra, Rhyming
Character Themes: Cooperation, Humor, Joy

Myers, Walter Dean, *Blues Journey*. Illustrated by Christopher Myers. Holiday House, 2003. ISBN: 0823416135 (hardcover) (Grades 8–12)
Perhaps such a perfectly interpreted blending of artistic text and illustration could come about without the bonds of family, but it would be difficult to imagine. An icon in young adult novel writing, Walter Dean Myers breaks away from his established genre to join his artistically talented son, Christopher, in taking readers on the journey that is the birth of the blues, from rural fields to urban streets. An author's note introduces the work with factual information allowing the text to flow simply from lyrics. Clean lined collages, in black, white, blue, and brown reflect the varying moods of the "call and response" lines. Although perhaps not a book that would be chosen by the younger audience, this will be a favorite among jazz and blues buffs, whether adolescent or adult.
Awards: ALSC Notable Children's Book, BCCB Blue Ribbon, Boston Globe-Horn Book Honor Award, Lee Bennett Hopkins Poetry Honor Award
Related Subjects: African-Americans, Jazz, Music
Character Themes: Creativity

Myers, Walter Dean, *Harlem: A Poem*. Illustrated by Christopher Myers. Scholastic, 1997. ISBN: 0590543407 (hardcover) (Grades 9–12)
Walter Dean Myers celebrates the rich and hope-filled history of this unique community in a single poem presented as a picture book. With well-chosen words, Myers has created a living, breathing tapestry of color and sound. The reader smells the food, sees the street games, and hears the worship and the jazz filling the city blocks. Unity and diversity live together here. The brightly colored collages of Christopher Myers display a raw energy, providing a powerful backdrop to the spare words of the poet. Although published in picture-book format, this is not just a book for children. The older the readers, the greater understanding they will have of the images and the legacy presented.
Awards: Caldecott Honor, Coretta Scott King Award, Boston Globe-Horn Book Honor Award
Related Subjects: African-Americans, Food, Harlem, Hope, Jazz, Urban life, Worship
Character Themes: Diversity, Unity

Nye, Naomi Shihab, *19 Varieties of Gazelle: Poems of the Middle East*. Greenwillow Books, 1994. ISBN: 0060097655 (hardcover) (Grades 7-12)
Gifted poet and winner of numerous prestigious awards, Naomi Shihab Nye offers here her signature style depicting life in Jerusalem, and the West Bank,

interwoven with that of Arabic families in America. Although the collection was first published in 1994, Nye added an introduction in the wake of September 11, 2001, reflecting the pain of the peaceful Middle Eastern population who grieved the loss of fellow Americans that fateful day. Readers learn of religion, foods, climate, and family life while reading of joy, celebration, grief, and loss experienced by the Arab community. This collection offers an intimate glimpse into the soul of a segment of culture that has been battered not only by other races, but by its own people, as well. Since poetry appeals to the imagination and emotions, this small volume offers ripe fruit to share in racial understanding.

Awards: National Book Award Finalist, Outstanding Books for the College Bound: Poetry, Tayshas Reading List (Texas)

Related Subjects: Arab-Americans, Middle East—Fundamentalism, Foods, Family, Family, Foods, Middle East

Character Themes: Ethnic pride, Love, Loyalty, Self-expression

Nye, Naomi Shihab (compiler), *This Same Sky: A Collection of Poems from around the World.* **Four Winds Press, 1992. ISBN: 0027684407 (hardcover) (Grades 8–12)**
Wanting to expose American readers to what lies beyond their normal borders, Nye has included only works by poets from outside the United States. Contributions from 129 writers support the compiler's premise that there are emotions common to all people no matter where they live. Some selections were originally written in English and others are translated. Families, nature, human growth, and self-discovery are all appropriate subjects covered in the six chapters. A world map giving the location of contributors and brief anecdotes about them are included.

Awards: ABA Book Sense Pick, ALSC Notable Children's Book, *Booklist* Editors' Choice

Related Subjects: Family, Nature, Self-concept

Character Themes: Hope, Love, Self-acceptance

Okutoro, Lydia Omolola (compiler), *Quiet Storm: Voices of Young Black Poets.* **Hyperion Books for Children, 1999. ISBN: 0786804610 (hardcover) (Grades 9–12)**
Okutoro has included young poets of various African heritages in this collection with ages ranging from thirteen to twenty-one. Sections are grouped by theme and are introduced with works by recognized poets such as Langston Hughes and Nikki Giovanni. Writing quality remains high in spite of the youth of the contributors, and the broad range of issues addressed will appeal to people of all cultures. Despite the serious nature of many of the

poems, the tone of the collection remains positive and upbeat. Background information is given about each of the fifty poets included.

Awards: ALA Best Book for Young Adults

Related Subjects: African-Americans, Cross-cultural relations, Friendship, Heritage, Prejudice

Character Themes: Ethnic pride, Hope, Self-acceptance

Panzer, Nora (editor), *Celebrate America in Poetry and Art*. Illustrations from the National Museum of American Art, Smithsonian Institution. Hyperion Paperbacks for Children, 1999. ISBN: 0786813601 (paperback) (Grades 7–12)

This tidy collection offers readers a museum excursion accompanied by some of the most accomplished verse makers and artists in this country. Maurice Kenny writes of Native Americans alongside George Catlin's paintings of the same. Carl Sandburg is teamed with George Inness as they view Niagara Falls. William Johnson's illustrations of battle accompany Joseph Seaman Cotter Jr.'s sonnet saluting the African-American soldier. Times of peaceful musings as well as terrible days of conflict are depicted in this small collection. Finding its place in the study of history, geography, literature, and art, this little gem has the potential of becoming a treasure on the library shelf.

Awards: Jefferson Cup Honor Award (Virginia)

Related Subjects: America, Art, Diversity, Education, Geography, United States—History

Character Themes: Courage, Inspiration, Learning, Patriotism, Pride

Paolilli, Paul, and Dan Brewer, *Silver Seeds*. Illustrated by Steve Johnson and Lou Fancher. Penguin Group/Viking, 2001. ISBN: 0670889415 (hardcover) (Grades 4–8)

Two children follow the pleasures of nature expressed through acrostic poetry from Dawn to Night. Each poem is accompanied by two full pages of illustration designed to be the perfect companion for the simple lines. The youthful guides lead readers through their world, appearing on nearly every page enjoying a variety of natural wonders from the bright and beautiful Hummingbird to the gray tones of ethereal Fog. Teachers will find this lovely picture book an apt introduction to one of the simplest forms of poetry or a creative addition to science units. Librarians will count this among their favorite books to read aloud, especially with the large and expressive illustrations.

Awards: Junior Library Guild Selection, Minnesota Book Award Finalist

Related Subjects: Acrostic poetry, Science

Character Themes: Appreciation of nature

Prelutsky, Jack, *A Pizza the Size of the Sun*. Illustrated by James Stevenson. Scholastic, 1997 (orig. 1994). ISBN: 0590374699 (paperback) (Grades 4–8)
For readers who have never encountered the originality of Jack Prelutsky, this volume is a welcome introduction. For the audience who has previously read his quirky poems, there may already be grins of anticipation. Much like Dr. Seuss and Shel Silverstein, Prelutsky demonstrates the ability to get inside the mind and impish nature of a child, writing as though the small person's view of the world is much more reasonable than that of the adult. Surprise endings, incongruity, wordplay, and vocabulary elevated enough to challenge but not to daunt young readers fill the pages with varied offerings that entertain and tickle readers' ribs in the process.
Awards: *Booklist* Editors' Choice, Horn Book Fanfare, IRA Young Adults' Choices
Related Subjects: Family, Food, Pets
Character Themes: Creativity, Humor

Roessel, David, and Arnold Rampersad (editors), *Poetry for Young People: Langston Hughes*. Illustrated by Benny Andrews. Sterling Publishing, 2006. ISBN: 1402718454 (hardcover) (Grades 6–12)
Beginning with a biographical chapter, Roessel and Rampersad's collection of twenty-six poems is an excellent introduction to the famous poet of this title. Working during the period of the Harlem Renaissance, Langston Hughes gave voice to the African-American experience in America that is still relevant today. Although some accused this icon of writing poetry that was too simple, Hughes remained true to his vision of himself as a "folk poet." Cubist illustrations effectively convey the mood of each poem. An explanation of terms is included on each page. This volume is one of a number of books in the Poetry for Young People series. Some of the other authors available in this format include Robert Browning, Robert Frost, Henry Wadsworth Longfellow, and Walt Whitman.
Awards: Coretta Scott King Award
Related Subjects: African-Americans, Civil rights, Cross-cultural relations, Family—Relationships, Harlem, Heritage
Character Themes: Creativity, Dedication, Talent

Rosenberg, Liz (editor), *Earth-Shattering Poems*. Henry Holt & Co., 1998. ISBN: 0805048219 (hardcover) (Grades 9–12)
Poems of love, loss, pain, and joy have been collected by Liz Rosenberg in this small volume. Beginning with Sappho, born in Greece in 620 B.C., to

twentieth-century poets such as Langston Hughes and Sylvia Plath, the works represented extend from ancient China to modern America. These poems are a good match for the stormy days of youth when emotions run from extreme joy to great sorrow in rapid rotation. Some are dark, some joyful, but all speak to those earth-shattering moments we all experience. Biographical notes about each poet lend insight to the poems chosen.

Awards: New York Public Library Book for the Teen Age, Riverbank Review Book of Distinction, Outstanding Books for the College Bound: Poetry (YALSA)

Related Subjects: Emotions, China, Russia, Sorrow, Spain

Character Themes: Joy, Love

Rylant, Cynthia, *Waiting to Waltz: A Childhood*. Illustrated by Stephen Gammell. Atheneum, 2001. ISBN: 0689842929 (hardcover) (Grades 6–12)

Rylant takes the reader on a trip through her memories of growing up in a small town in West Virginia. The personality quirks of those who made up her life are revealed, but a sense of respect for their individuality is maintained. No desire for escape drives these verses, but rather an appreciation of the Appalachian culture and a lighthearted humor combine with glimpses of life's serious issues. Offerings will prompt readers to remember the joys and fears of their own growing years. Stephen Gammell's soft black-and-white sketches reinforce the feeling of nostalgia.

Awards: ALA Best Book for Young Adults

Related Subjects: Appalachia, Childhood, Death, Family, West Virginia

Character Themes: Humor, Respect for others

Smith, Charles R. (author and photographer), *Rimshots: Basketball Pix, Rolls, and Rhythms*. Puffin/Penguin Group, 1999. ISBN: 0140566783 (paperback) (Grades 6–12)

A thin poetic masterpiece, styled by basketball lingo in words of color and pictures of black and white, this volume is a must-have for middle and high school settings. Although there are some pages of narration, most images are created by the combination of carefully crafted poetry inspired by the sport born out of rhythm, embellished by on-the-street photographic vignettes. Readers can almost hear the slap of the ball on the asphalt or tile, feel the urgency of the benched player to get in and score, experience the adrenaline rush of the showy three-pointer, and smell the heat of the game. These lines and images could only have been created by one who is passionate on the court, and who has relived those moments with carefully chosen words and pictures.

Awards: Parents' Choice Silver Honor Award
Related Subjects: African-Americans, Athletes, Basketball, Cross-cultural relations, Inner city, Sports
Character Themes: Competition, Determination, Enthusiasm, Inspiration, Joy, Teamwork

Sones, Sonya, *Stop Pretending: What Happened When My Sister Went Crazy*. Scholastic, 2000. ISBN: 0439250706 (paperback) (Grades 8–12)
On Christmas Eve, Cookie's big sister has a nervous breakdown and must be hospitalized. In powerful verse, the younger sister chronicles her family's struggle with its missing member. Parents fight; peers ridicule. As time passes, Cookie continues to visit Sister in the mental ward, journaling her feelings of pity, anxiety, and anger. Sister seems to remain untouched. When John enters Cookie's life as her first love, he—thankfully—provides just the support that is needed, even visiting Sister in the hospital. When Cookie is given a camera, she takes it to the hospital, and the two girls begin to connect in a new way. Medication, shock therapy, isolation, and loving support result in a glad ending for the entire family. This unique novel has won wide acclaim.
Awards: ALA Best Book for Young Adults, Christopher Award, Claudia Lewis Award, Gradiva Award, IRA Young Adults' Choices, Myra Cohn Livingston Award
Related Themes: Family—Relationships, Mental illness, Siblings
Character Themes: Honesty, Love, Loyalty, Survival

Steptoe, Javaka (compiler and illustrator), *In Daddy's Arms I Am Tall: African Americans Celebrating Fathers*. Lee & Low Books, 1997. ISBN: 1880000318. (hardcover) (Grades 3–12)
With titles like *Tickle, Tickle* by Dakari Hru, and *The Farmer* by Carole Boston Weatherford, poems in this collection give voice to the joy and the deep respect engendered in children by their African-American fathers. Poems supplied by both new and established writers explore the dreams, the love, and the steadfastness of the parents honored in this variety of verses. The various techniques employed in Steptoe's innovative illustrations, such as collage, torn paper, pastel, and appliqué, give a three-dimensional quality to the pages.
Awards: ALSC Notable Children's Book, Coretta Scott King Award, *Parenting Magazine* Best Book of the Year, Texas Bluebonnet Award
Related Subjects: African-Americans, Family—Relationships, Parents
Character Themes: Ethnic pride, Family love, Humor, Respect

Williams, Vera B. (author and illustrator), *Amber Was Brave, Essie Was Smart.* **Greenwillow Books, 2001. ISBN: 0060571829 (paperback) (Grades 3–6)**

When their father is sent to jail for passing a bad check, Amber and Essie's mother has to work long hours to pay the bills, leaving them alone in the apartment for many hours. As the older sibling, Essie takes seriously her responsibility to comfort and care for the younger Amber. Together they encourage and cheer each other, making the best of a difficult time. This little book of poems is both sad and happy. It does not shy away from the struggles of poverty, yet conveys the warmth and hope of shared affection. The spare pencil illustrations are a perfect accent.

Awards: *Booklist* Editors' Choice, Boston Globe-Horn Book Honor Award, Claudia Lewis Award, Josette Frank Award, *School Library Journal* Best Book
Related Subjects: Parents, Poverty, Siblings
Character Themes: Coping, Family love, Kindness

Wong, Janet, *Behind the Wheel: Poems About Driving.* **Margaret K. McElderry Books, 1999. ISBN: 0689825315 (hardcover) (Grades 10–12)**

Getting that almighty piece of paper known as the driver's license is, in America, a rite of passage akin to no other. Rural or urban dwellers facing metropolitan bustle or village cruising meet challenges to be conquered by the untried cavalier of the road. Freedom and responsibility share the ride as expense and adventure turn the wheel. Janet Wong takes the position most vulnerable and speaks with the tongue of the teen, critiquing the skills of the older generation, trying to appease peers, and experiencing the dreaded encounter with the police. Realism governs poetic expression in this set of verses that will find a home in the heart of the novice driver, the parent who sits in the "suicide seat," friends who ride along, and the law enforcement officer who really does just want to keep the road safe.

Awards: ABA Book Sense Pick, Quick Pick for Reluctant Young Adult Readers (YALSA)
Related Subjects: Adventure, Coming of age, Driving, Family, Fun, Peers, Self-concept
Character Themes: Humor, Independence, Maturity, Respect for authority

Wong, Janet S. (author and illustrator), *A Suitcase of Seaweed and Other Poems.* **Margaret K. McElderry Books, 1996. ISBN: 0689807880 (hardcover) (Grades 6–10)**

Three different cultures are interwoven in a poetic tapestry as the author blends her Korean, Chinese, and American backgrounds. The confusion that results from these conflicting influences is effectively expressed in thirty-six short poems. Readers from various ethnic backgrounds may sympathize with the writer's struggles to respect her Asian heritage and yet fit in to the American way of life. They may recognize the types of prejudice she has encountered and gain courage from her attempts to forge her own sense of personhood in the midst of it all.

Awards: Appeared on 5,000 subway and bus posters for New York City Metropolitan Transit Authority's "Poetry in Motion" program, William Allen White Children's Book Award Master List (Kansas)

Related Subjects: Asian-Americans, Family

Character Themes: Flexibility, Self-acceptance

Woodson, Jacqueline, *Locomotion*. G. P. Putnam's Sons, 2003. ISBN: 0399231153 (paperback) (Grades 6–12)

As Lonnie Collins Motion learns about writing poetry from his gifted fifth-grade teacher, his story gradually unfolds for the reader. His thoughts on poverty, the death of his parents in a fire, and life in a foster home are voiced along with the normal relationships among sixth-grade boys. Through Lonnie, or Locomotion, as he is called, Woodson unveils a story of grief and loss set in an urban environment. Lonnie, however, is a survivor, and poetry provides a vehicle for his healing. Similar in style to Sharon Creech's *Love That Dog*, these sixty poems hold appeal for a wide range of ages.

Awards: Boston Globe-Horn Book Honor Award, Coretta Scott King Award, National Book Award Finalist

Related Subjects: Bibliotherapy, Death—Parents, Orphans, Poverty, Urban life

Character Themes: Integrity, Survival

Yolen, Jane, *O Jerusalem*. Illustrated by John Thompson. Blue Sky Press, 1996. ISBN: 0590484265 (hardcover) (Grades 7–12)

Jerusalem is a turbulent city that has incited the passions of many people for centuries. Jane Yolen and John Thompson have captured the passion of all three religions that claim this hallowed ground through poetry, prose, and illustration. The feelings and faith of Jews, Christians, and Muslims are presented in a balanced manner. Historical background is presented in prose selections that deepen the meaning of each poem. Young adults who witness scenes of violence and war in the Middle East on televised news may have a deeper understanding of the underlying conflicts in the area after reading this book. Thompson's acrylic illustrations effectively support the thrust of the poems, adding significance to this work.

Awards: ALSC Notable Children's Book

Related Subjects: Jerusalem, Middle East, War

Character Themes: Faith, Loyalty, Respect

CHAPTER EIGHT

Traditional Literature

Adults and children worldwide love to hear a tale well told. Religion, art, music, drama, and politics all utilize the power of story. From the beginning of time, civilizations have relied on narratives to transmit values from one generation to another. The significance of the tales shared varied from culture to culture. Some stories were believed to be true explanations for natural phenomena; others were simply enjoyed for the sake of entertainment. Some were vital to the foundations of government; others were designed to control children when they were getting too rambunctious. The earliest method of passing along these nuggets of culture was by word of mouth. The storytellers often held the same, or nearly the same, rank in the village as the chief, since they bore the burden of preserving heritage. The arrival in the village of such an important person was heralded with excitement and expectation around the fireside or in the marketplace. Adults and children eagerly left their tasks to come and look, listen, and respond.

With the invention of the printing press, stories became mobile without a teller. *Aesop's Fables*, first told about 500 B.C., was deemed worthy of printing in 1484, early in the history of that world-changing machine. Aiding in the spread of the printed word was the first edition of the Mother Goose tales in the seventeenth century, and the Grimm's collection in the nineteenth. While the Grimm brothers were immortalizing their culture in Germany, Asbjornsen and Moe were following suit in Norway. Joseph Jacobs scanned the countryside in England, while Andrew Lang, a Scotsman, chose to go worldwide with his search. Hans Christian Andersen and George MacDonald used the successful genre to create their own stories, borrowing the conventions of traditional stories.

It is important to note that, from the beginning, traditional or folk litera-ture was not created for a youthful audience, but was adopted by children and young adults because of their delight in the hearing. So, what are the stories that held such appeal for a young audience? Folk literature, as this ancient lore is called, includes myths, legends, epics, tall tales, fables, and folk tales of many varieties including those involving magic—best known as fairy tales. In contemporary society this enormous body of entertainment is available in a wide variety of reading levels, from adult to novice reader. Stories are avail-able in collections that span the world, or focus on a single people group. Volumes may number in the hundreds of pages, or be told as a single story in picture-book format.

Both the esteemed Newbery and Caldecott Awards list winners and honor books in the folk literature genre. The Boston Globe-Horn Book, the Coretta Scott King Award, and the Pura Belpré Award also list traditional se-lections among their winners.

Traditional literature lies at the root of all stories. Somehow there is uni-versal kinship in the age-old battles between good and evil that speaks across time and generations. There is just something both thrilling and comforting about hearing or reading the nostalgic line, "Once upon a time. . . ."

Andersen, Hans Christian, *The Ugly Duckling*. Illustrated by Jerry Pinkney. HarperCollins, 1999. ISBN: 068815932X (hardcover) (Grades PreK–2)
Jerry Pinkney gives the reader a rich watercolor adaptation of this favorite fairy tale. When a large, oddly shaped egg hatches in mother duck's nest, she believes it is a turkey chick and tries to raise it as her own. The other ducks, however, are not so accepting. After being chased, pecked, and kicked, the ugly duckling runs away from the pond, taking refuge in the cottage of an old woman. After a long, cold winter the duckling again ven-tures into the world and sees a flock of beautiful white birds. Much to his surprise, they welcome him into their fold as one of their own. This is an excellent book to use with children who feel ostracized for their differ-ences. The meticulous detail and lush colors of Pinkney's images enhance this enchanting tale.
Awards: Caldecott Honor
Related Subjects: Birds—Swans, Fairy tales, Self-concept
Character Themes: Self-acceptance

Arnold, Marsha Diane, *Heart of a Tiger*. Illustrated by Jamichael Henterly. Dial Books for Young Readers, 1995. ISBN: 0803716958 (hardcover) (Grades 1–3)
When the animals of the jungle reach the age of one year, they choose names for themselves. In order for the name to be accepted, all of the animals must agree that it fits the wearer. Little Grey House Kitten Number Four wants a strong name like the Bengal tiger he admires. In spite of the ridicule of the other animals, Number Four follows Beautiful Bengal in order to learn his ways. In a moment of crisis, the little gray cat exhibits wisdom, ingenuity, and courage to save the life of the one he admires. All the animals agree that he has earned the right to be called Bangali Sher Ka Dil—Heart of a Tiger. The watercolor illustrations of the Indian jungle in green and gold tones are lush and lovely.
Awards: IRA Children's Book Award, Show Me Readers Award (Missouri), Marion Vannett Ridgway Award, Young Hoosier Book Award (Indiana), Washington Children's Choice
Related Subjects: Folk literature, Heroes, India, Jungles, Names, Self-concept
Character Themes: Courage, Ingenuity, Perseverance, Self-respect

Artell, Mike, *Petite Rouge: A Cajun Red Riding Hood*. Illustrated by Jim Harris. Dial Books for Young Readers/Penguin Putnam, 2001. ISBN: 0803725140 (hardcover) (Grades 4–8)
When Petite Rouge, accompanied by her cat, TeJean, glides off in the little pirogue to grand-mere's house on the bayou, the young duck knows that danger lurks in the murky waters. Soon she is confronted by "dat ol' gator, Claude" and boldly establishes her authority by threatening the bully with bodily harm if he doesn't go away. As is true to the traditional Little Red Riding Hood story, the villain knows a shortcut, and Claude is soon in possession of grand-mere's bed. However, TeJean and Petite Rouge are not to be defeated, nor eaten, and ol' Claude comes to a unique and spicy end. Although the story line follows that of the familiar tale, Petite Rouge, Claude, and other characters speak in dialect with narration in the lilting rhythm of Cajun music. One can almost hear accordion accompaniment in the background. Readers who are ready for a fresh taste to familiar fare will find this story delicious.
Awards: Louisiana Young Readers' Choice
Related Subjects: Alligators, Cajun culture, Folk literature
Character Themes: Humor, Ingenuity, Teamwork

Birdseye, Tom (reteller), *Soap! Soap! Don't Forget the Soap! An Appalachian Folktale.* **Illustrated by Andrew Glass. Holiday House, 1993. ISBN: 0823410056 (hardcover) (Grades K–3)**

Plug Honeycut gets himself into a passel of trouble when he can't remember what his mother told him to buy at the store. Instead of saying, "Soap, Soap, don't forget the soap," he begins to repeat whatever is said to him. Inadvertently, he insults a whole series of people with the phrases he hears. Finally, when the mayor's wife threatens to wash his mouth out with soap, he remembers the purpose of his trip. He returns home, dirtier, but wiser for his adventure. This highly amusing tale is enhanced by the charming illustrations of Andrew Glass.

Awards: Black-Eyed Susan Book Award (Maryland), Golden Sower Award (Nebraska), Washington Children's Choice

Related Subjects: Appalachia, Folk literature

Character Themes: Discretion, Forgetfulness, Humor, Responsibility

Bryan, Ashley (author and illustrator), *Beautiful Blackbird.* **Atheneum Books for Young People, 2003. ISBN: 0689847319 (hardcover) (Grades K–2)**

When the birds gather together, Blackbird is voted the most beautiful in the forest. Despite their bright colors of red, green, yellow, purple, orange, pink, and blue, the other birds are discontent and persist in asking Blackbird to share some of his attractive shade with them. Protesting that real beauty comes from within, Blackbird, nonetheless, gives in and paints black stripes and spots on each of the vibrantly hued birds. In this picture book, Bryan has adapted a traditional story of the Ila-speaking people of Zambia, illustrating it with cut-paper artwork. Repetition and rhyme give a lilting cadence to the text.

Awards: Coretta Scott King Award

Related Subjects: Africa, Birds, Colors, Folk literature

Character Themes: Beauty, Vanity

Climo, Shirley, *The Persian Cinderella.* **Illustrated by Robert Florczak. HarperCollins, 1999. ISBN: 0060267631 (hardcover) (Grades 4–8)**

In the land of Persia was born a beautiful child called Settareh for the star-shaped birthmark on her cheek. Shortly after her birth, Settareh's mother died, and the tiny child was cared for by other female family members until her father remarried. In this country, the women—aunts, cousins, and later Settareh's stepmother—lived in the women's part of the house, and the child rarely saw her father. Mistreated by stepsisters and stepmother alike, Settareh suffered loneliness until one day when her father came and gave her a gold coin to buy beautiful clothes for the New Year gala to be given at the Royal Palace. While others were buying expensive cloth to create exotic garments, Settareh gave some of her money to a beggar woman and bought an enchanted jug with her remaining coins. The rest of the story is similar to the universal Cinderella stories, embellished with a death-rebirth element, which provides a surprise ending. As always, Climo engages readers with her culturally accurate retelling. Florczak's exquisitely drawn illustrations add to the richness and beauty of the text to make this volume a valuable edition to a Cinderella collection.

Awards: CBC/NCSS Notable Children's Trade Book in Social Studies
Related Subjects: Cinderella stories, Folk literature, Persia (Iran), Storytelling
Character Themes: Kindness, Self-acceptance

deAngeli, Marguerite (collector and illustrator), *Book of Nursery and Mother Goose Rhymes*. Little, Brown & Co., 1970 (orig. 1953). ISBN: 9993636797 (hardcover) (Grades PreK–3)
This rhyme-packed volume embodies the meaning of traditional verses for children. With 376 rhymes and more than 260 illustrations, readers would have difficulty imagining what could have been omitted in the Mother Goose genre. Before introducing the selections from her own American and English roots, deAngeli shares personal experiences in the Foreword that will resonate with many adult readers. Poor indeed is the child who has not been read to from this volume, or one like it. Each page is graced with wistful illustrations, either nostalgically rendered in black and white, or tinted with the artist's gentle watercolors. Although oversized, this volume should grace the shelves of every primary library and home nursery. It is truly a treasure trove of verses that creates precious memories.

Awards: Caldecott Honor
Related Subjects: Childhood, Folk literature, Nature
Character Themes: Humor, Thrift, Wisdom

Demi (author and illustrator), *One Grain of Rice: A Mathematical Folktale*. Scholastic, 1997. ISBN: 0590939998 (paperback) (Grades 1–4)
In times of abundance, the raja claims a heavy tax of rice with the promise that in hard times he will distribute it back to his people. When famine comes, however, he selfishly refuses to honor his promise, and keeps that rice for himself. When young Rani sees rice leaking from one of the raja's sacks as it is carried away by his elephants, she catches the rice in a bowl and

returns it to the ruler. For this good deed she is offered a reward. Cleverly she asks for the gift of one grain of rice, which will be doubled every day for thirty days. Not even the raja suspects that as a result, she will end up with over a billion grains of rice, which she then returns to the people. This is a beautifully illustrated story that demonstrates the mathematical power of doubling.
Awards: Show Me Readers Award (Missouri), Black-Eyed Susan Award (Maryland), Capitol Choices (Washington, D.C.)
Related Subjects: Famine, Folk literature, India, Mathematics, Multiplication
Character Themes: Cleverness, Courage, Honesty, Integrity, Thoughtfulness, Unselfishness

Hyman, Trina Schart (reteller and illustrator), *Little Red Riding Hood*. Holiday House, 1983. ISBN: 0823404706 (hardcover) (Grades 3–5)
This retelling of the classic story is noteworthy for the lessons that shine through, as well as Hyman's signature art. Little Red Riding Hood still talks to a stranger, even though he is fearful in appearance, telling him entirely too much about her destination. She then proceeds to follow his advice about picking flowers that are off the safe path. Children will not miss the lesson and will be grateful to the brave woodsman who rescues Little Red and Grandmother. The renowned illustrator embellishes each page with decorative borders of lovely flowers, belying the danger of the child, yet including enough contrasting light and dark to provide a sinister foreshadowing. Taken together, this is the edition of the story that should grace every library shelf.
Awards: Caldecott Honor
Related Subjects: Folk literature, Wolves
Character Themes: Kindness, Obedience, Survival

Isaacs, Anne, *Swamp Angel*. Illustrated by Paul O. Zelinsky. Dutton Children's Books, 1994. ISBN: 0525452710 (hardcover) (Grades 3–6)
From birth, when she is described as "only slightly taller than her mother," Angelica Longrider is unusual. At two years old she builds her first log cabin, but this amazing feat is merely a prelude to the encounter that established her fame—wrestling ole Thundering Tarnation, a giant of a bear. This humorously illustrated tall tale offers explanation for the formation of the Great Smoky Mountains in Tennessee, the Shortgrass Prairie in Montana, and even the celestial constellation of the Great Bear. Listening and reading audiences will enjoy this rollicking tale interspersed with figures of speech to delight anyone who loves wordplay.
Awards: Boston Globe-Horn Book Honor Award, Caldecott Honor, Emphasis on Reading Winners (Alabama)

Related Subjects: Giants, Great Smoky Mountains, Tall tales
Character Themes: Competition, Courage, Determination, Humor

Lester, Julius, *John Henry*. Illustrated by Jerry Pinkney. Dial Books, 1994. ISBN: 0803716060 (hardcover) (Grades K–4)
On the day he was born, the animals from the forest gathered around to see John Henry. At two days old he was out chopping wood for his family and before long, this young giant decided it was time for him to go into the world. Given two 20-pound sledgehammers by his daddy, he found a crew building a railroad line through the mountains. Not only did John Henry outshine all the other men on the crew, he decided to challenge the steam drill to a race through the miles of rock. Pinkney's richly colored illustrations add energy and beauty to this African-American legend.
Awards: ALSC Notable Children's Book, Boston-Globe Horn Book Award, Caldecott Honor, Newbery Honor
Related Subjects: African-Americans, Folk literature, Giants, Heroes, Tall tales
Character Themes: Ambition, Diligence, Humor, Resolve, Strength

Lester, Julius, *The Tales of Uncle Remus: The Adventures of Brer Rabbit*. Illustrated by Jerry Pinkney. Dial Books, 1999. ISBN 0803724519 (hardcover) (Grades K–3)
Julius Lester has reduced the heavy dialect of the original tales by Joel Chandler Harris to make them more accessible to young modern readers. Though some of the references are contemporary, Brer Rabbit remains a troublemaker who consistently turns the tables on his antagonists Brer Fox and Brer Wolf. Jerry Pinkney's beautiful illustrations reinforce the humorous tone of these timeless stories. Adults will enjoy reading these chronicles aloud as much as children will enjoy listening to them.
Awards: ALSC Notable Children's Book, *Booklist* Editors' Choice, Coretta Scott King Honor Award
Related Subjects: Folk literature, Rabbits, Trickster tales
Character Themes: Creativity, Humor, Ingenuity

Martin, Rafe, *The Boy Who Lived with the Seals*. Illustrated by David Shannon. Putnam & Grosset, 1993. ISBN: 0698113527 (paperback) (Grades 1–4)
When their young son wanders off and cannot be found, a Chinook mother and father assume he is lost. Then they hear of an island where the seals love to sun themselves. Among these seals, there is a boy. Brought back to his

tribe, the boy's parents teach him again the ways of their people, but he remains restless. He exhibits an extraordinary gift for making canoes with beautiful designs of the sea and finally tells them stories of his life with the seals. One day when crossing the great River with his parents, he can resist the call of the seals no longer and rejoins the sea creatures. Ever after, when the parents travel to their summer camp, a beautiful canoe is found waiting for them on the shore.

Awards: *Booklist* Editors' Choice, CBC/NCSS Notable Children's Book in Social Studies
Related Subjects: Feral children, Folk literature, Loss of child, Native Americans—Chinook, Sea, Seals
Character Themes: Family love, Talent

McKissack, Patricia C., *Mirandy and Brother Wind*. Illustrated by Jerry Pinkney. Alfred A. Knopf, 1988. ISBN: 0394887654 (hardcover) (Grades 4–8)
A family photograph and its accompanying story inspired Patricia McKissack to craft this winsome tale of her grandparents' participation in the tradition known as the "cake walk." Spirited young Mirandy, determined to win the prize in the juniors' competition for the coveted sweet, believes that the best partner she could have is Brother Wind. Her enthusiasm in catching and imprisoning the elusive natural phenomenon carries her through Ma Dear, Grandmamma Beasley, Mr. Jessup, and finally to the conjure woman, Mis Poinsettia. However, each suggestion must have the approval of her friend Ezel. In the process of her pursuit, Mirandy learns, or thinks she learns, that Ezel has asked another girl, Orlinda, to be his partner for the cakewalk, much to Mirandy's chagrin. Finally, the time arrives for the wondrous event. All ends perfectly with everyone getting their just desserts, and leaving readers with a smile. Jerry Pinkney's lilting watercolors sweep readers right into Mirandy's cause, and the dance.

Awards: Caldecott Honor, Coretta Scott King Award
Related Subjects: African-Americans, Dance, Heritage, Storytelling
Character Themes: Determination, Enthusiasm, Humor

Mosel, Arlene (adapter), *Tikki Tikki Tembo*. Illustrated by Blair Lent. Scholastic, 1968. ISBN: 0590416227 (paperback) (Grades 3–7)
The ancient and humorous explanation of why the Chinese give their children short names continues to entertain audiences of all ages. Chang, the second son, whose name meant "little or nothing" and his brother, firstborn Tikki tikki tembo-no sa rembo-chari bari ruchi pip peri pembo, which meant

"the most wonderful thing in the whole wide world" are inseparable play-mates. Each is inspired by mischief and a spirit of adventure, and each takes his turn falling into the well. Length of name, however, nearly makes a fatal difference in length of life for the favored son. Librarians with deft mastery of syllables will enjoy reading this story aloud to primary students. Teachers in the elementary grades will find the tale a happy addition to units on Asia.
Awards: ALSC Notable Children's Book, Boston Globe-Horn Book Award
Related Subjects: China, Folk literature, Siblings
Character Themes: Humor, Loyalty

Perrault, Charles, *Puss in Boots*. Illustrated by Fred Marcellino. Translated by Malcolm Arthur. Farrar, Straus & Giroux, 1990. ISBN: 0374361606, (hardcover) (Grades 4–8)
At the death of his father, the youngest of three sons is left only a cat, while his two older brothers are bequeathed a mill and a donkey with which to make their fortunes. The poor unfortunate youth thinks aloud that after he has killed and eaten his inheritance, he will have nothing. However, Puss has something to say about his fate, as well as that of his master. As the tale unfolds, both become wealthy and famous through the cunning of the well-dressed feline. Subtle humor, sprinkled throughout the traditional tale, blends with large and rather dreamy pastel paintings adorned with their own shades of amusement to make this centuries-old story a contemporary favorite.
Awards: Caldecott Honor
Related Subjects: Cats, Folk literature, Storytelling
Character Themes: Ingenuity, Loyalty

SanSouci, Robert D., *The Talking Eggs*. Illustrated by Jerry Pinkney. Dial Books for Young Readers/Penguin Books, 1989. ISBN: 0803706197 (hardcover) (Grades 4–8)
Adapted from a Creole folktale, this story of good sister Blanche, bad sister Rose, and a bad mother demonstrates the importance of respect, obedience, and kindness while entertaining readers with elements of fantasy and suspense. When overworked and unappreciated Blanche meets a mysterious old lady in the woods, her drab life blossoms, because her heart is kind and she understands the importance of obedience. When spoiled and mean-spirited Rose meets the same lady, she responds out of the desires of her selfish heart; both Rose and her mother are rewarded accordingly, and Blanche is vindicated. Jerry Pinkney's lively illustrations capture the mood and character of both girls, and effectively draw contemporary readers into this traditional story with its timely moral.

Awards: Caldecott Honor, Colorado Children's Book Award, Coretta Scott King Honor, Diamond Award (Delaware), Georgia Children's Book Award
Related Subjects: Cajun culture, Folk literature
Character Themes: Kindness, Obedience, Respect

Schroeder, Alan, *Smoky Mountain Rose: An Appalachian Cinderella Story*. Illustrated by Brad Sneed. Puffin, 2000. ISBN: 0140566732 (hardcover) (Grades 4–8)
When Rose's Ma dies and her Pa marries Gertie, the new stepmother brings with her two daughters, Annie and Liza Jane, who are so mean that they would "steal flies from a blind spider." When her Pa dies, life becomes unbearable for the orphan. So begins this mountain version of the *Cinderella* story. The Schroeder tale is loosely based on the 1697 Perrault version, with the setting offering dialect, foods, animals, and values appropriate to the Appalachian culture. Our hero is Seb, who throws a shindig at which Rose makes her dramatic entrance and exit. A huge sow works her magic as the fairy godmother; a "mushmelon" becomes the coach; but the glass slipper remains the same, as does the thrill of romance. Rose proves herself to be a true "sweet thing" when she forgives her stepfamily and all live happily ever after. Sneed's lively illustrations add exactly the right spark to complete this unique retelling.
Awards: Kentucky Bluegrass Award
Related Subjects: Appalachia, Cinderella stories, Folk literature
Character Themes: Diligence, Forgiveness, Humor

Stevens, Janet (author and illustrator), *Tops and Bottoms*. Harcourt Brace, 1995. ISBN: 0152928510 (hardcover) (Grades 2–4)
Rabbit has a very large family to support with no land on which to grow his vegetables. Striking a deal with his lazy neighbor Bear, Hare agrees to do all the work, and Bear can choose the part of the crop he wants to keep—either the tops or the bottoms. However, when Bear chooses tops, clever Hare plants carrots. When Bear chooses bottoms, Hare plants lettuce and celery. When Bear thinks he has figured out the trick and demands both the tops *and* the bottoms, Hare plants corn and gets the middle. In the end, Bear learns the benefits of hard work, and Hare has enough money from the crops to buy his own land.
Awards: ABA Book Sense Pick, American Horticultural Society "Growing Good Kids Award" for Excellence in Children's Literature, Bill Martin Jr. Picture Book Award (Kansas), *Booklist* Editors' Choice, Caldecott Honor, IRA Teachers' Choices

Related Subjects: Animals, Bears, Folk literature, Rabbits, Trickster tales
Character Themes: Cleverness, Work ethic

Wilde, Oscar, *The Selfish Giant*. Illustrated by Lisbeth Zwerger. Scholastic, 1984. ISBN: 0590444603 (paperback) (Grades 4–8)
This literary folktale reveals a powerful story of sharing and joy. A garden, owned by a giant, has become the favorite playground for village children in the absence of its owner. However, when the Giant returns, he chases the children out of his garden and posts a "No Trespassing" sign. As the seasons change, only snow, frost, and hail will come to the garden because of the coldness of the Giant's heart. However, children are persistent, and when a small hole appears in the wall, back they creep. Birds, blossoms, and balmy breezes reach all except one corner, where a little boy cries because he cannot reach a tree to climb. With melting heart, the Giant lifts the child to its branches. Spring breaks forth not only in the garden, but in the Giant's lonely, selfish heart. With transformed spirit, the Giant welcomes back the children. Although the little boy has disappeared, he does return with a profound message for the Giant, as well as for readers.
Awards: Hans Christian Andersen Award (IBBY)
Related Subjects: Folk literature, Gardening, Giants, Seasons
Character Themes: Joy, Sharing

Wood, Audrey, *Heckedy Peg*. Illustrated by Don Wood. Harcourt Brace, 1978. ISBN: 0152336788 (hardcover) (Grades 3–7)
This startlingly beautiful book chronicles a tale of the power of a mother's love, the naiveté of children, and the subtlety of evil. When the mother of seven youngsters, named for days of the week, goes to market, she leaves her little family with only two instructions: do not let in strangers, and do not touch the fire. She promises rewards for all. Of course, as soon as the authority figure is out of sight, trouble begins. With striking use of light and dark paintings and dramatic pacing of text, the Woods take readers into the depths of despair and raise them to the heights of a world turned out right. Victory comes because a mother listened, even when her children did not. This versatile volume offers suspense and satisfaction across age levels, in a variety of settings.
Awards: Flicker Tale Children's Book Award Nominee (North Dakota), Irma Simonton Black and James H. Black Award for Excellence in Children's Literature (Bank Street), Young Hoosier Book Award (Indiana)
Related Subjects: Family—Relationships, Good vs. evil, Siblings
Character Themes: Love—Maternal, Obedience

Yolen, Jane (collector), *Mightier Than the Sword: World Folktales for Strong Boys*. Illustrated by Raul Colón. Harcourt, 2003. ISBN: 0152163913 (hardcover) (Grades 4–9)

The author has chosen fourteen folktales from around the world featuring boys who gain victory over their enemies by intelligence and cleverness rather than physical force. Indeed, it is often the youngest and weakest of the young men who exhibits the strongest character and thus becomes the hero. One full-page illustration portrays a scene from each story. Selections come from such diverse areas as China, Germany, Angola, Israel, and Afghanistan while notes in the back of the book explain any adaptations that Yolen has made to the tales. Also included is a bibliography of sources. This title can be used as a companion to Yolen's *Not One Damsel in Distress*.

Awards: Aesop Prize

Related Subjects: Folk literature, Heroes, Parents

Character Themes: Compassion, Courage, Ingenuity, Sacrifice, Wisdom

Zelinsky, Paul O. (author and illustrator), *Rapunzel*. Dutton Children's Books, 1997. ISBN: 0525456074 (hardcover) (Grades 5–8)

In this eclectic retelling of a familiar tale, Zelinsky has integrated elements from both French and Italian traditions, as well as from the landmark Grimm collection. Lavishly illustrated, the story almost tells itself through the rich textures, expressive characters, and elaborate details. In this version, Rapunzel is cared for by an overly protective sorceress who, enraged when she discovers that her charge is going to have a baby, drives her out into the wilderness to survive alone. When the prince arrives, he is frightened into a fall from the tower, and blindness results. All ends well when after a year, the prince finds his beloved family and healing tears restore his sight. Flowing narrative provides a perfect partner for the elegant artwork.

Awards: Caldecott Medal

Related Subjects: Folk literature, Princes, Storytelling

Character Themes: Love, Sacrifice

INDEX A

Title/Author/Illustrator/Translator

Book Awards

INDEX C

Character Themes Terms

INDEX D

Related Subjects Terms

Civil rights, 95, 101, 107, 138, 143, 155; Segregation, 93, 115
Civil War, 71, 85, 98, 144, 149; Confederate, 144; Union, 102
Civilian Conservation Corps, 77
Clock makers, 99
Clouds, 137
Coal mines, 95
Coastal life, 128
Coleman, Elizabeth, 72
Colorado, 11, 92
Colors, 133, 164
Columbine High School, 92
Columbus, Christopher, 98
Coming of age, 55, 147, 158
Communication, 41, 147
Composers, 92
Concept Book, 115
Connecticut, 9, 70
Conservation, 30, 100
Cooking, 23, 110
Cotter, Joseph Seaman, Jr., 154
Cotton mills. See Textile mills
Counting, 114, 151
Cows, 119
Creative Writing, 11
Crickets, 12
Crockett, Davy, 98
Cross-Cultural relations, 27, 70, 80, 88, 96, 101, 105, 107, 115, 117, 126, 130, 132, 138, 139, 154, 155, 157
Cross-Generational Relationships, 19, 23, 24, 27, 28, 32, 34, 36, 38, 41, 43, 66, 74, 84,88, 89, 93, 96, 115, 123, 130, 143
Cruelty. See Abuse
The Crystal Palace, 97

Dance, 120, 168
Deafness, 70
Death, 13, 22, 23, 43, 86, 147, 148, 149, 156; Parent, 3, 11, 36, 67, 69, 74, 79, 97, 159; Child, 72

Denmark, 66
Diaries, 30
Dickinson, Emily, 61
Dinosaurs, 98
Diplomats, 103
Diversity, 5, 27, 37, 117, 147, 151, 152, 154
Divorce, 149
Dogs, 4, 20, 21, 24, 46, 52, 60, 61, 73, 87, 118, 122, 123, 124, 131, 134, 144; Newfoundland, 72, 104
Dolls, 2, 5, 51, 57
Dolphins, 30
Douglass, Frederick, 142
Dragons, 59
Dreams, 137
Dreidels, 132
Driving, 158
Dunbar, Paul Laurence, 142
Dust Bowl, 74
Dyslexia, 131

Easy Reading 115, 118, 122, 126
Ecology, 8, 38, 60, 77, 96, 100, 118, 145
Ecosystems, 96
Education, 55, 78, 154
Edward I, 90
Egypt, 82
Elephants, 12
Ellington, Duke, 106
Ellis Island, 74, 80
Emotions, 51, 121, 148, 156
Empire State Building, 137
Endangered species, 29, 96, 102, 127
England, 6, 12, 14, 56, 64, 65, 90, 95, 100
Epidemics, 76, 103
Ethnic cleansing, 68
Exile, 85
Explorers, 104, 109
Exploring, 5, 110, 118

Failure, 42
Fairy Tales, 50

Peter Pan, 50
Peterson, Roger Tory, 96
Pets, 4, 20, 21, 43, 60, 73, 106, 123, 155
Philadelphia, 103
Photography, 95, 107, 112, 137, 150
Physical handicaps. *See* Special Needs
Pigs, 34, 56
Pilgrims, 149
Pirates, 50, 58
Plantations, 101
Plath, Sylvia, 156
Poetry, 61, 98, 120
Poland, 103
Police, 131
Polio, 78, 99
Pond life, 133
Postal Service, 52, 89
Pottery, 84
Poverty, 11, 13, 38, 67, 158, 159
Prairies, 65, 80, 115, 117
Prayer, 136
Prejudice, 15, 16, 31, 32, 36, 40, 72, 81, 93, 95, 101, 103, 108, 118, 126, 130, 143, 151, 154
Prelutsky, Jack, 150
Presidents, 135
Pride, 13, 51, 129
Prince Edward Island, 11
Princes, 172
Princesses, 54
Prison, 68
Problem solving, 6, 25, 89
Prodigy, 25, 72
Promises, 48
Proverbs, 48, 49
Psychology, 45

Quakers, 101, 110
Queen Victoria, 97
Quests, 9, 41, 61
Quilting, 139

Rabbits, 3, 8, 49, 167, 171
Raccoons, 106
Railroads, 67, 89
Rain Forests, 118
Ranching, 11, 13, 39, 128
Range wars, 80
Rats, 125
Reading, Joy of, 49, 78, 124, 131
Redemption, 51, 138
Refugees: Political, 36
Rehabilitation, 35
Rejection, 27, 56, 67, 86, 151
Relationships, 82
Religion, 35, 43, 81
Restitution, 35, 62
Revere, Paul, 98
Revolutionary War, 86; United States 99, 149
Rey, H. A., 93
Rey, Margaret, 93
Rhyming, 121, 151
Rhythm, 120
Rigg, S.C., 144
Robinson, Bill, 120
Roosevelt, Theodore, 100
Rudolph, Wilma, 99
Runaways, 3, 30
Running, 99
Rural life, 21, 110
Rush, Benjamin, 103
Russia, 109, 132, 156
Ruth, Babe, 114

Safety, 131
Sailing, 8
San Francisco, 5
Sandburg, Carl, 154
Sappho, 155
Scandinavia, 116
School, 22, 25, 33, 40, 42, 66, 75, 92, 97, 118, 121, 126, 131, 132, 147, 148
Science, 43, 79, 94, 105, 112, 123, 127, 133, 137, 145, 146

Underground railroad, 101, 136, 139
Unemployment, 22
United States: History, 68, 71, 76, 79, 86, 94, 111, 135, 144, 154
Urban life, 27, 45, 123, 150, 152, 157, 159

Vacations, 19
Venice, 53
Vermont, 73, 78
Veterinarians, 105
Victorian Era, 6
Villages, 9, 20, 55, 73, 75, 128
Violins, 37, 44
Virginia, 85, 89
Vocabulary, 22, 120
Vocations, 78
Voyages, 9

Waitressing, 18
Wales, 20, 64, 100
War, 53, 144, 149, 160
Washington, George, 99, 103
Washington State, 75
Water, 112
Weather, 104, 137 150
Weatherford, Carole Boston 157

The West, 128, 149
West Virginia, 134, 156
Whales, 60
Whitman, Walt, 98, 155
Wick, Tempe, 86
Wilderness, 20
Wildlife, 8
Williams, William Carlos, 144
Winter, 116, 117, 127
Wisconsin, 18
Wolves, 166
Women, 72, 84, 101, 102, 119
Woodcarving, 138
Wordless books, 117, 124, 137, 138
World War I, 80, 106
World War II, 14, 76, 79, 81, 87, 93, 103, 110
Worship, 152
Worth, Valerie, 144
Wrestling, 143
Writers, 102, 120, 149
Wyoming, 39

Yellow Fever, 103
Yolen, Jane, 150

Zoos, 105

About the Authors

Rachel E. Schwedt is librarian for the Curriculum Library and cataloger at the Liberty University Library in Lynchburg, Virginia.

Janice Ayers DeLong is associate professor of English in the Department of English and Modern Languages, School of Communications at Liberty University in Lynchburg, Virginia.